FLAWS
IN THE
SOCIAL
FABRIC

FLAWS IN THE SOCIAL FABRIC

Homosexuals and society in Sydney

DENISE THOMPSON

George Allen & Unwin
Sydney London Boston

First published in 1985
George Allen & Unwin Pty Ltd
8 Napier Street, North Sydney, NSW 2060, Australia

George Allen & Unwin (Publishers) Ltd
Park Lane, Hemel Hempstead, Herts HP2 4TE, England

Allen & Unwin Inc.
Fifty Cross Street, Winchester, Mass 01890, USA

National Library of Australia
Cataloguing-in-Publication entry:
Thompson, Denise, 1940– .
Flaws in the Social Fabric.

Bibliography.
Includes index.
ISBN 0 86861 676 1.
ISBN 0 86861 684 2 (pbk.).

1. Homosexuals—New South Wales—Sydney—
History. 2. Sydney (N.S.W.)—Social conditions.
I. Title
306.7'66'099441

Library of Congress Catalog Card Number: 84-72058

Typeset in 10/11 Bembo by Graphicraft Typesetters, Hong Kong
Printed in Hong Kong

CONTENTS

For Chris Burvill

ACKNOWLEDGEMENTS

THE following people gave invaluable advice, information and assistance during the research for Part I: Elaine Alinta, Jo Beaumont, Terry Bell, Tim Carrigan, Mike Clohesy, Jan Davis, Ken Davis, Peter de Waal, Col Eglington, Paul Foss, John Gould, Richard Jessop, Craig Johnston, Robyn Kennedy, John Lee, Margaret McMann, Di Minnis, Meagan Morris, Robyn Plaister, Chris Poll, Sue Rawlinson, Pam Stein, John Ware, and Lex Watson.

As well, I would like to thank especially: Chris Burvill, who was research co-ordinator at the ADB during the time I was writing the report; Paul Stein QC, who was President of the ADB at that time; and my mum, Betty Perry, who did so much of the typing as short notice in the last panic to get the manuscript to the publisher.

INTRODUCTION

THIS book is something of a hybrid. The initial impetus for its publication came from the NSW Anti-Discrimination Board (ADB) during 1980 when the Board's report, *Discrimination and Homosexuality*, was still being written.[1] I started researching and writing a history of the gay movement during the eleven months between my two periods of employment with the ADB.[2] When I returned to complete the report, I attempted to incorporate some of the material I had gathered in the meantime, only to find myself faced with a number of difficulties. In the first place, I found that no matter how hard I tried to adapt gay liberation discourse into terms appropriate for a government report, it simply would not 'fit'. Time and again, I found that the taken-for-granted rhetoric of the gay movement sounded bizarre or meaningless when the only question at issue was that of guaranteeing rights for 'homosexuals' by means of narrowly defined legislative enactments and administrative procedures.[3] The ADB's terms of reference confined the research project to a civil rights framework, and limited its endeavour to the tasks of establishing that discrimination against 'homosexuals' existed, and of elucidating the kinds of discrimination which, for the most part, 'homosexuals' themselves considered to be of major concern.[4]

This civil rights approach, while not in outright conflict with an approach which takes the gay movement as its starting point, remains restricted in the scope of what can be considered within that framework. While it can be argued that, in fact, the only issue raised by the gay movement which has made any impact at all, *is* the demand for civil rights, yet that issue was by no means central to the gay liberation debate. It may have been the only issue around which it was possible to organise and develop strategies, but there were times in the

1

gay movement's history when the issue of civil rights was explicitly disavowed in favour of 'revolution'. Within this framework, the state, even under a democratically elected government, is the main enemy, as the most readily identifiable source of social power. In contrast, the demand for civil rights leaves the status quo intact. 'Rights' are dependent on the magnamimity of the powers that be, and are granted to those who are powerless to redress their own wrongs. Within this context, the state, as the source of the legislative enactment of 'rights', is beneficent. And the polemics of 'revolution' sit uneasily within the confines of a government report. Every attempt I made to translate gay liberation rhetoric into 'a case for the defence' failed as soon as I moved away from the task of exposing and bringing into question the social outcast status of 'homosexuals'.

Admittedly, the gay liberation debate involved more than a mere polemics of 'revolution', and it *was* possible to include in the ADB report an historical overview of the concept of 'homosexuality',[5] drawing on the results of the work done by one gay scholar, Jeffery Weeks. But the purposes of that inclusion had to remain limited—to demonstrate that what today is taken for granted about 'homosexual-ity' is of fairly recent historical origin, as are the forms taken by the social condemnation of those individuals identified as 'homosexual'. It was not possible to follow up the major insight arising out of the findings of this work—a rendering of the concept of 'homosexuality' highly problematic—because the ADB's terms of reference already presupposed the existence of individuals identifiably 'homosexual'. To bring that into question in the report would have been pointless since it would have brought into question the category of individuals to which the report addressed itself—unless it had been possible to engage in debate about issues which are far from resolved. But a government report was hardly appropriate as a forum for continuing debate.

The final difficulty I experienced in writing the ADB's report related to my own interests in the phenomenon of (male) 'homosex-uality'. As a lesbian feminist I can only write a *critical* account of a movement which, from the point of view of lesbians, inexorably reproduced the predominance of male interests prevailing within the present social order, despite some goodwill on the gay liberationists' part and a number of well-intentioned attempts to do otherwise. But a critical approach to gay liberation, even though not directed against the civil rights arguments, nor intended to belittle or dismiss the aims of the movement, would have gone far beyond the ADB's terms of reference and, once again, undermined the main argument. It is true that there were no barriers as far as the ADB was concerned to pointing out that discussions of 'homosexuals' and 'homosexuality' tended to refer to men only and to omit women from consideration, even to the extent of implicating the gay movement itself in that practice. But it was not possible to develop that point at any length. In the first place, and on a pragmatic level, it could not lead to any recommendations for implementation by the NSW Government (or anyone else for that matter).

But more cogently, the concept of 'homosexuality' itself set limits to the extent to which it was possible to discuss the situation of lesbians. Because the data investigated within the category of 'homosexuality' tended to confine the scope of its reference to the male, so did the ADB's report. Time and again in writing up the data, I would find myself writing only about men. The device of including *male* in brackets before 'homosexuality' very quickly became tedious.[6] And explanations suggesting reasons for the omission of lesbianism from the scope of the discussion could not be repeated indefinitely. The only solution I could see would have been to set up a separate discourse on lesbianism. This solution was suggested by one of the ADB's kindlier critics,[7] on the grounds that interpolations on lesbianism were a diversion from the main argument. But such a 'separatist' solution was not available because within the civil rights framework there was nothing more which needed to be said about lesbians than could be said about homosexual men; both were entitled to be treated on terms of equality with the rest of the population. What could be said about women had already been said about men. As long as the discussion was confined to the civil rights framework, a separate discourse was redundant.

As a consequence, the dilemma remained. In researching and writing the report we could do no more than make well-intentioned moves in the direction of rectifying the inequalities inherent in the situation of women in relation to men, even though the result was no more than a minor improvement on the status quo where the omission of lesbianism is either not acknowledged, or is given a regretful token acknowledgement without being rectified. To the extent that this book reproduces the emphasis of the ADB's report, it reproduces the predominance of the male. This is a situation which I find unsatisfactory: while I have a general interest in the topic of 'homosexuality', and that has carried me through, this is not really the book I want to write.

The obvious question then is: why did I write it? The short answer is that I was given the opportunity. Having taken it up, I have also taken the opportunity to write about issues which interest me, rather than allowing the limitations of the original text—the ADB's report, *Discrimination and Homosexuality*—to appear unchallenged. However, that has meant that this book contains a number of discourses which

3

have nothing to say to each other, unless dismissively. Gay liberation sits uneasily with civil libertarianism, Christian theology, and medical science, while lesbian-feminism glowers watchfully from the shadows. Coexistence is tenuously maintained with a thin strand of rationality. My own interests have been made manifest, but they cannot provide coherence because they do not take precedence. Such is the price of universal tolerance.

Part I of the present book is therefore new; Part II is chapters 2 and 3 of *Discrimination and Homosexuality* with some excisions and some introductory material.

I
THE GAY MOVEMENT

1

CAMP
NSW

P ART I is intended to give a brief overview of some of the main events in the history of the gay movement in Sydney. It is by no means an exhaustive account. But then it is possible that the minutiae of events would hold interest for no one but the participants. If gay liberation raised issues of wider relevance than the experiences of a few hundred individuals, that relevance will not be elucidated by a detailed account of what happened when and who said what to whom. Nevertheless, I feel there is a need to document some highlights, at least, of gay liberation in Sydney, since very little is available in a readily accessible form.

The present exposition is the work of one author, and not a collective effort. As a number of people I spoke to in the course of researching this chapter remarked: 'You ask three different people what happened, and you'll get three different stories.' In a sense, this account is yet another 'different story', filtered through my own set of experiences, perceptions and interests. I was not involved in the early days of gay liberation, and only peripherally involved since 1978. That could be seen as a disadvantage, since personal experience of the events and issues gives a deeper understanding. However, those who *were* involved have an unfortunate tendency to explain what happened in terms of conflicts arising out of personal antipathies between specific individuals. While those explanations are true enough as far as they go, for a number of reasons (not the least of which are the laws of libel), I have avoided them. I have preferred, instead, to analyse the wider implications of the conflicts.

The question of what is and is not to be included in a 'gay movement' is a vexed one, on which there is probably less consensus at the present time than there has ever been. If sheer numbers are the only criterion, then the following account should have included the social clubs whose numbers have proliferated since 1970, and whose membership would add up to thousands of 'homosexuals' of both sexes. On that same criterion, it should also have included the (male) 'gay community', whose activities are centred on the commercial bar scene in Oxford Street, Darlinghurst. Again, taking only numbers of people involved into account, the gay church groups—particularly Acceptance, the Catholic group, and the Metropolitan Community Church, the interdenominational group—play an important part in the lives of many homosexuals.

But I have excluded from the category of 'gay movement' all of the above, along the CAMP NSW since the end of 1978, because the concept of a 'movement' implies a deliberate political stance. Whether that stance is 'reformist' (in the narrow sense of 'political', that is, working to influence state institutions) or 'revolutionary' (in the sense of advocating a 'total' restructuring of the social order), the aim is social change. (Whether or not that aim is actually achieved is irrelevant—political movements remain political even when unsuccessful.) In contrast, the above-mentioned groups are apolitical, even to the extent, in some cases, of condemning agitation for the repeal of laws against male 'homosexual' acts as 'rocking the boat'. Not that either post-1978 CAMP, or the church groups, have demonstrated an aversion to the campaigns against those laws. The present executive of the Gay Counselling Service of NSW (as CAMP has recently become known) has expressed support for the campaign, although at the same time expressing reservations about the wisdom of street demonstrations in the light of their current emphasis on the social acceptability of 'homosexuals'. Moreover, the church groups have at times displayed a militancy which would have done justice to the most radical of gay activists. But the line between political and non-political must be drawn somewhere. The fact that the distinction is always just a more or less useful convention leaves the way open for further debate.

But there is also a further distinction which must be made (since it is a distinction which was drawn by the participants in the gay liberation debate), and that is between the two categories of 'political' referred to above: the 'reformist' and the 'revolutionary'. The contemporary debate placed CAMP into the former category, and the various groups which called themselves 'gay liberation' into the latter (the difference in nomenclature was not an accident). This difference in political emphasis (or divergence in political intention) was the source of much acrimonious debate in the first few years of the gay movement in Sydney. However, as the first rush of radical enthusiasm seeped away in the face of the immensity of the task, while at the same time the ideas of gay liberation came to permeate much of CAMP's

8

political practice, the distinction wavered and disintegrated. But the distinction between a political 'gay movement' and an apolitical 'homosexual' constituency not only remains cogent, but has intensified in the light of the ease with which the male 'gay community' has settled into a niche within the status quo.

The gay movement in Sydney (indeed, in Australia) must be dated from that meeting in July, 1970, when John Ware and Christabel Poll set up CAMP Inc. This was not the first time that homosexuals[1] had organised in mutual support groups. Social groups and support networks for male homosexuals had existed in Sydney since at least the twenties and thirties.[2] However, the existence of these groups was known only to the initiated few. In contrast, the primary motivation in setting up CAMP Inc. was to reach out beyond the confines of a homosexual support group, by educating the 'thinking public', and challenging the received opinion that homosexuals were 'mad/bad/sick' by admitting one's homosexuality openly and publicly and without shame, and demonstrating to people of goodwill that homosexuals were 'ordinary folk just like you and me'. It was this emphasis on 'coming out' as the primary aim of CAMP Inc. which qualified it as a political organisation, and hence for a place in the history of the gay movement.

The name, CAMP Inc., and the phrase for which it was an acronym—the Campaign Against Moral Persecution—was suggested by Michael Cass (Widdup, 1971), at that time John's lover of eight years. The original suggested name, 'Queen's Dykes', had been staidly vetoed by the lawyer who attended that first meeting, on the pedantic grounds that it would conflict with the legal use of the term 'Queen's' as in 'Queen's Counsel'.

That the first homosexual organisation in Australia to 'come out' publicly, should have called itself 'camp' rather than 'gay' (the term which was already in common use among those who were influenced by events in the United States) was not only due to the aptness of Michael's coining, but also to a deliberate stance on the part of CAMP Inc.'s initiators. John and Chris were opposed to jumping on the American bandwagon in the wake of the 'Stonewall Riot' (see p. 122). They insisted that an Australian homosexual movement arose in a specifically Australian context. While they had no particular objection to the term 'gay'—Chris Poll called an article 'Gay Liberation'—they saw no reason why an Australian movement should automatically follow patterns set elsewhere, in response to different conditions. They held that there was no equivalent in Australia of the long-established groups in the United States, such as the Mattachine Foundation and the Daughters of Bilitis, which, even if staid and

9

conservative, were at least living proof to homosexuals that organisation was possible, and which had already spent a number of years slowly and laboriously educating the American public. Neither was there any equivalent of 'the highly volatile American political and social scene'. For this reason, John and Chris were convinced of the inadvisability of such tactics as 'gay pride' marches chanting 'Two, four, six, eight, gay is just as good as straight'. While in complete agreement with the sentiment, Chris argued that, in the short term, there were more appropriate tactics:

> as far as the wider society is concerned, we should concentrate on providing information, removing prejudice, ignorance and fear, stressing the ordinariness of homosexuality and generally reassuring and disarming those with hostile attitudes. Concerning homosexuals, we think a policy of development of confidence and lessening of feelings of isolation and guilt, where they exist, is vital. (Poll, 1970:   )

Whatever the inadequacies of CAMP Inc.'s initial radicalism—for example, a naive trust in the efficacy of education and rational persuasion, and in the inherent goodwill of the 'public'—those limitations became obvious chiefly with hindsight (although the awakening was not long delayed). For although CAMP Inc. was criticised from the very beginning as 'insular', 'reformist', 'conservative', 'bourgeois', its critics were able to provide very little in the way of an alternative program. The fact is that CAMP Inc. was set up in a political vacuum as far as 'sexual politics' was concerned. The vanguard of the 'permissive sixties' was the rampantly heterosexual Sydney 'push', whose machismo was enhanced rather than diminished by the preoccupation with more and better 'fucks' (as many of the women found to their cost). Women's Liberation had just started, and the feminist critique of the rigidity of gender roles promised further insights into the reasons for homosexual oppression. But the 'women's libbers' were determinedly excluding men from their debates (John Ware himself was visited with the wrath of the Furies when he tied himself to a chair to prevent his expulsion from the Women's Commission in March 1973), and were far from happy with accusations that they were all lesbians. And the Left was convinced that homosexuality was a symptom of 'bourgeois decadence'.

But the Humanist Society and the Council for Civil Liberties were on side. While these two organisations have frequently been criticised for their 'wishy-washy small-l liberalism'—hence the epithets 'reformist' and 'bourgeois'—they had, nevertheless, shown at least some awareness of the problems homosexuals faced. The former had already made a number of attempts to set up homosexual law reform groups in each state. And the latter provided a lawyer who attended

CAMP Inc.'s inaugural meeting in July, 1970, to advise on possible legal problems.

Not only was CAMP[3] the first homosexual organisation in Australia to define itself as primarily political, in the sense that it was set up with the expressed aim of bringing about social change (no matter how 'reformist' its intentions and methods may have seemed to its critics); it is also Australia's longest-lived homosexual organisation, having been in continuous existence since 1970. That continuity, however, is more apparent than real. While it is true that CAMP has continued without a break as a structured organisation for the whole of that time, its history nevertheless falls into three distinct phases.

The first phase lasted until about the second half of 1971, and was characterised by an easy-going approach which had a lot to do with John and Chris's personal styles. The second phase—from 1972 to the end of 1978—was characterised by a more structured framework for CAMP's activities, with a constitution and a balance sheet, annual general meetings and elections of office bearers, an executive with a secretary and a treasurer and two co-presidents (from April 1972, when Lex Watson and Sue Wills were elected the first of CAMP's co-presidents, to February 1976, when the offices of co-president were abolished because of their hierarchical implications). This phase was also chracterised by an ever-increasing amount of political activity (at least until 1977)—lobbying of and submissions to governments and governmental inquiries, public-speaking engagements, media coverage, demonstrations, etc. The third phase, from the end of 1978 to the present, was ushered in with the enforced withdrawal of the 'political heavies' from CAMP. It was characterised by a decreasing emphasis on political activity, in favour of a primary emphasis on CAMP (or the Gay Counselling Service, as it has recently become known) as a predominantly welfare-oriented organisation, a charity, and a counselling service.

But in the days when Chris and John were the leading lights, ably abetted by a number of like-minded cronies, CAMP Inc. teetered gently on the brink of anarchy. They were a happy-go-lucky lot, who survived more on bonhomie and booze than a fierce commitment to ideological purity. As one of those cronies, Jo Beaumont,[4] said recently: 'none of us thought that anything we did was all that terribly important.' Some sense of the style of those early days comes across in a letter to the editor which Jo wrote in November 1971. The letter was a response to a correspondent who had expressed his 'dismay' at Professor Henry Mayer's support for 'blatant and open homosexuality, at a time when Australia's moral fibre is continually under attack'. The writer had concluded his letter with the opinion that 'open endorsement does little for the unfortunates or for society at large. Homosexuals should be punished and not condoned'. Jo replied:

> As a normally tolerant homosexual woman I find [the correspondent's] statements about homosexuality to be disturbing in their bigoted sincerity. Perhaps he doesn't realise that we are ordinary people with eight fingers, a laugh and two thumbs. In addition, we have the usual quota of intrinsic human dignity. We are not asking for it Mr . . ., we're telling you that we've got it. It only remains for you, and others like you, to remove your tangled moral blindfolds. A bit of your 'Christian culture', in the form of Christian charity, mightn't go amiss either. We don't want your 'pity for for our unfortunate plight'—you're the fellow with the hang-ups.[5]

At the first annual general meeting, on 6 February 1971, no minutes were kept, and John and Chris tried, unavailingly, to do away with the formal meeting practice of seating a Chair and speakers face-to-face with, and separated from, the audience.[6] They did, however, manage to 'upset most of the audience by being unbusinesslike', and by sharing a flagon (Widdup, 1971). Chris was more inclined to sum up the situation in an apt phrase than to engage in detailed theoretical analysis:

> Everyone tends to think that we are entirely to blame for being homosexuals, that it's some ridiculous thing we've taken up to be tiresome. Another projection of people's fantasies about the thing is that lesbians use all sorts of bizarre apparatus because they haven't got etceteras.
> As far as I know anyway, this is a complete myth.[7]

Neither she nor John was happy with the formality of meeting procedures. She is recorded in the minutes of the general meeting of 15 September, 1971 as having 'attacked the whole idea of a structure, of a need for leaders and led'. And, as Lex Watson remarked recently: 'John didn't want to run anything.'

Nevertheless, John's and Chris's vague and unformulated objections were eventually overridden. As Dennis Altman put it at the September 15 meeting, CAMP's 'financial obligations, social obligations, and a need for public spokesmen [sic]' demanded a formal organisation. Other members had already pointed out at the seventh general meeting in August, the need for the finances to be placed on 'a thoroughly business-like basis', and argued that a constitution 'was necessary for the image of the organisation . . . because at present no one was formally responsible for anything, and some form of structure was becoming vitally necessary'. (Foss, 1972)

The most radical and courageous tactic employed by the members of CAMP Inc. in the early days (or by some of them) was 'coming out'. In this, John Ware and Christabel Poll led the way. In the *Australian* of 10 September 1970 there was an interview with John (with picture). On 19 September there was another interview, with Chris, John and Michael (again with a photo, although Michael had his back to the camera—he had already lost one job because of his homosexuality, and he felt that he couldn't afford to take any more chances at that time). The ABC asked for interviews, and even the *Courier Mail* printed the information CAMP sent them as a letter. As a result of this publicity, John and Chris received 'hundreds of letters' from all over Australia. They contacted those correspondents who lived in Sydney and who sounded enthusiastic, and invited them to a party at John's flat on 21 November 1970.

It was this 'coming out' tactic which was the trademark of CAMP Inc.'s early political style. Its importance was stressed many times in the pages of its journal *CAMP Ink*. For example, an editorial in the September 1971 issue expressed it thus:

> There seems to be a consistent refusal on the part of many homosexuals to admit the necessity for them to acknowledge openly that they are homosexual . . . This often encountered attitude . . . has in fact threatened the Campaign Against Moral Persecution . . . by trying to force on C.A.M.P. the external appearance of being a heterosexual society concerned with those poor creatures, the homosexuals . . . The refusal of most homosexuals to 'come out' reinforces community values . . . Homosexuals and all other minority groups by the way they act in public frequently reinforce the illusion that there is but one set of values and norms for society to abide by. Is it any wonder that society seeks to enforce this illusion and to dismiss any statement to the contrary as the unrepresentative raving of a *few* queers?

On the cover of the 1971–72 issue of *CAMP Ink*, 35 members, mostly from Sydney with a few from interstate, 'came out' with photos, although no names (space was limited).

Without doubt, the 'coming out' tactic was at first a startling challenge to received opinion about the nature of homosexuality and homosexuals, as well as being a radicalising experience in the personal lives of those homosexual individuals who threw down the gauntlet to entrenched conservative interests and, in the short term, lost the skirmish. It was also (and still is) a prerequisite for further political action, and to the extent that CAMP provided the opportunity for its members to 'come out', its place in the history of gay liberation is assured. But the majority of CAMP's members wouldn't (or couldn't) 'come out'. This involved the organisation in a recurrent dilemma. On the one hand, there was CAMP's political role as a movement of homosexuals working for social change (or at least reform)—a role which was of primary importance in its initial setting up, as John and Chris made clear in their first editorial in the first issue of *CAMP Ink*:

A few of the homosexuals who have written to us asking for details of CAMP Inc. have written back and said that they do not want to join because they could see NOTHING IN IT FOR THEM. This attitude is difficult to understand and disheartening when encountered . . . The overall aim of CAMP Inc. is to bring about a situation where homosexuals can enjoy good jobs and security in those jobs, equal treatment under the law, and the right to serve our country without fear of exposure and contempt.

Will those who claim there is NOTHING IN IT FOR THEM, have us believe that they already enjoy those rights? Their secretive actions surely give the lie to this . . . Homosexuals deserve to live as well as other Australians . . . It is time we went after those things.

On the other hand, CAMP had to accommodate those of its members who were unwilling (or unable) to face the risks involved, and who wanted no more than a social-support group which made no demands. To the extent that CAMP capitulated to this, in the interests of keeping the membership numbers up, and of providing what the majority of the members wanted no matter how limited the perspective, some of the criticisms of CAMP were justified.

But even beyond this dilemma, 'coming out' was itself limited as a political tactic, unless it went beyond the personal courage of particular individuals and developed into collective action. At an early stage of this first phase of CAMP's existence, it looked as though this was a step which the members were reluctant to take. One of CAMP's more considered critics quoted a number of statements emanating from CAMP, which appeared to demonstrate such a reluctance (Foss, 1972). One of these statements appeared in an editorial in the January 1971 issue of *CAMP Ink*:

We do not advocate that homosexuals in Australia should immediately march down the street carrying Gay Liberation placards, but we do feel that it should be recognised by all homosexuals that it is a necessary step to be taken eventually—maybe not for twenty years—but we must now work towards the day when we can walk down the street openly as homosexuals.

This critic was of the opinion that advice like this was self-defeating because it placed unwarranted limitations on future tactics. He also felt it was due to a 'nationalistic cringe mentality' (since the 'Gay Pride' march was a tactic employed by Gay Liberationists in the United States), and to an unwillingness to alienate the more conservative members of CAMP. However, this editorial bears a remarkable resemblance to the first paragraph of Chris Poll's 'Gay Liberation' article, which was intended to imply no more than that the occasion for such tactics had not yet arisen in Australia. That Chris's analysis was mistaken does not mean that it was based on such craven motives. Indeed, if the holding of demonstrations is any criterion, that advice was shortly to be disregarded anyway. And CAMP's first collective 'coming out' had the distinction of being the first homosexual demonstration in Australia (although it wasn't, strictly speaking, a 'Gay Pride' demonstration).

The demonstration occurred in Sydney outside the Ash Street, headquarters of the Liberal Party, on 6 October 1971. The occasion was the preselection for the federal seat of Berowra. The sitting member, Tom Hughes, former Federal Attorney General, was being challenged by Jim Cameron, who held the State seat for the area. The ostensible reason for Cameron's challenge was the fact that Hughes did not live in the area. But according to *CAMP Ink*, the real reason was that Cameron believed Hughes to hold 'dangerously liberal views'. One aspect of Hughes' small-l-liberalism was his cautious support for homosexual law reform. In May of the year before he had been reported to say: 'In a pluralist society it is no part of the function of the criminal law to uphold and preserve the Judaeo-Christian ethic simply because that ethic exists.' CAMP's opposition to Cameron was based on his belief that the law had a moral obligation to enforce that Judaeo-Christian ethic. This opinion was expressed in a talk Cameron gave at Warrane College at the University of NSW, 'Beyond Permissiveness to a Meaningful Society'. In this talk he had inveighed at length against the moral decay and social disintegration presaged by such decadent signs of the times as homosexual law reform.

Cameron lost the preselection. Whether CAMP's 'gay' (pun intended) demo had any influence on the voting is not recorded. For it was a light-hearted affair, with helium-filled balloons, and grins on the faces of the Liberal Party stalwarts confronted with placards saying: 'Even Hughes is better than Cameron', 'Don't let the wowser spoil the Party. Keep Cameron out', 'Cameron hates homos, but he'll sure b-g-r the Liberal Party', 'Advance Australian Fairies', and a large bright pink banner saying simply 'QUEENS'.[8]

Nevertheless, having pointed out the problems involved in establishing a political enterprise for which there were very few precedents (and corrected the impression that the early CAMP Inc. was opposed to taking to the streets in protest), it must be admitted that CAMP Inc.'s attitude towards the 'wider society' was conciliatory. There was no attempt to develop an analysis of the social outcast status of homosexuals, beyond attributing it to the nasty attitudes or ignorance of misinformed individuals who had never been given the opportunity to get to know that homosexuals were no different from anyone else. The main emphasis was on educating the 'public' to the point of view that 'homosexuals and lesbians are no odd-ball minority—we're a very large sub-group in the society' (as John Ware put it in the second interview in the *Australian*).

> The stereotyped idea of the homosexual is the hand-flapping tinsel and tat gay young queen ... He's only a minority. The typical homosexual is the man living next door to you whom you might know for years until you began to guess the truth.

It could be argued that the conciliatory nature of John's remarks, as they were quoted in the *Australian*, was due to the fact that they had to be tailored for the mainstream media, which never takes kindly to a radical questioning of 'the community's' values. It must also be admitted that what John said was channelled through an interviewer who responded to the sight of John and Michael, admitted 'queers' as they were, with the astounded comment that they were 'so completely all-male men'. However, that same attitude was evident in the original aims of CAMP Inc.

Those aims were stated in an article in the first issue of the journal *CAMP Ink*, in November 1970, 'W(h)ither CAMP Inc?'. They were: to set up branches all over Australia, with *CAMP Ink* as the communicating link between them;[9] to provide personal support for members; to establish contacts within the 'helping professions' to whom CAMP Inc. could refer people with serious problems; and to act as a centre for disseminating accurate information about homosexuality, by building up 'a large pool of qualified speakers to talk on any topic related to homosexuality to church groups, schools, universities, clubs, hospital personnel, etc.' This latter task CAMP fulfilled fairly consistently from that time until 1978.

In the light of these explicit aims, it would appear that CAMP Inc.'s critics were correct in their accusations of 'reformism'. CAMP's aims were limited to working within the status quo, and leaving the social order intact. In (partial) defence, it must be pointed out that CAMP achieved far more, little though it was, than the advocates of revolution. At the same time, CAMP's failure to go beyond piecemeal reforms within the terms laid down by the adversary finally caught up with it.

Nevertheless, during the next phase of its existence, CAMP's political activity went from strength to strength. When Lex Watson and Sue Wills were elected co-presidents in April 1972, they reaffirmed that CAMP was a political organisation, 'unlike all the previous and current social clubs, dances, bars, steam baths and beats that cater to homosexuals in Sydney' (Watson & Wills, 1972). The example they used as 'the beginning of our political activities' was David Widdup's campaign in the November 1972 federal election, for the seat of Lowe (with the slogan: 'I've got my eye on Billy's seat'). The campaign was not intended by anyone in CAMP, least of all David himself, as a 'serious' attempt to divest the sitting member (William McMahon, who until the election was Prime Minister of Australia) of his position in parliament: It was yet another exercise in 'public education', and hence 'political' in a wider sense than involvement in the parliamentary process. (David polled 218 votes.)[11]

Another of the major activities of 1972 was the Sex Lib Week Forum in July at the University of New South Wales, at which Robin Winkler debated aversion therapy with Neil McConaghy (see p. 114). Sex Lib Week was also the occasion for CAMP's second demonstration, on the evening of Thursday, 27 July. (It was not the second time they had appeared publicly in the streets. In March, CAMP and Sydney Gay Liberation took part in the Women's Liberation march, and some members of CAMP had participated in Sydney Gay Liberation's demonstration earlier in July, outside the ABC offices, in protest at the banning of the TDT segment on gay liberation.) It was unquestionably a 'gay pride' march. Although the leaflet prepared for Sex Lib Week stated that the events of that week were to mark the passing of the English Sexual Offences Act five years before, that in itself deserved no celebration—it simply pointed to the fact that the situation in Australia was still as prohibitive as the English situation before 1967. The march itself was purely a 'coming out' affair. As one of the enthusiastic participants put it: 'we had "come out" to try to reach people. We'd forsaken the closets and left our ghetto. We marched' (Delaney, 1972).

It was also in 1972 that Peter Bonsall-Boone was sacked. On 31 October he and Peter de Waal, Sue Wills and Gaby Antolovich had appeared on the ABC's Chequerboard program, 'This Just Happens To Be Part of Me', where the two couples had talked about their respective relationships, and their 'general happiness and contentment as homosexuals' (as Bonsall-Boone put it). The next Sunday he received a phone call from the Rector's Warden of St Clement's Anglican Church, Mosman, where for the past four years he had worked as secretary, asking him to resign. On the following Sunday he notified the church that he refused to resign, and was sacked. The reason behind the sacking, he felt, was not the fact that he was homosexual—the people he had been working for had known that for months—but that he had declared it publicly and unashamedly. On Sunday, 12 November, CAMP combined with Sydney Gay Liberation to hold a demonstration in protest outside the church. None of the other three participants in the program experienced any problems. Peter de Waal even found that his union was prepared to support him if he was discriminated against as a result of his stand.[12]

The year 1973 was a disturbed one for CAMP. They had had to

17

move out of "393"[13] at the end of 1972 and were not to settle into other premises until the end of 1973. In the meantime, however, CAMP took a step which was to have important consequences for the organisation's subsequent development. That step was the setting up of Phone-A-Friend (PAF), a telephone counselling service for homosexuals, in April 1973. In February, CAMP had moved to its second premises at 10 David Street, Forest Lodge, but PAF was run from a member's private phone at first, because the phone was not installed at David Street, and CAMP's tenancy was precarious. (As it turned out, they had to vacate the premises in June, when the Leichhardt council objected to their operating in a residentially zoned area.)[14] At the end of 1973 CAMP moved into 33a Glebe Point Road. At CAMP Centre, as it was called, PAF found a permanent home— until 1981, when the Gay Counselling Service (CAMP's new name) moved to premises in Surry Hills, shared with the Fitness Exchange (a gymnasium for gay men), and Acceptance (the Catholic homosexual group). PAF also found a permanent telephone number listed under appropriate headings in the phone book, after it had been made clear to the bureaucracy that PAF was not a call-boy service.

There is no doubt that PAF was successful. By April 1975, after two years in operation, the service had received over 5000 calls, and had established cross-referrals with other counselling services, such as Life Line, the Wayside Chapel, and the Crisis Centre.[15] In comparison with the rest of CAMP's activities, PAF was more continuous, much in demand, and the first introduction for many people to the 'gay community'. It was obviously achieving something, and generated a sense of purpose among those who worked in it.[16]

But it would appear that its very success created problems, even as early as 1974. In March of that year, Lex Watson and Sue Wills resigned as co-presidents, and Gaby Antolovich as editor of *CAMP Ink*. In their letters of resignation (printed in the March 1974, issue of the *CAMP NSW Newsletter*), all three criticised PAF, and accused it of being a depoliticising influence in CAMP. Gaby felt that PAF was perpetuating the very 'establishment' which CAMP had supposedly rejected years ago, and that 'CAMP is becoming the biggest closet homosexuals have ever known'. Sue Wills deplored the 'elitism' of the PAF listeners who were thrust into the role of 'experts' towards the people who rang in. She objected to the provision of 'help' and 'communion' for homosexuals being seen as the dominant function of CAMP, at the expense of 'the activities designed to remove the oppression which makes this "help" and "communion" necessary'.

The new executive added the comment after these letters that it did not share the misgivings about Phone-A-Friend; nor could it 'vouch for the accuracy of the bases of some of the criticisms'.

The executive which was elected in April 1974 included Margaret McMann and Peter Bonsall-Boone as co-presidents, and Mike Clohesy as secretary.

Leaving aside the prophetic aspects of the criticisms levelled by Lex, Sue and Gaby (they were to be more than amply borne out in 1978) and subsequently, for the next three years at least, it looked as though they had been suffering from some phantom bee in their collective bonnet. Until 1977, CAMP's political activities not only continued undiminished, but actually increased in scope and intensity. The activities for 1974 are detailed in CAMP's 'Oppression on Reflection, '74', written by Mike Clohesy and Peter de Waal. During 1975, according to Peter Bonsall-Boone's co-presidential address to the February 1976 Annual General Meeting,[17] CAMP's involvement in political activity outdistanced even the high level of 1974. The most significant happening of that year, according to Peter Bonsall-Boone, was CAMP's submission to the Royal Commission of Enquiry into Human Relationships.

The submission was presented in September. In order to raise public awareness and discussion of the issues, CAMP distributed it with a news release to the media on October 6. One of the responses was an invitation to appear on the Channel 9 program, 'A Current Affair'. An interview with Mike Clohesy and Peter de Waal was screened on October 8. At the time Mike was employed as a teacher at a Marist Brothers' school. The day after the interview was screened he was called into the office of the principal, who told him that six parents had rung and complained about having a 'declared homosexual' as a teacher in the school. The principal, who was not unsympathetic, expressed satisfaction with Mike's teaching, and a desire that the issue should quietly fade away. He suggested that Mike take a few days off school, to allow time for the views of the church authorities to surface. When Mike contacted the principal again, he was told that the Catholic Education office (CEO) had issued instructions that he was to be dismissed immediately.[18]

The Royal Commissioners, on hearing that one of their witnesses had been dismissed as a result of publicity surrounding a submission, invited CAMP, and Mike Clohesy in particular, to give oral evidence before it on November 9. It also invited the CEO to give its version of the sacking. Instead of sending witnesses, the Catholic hierarchy of NSW instructed a firm of solicitors who briefed a Queen's Counsel and two barristers. The lawyers presented a submission calling on the Commission to rule that homosexuality was outside its terms of reference.[19] However, on December 19, the Commissioners handed down a decision which overruled the Catholic Church's objections. They argued that 'the reference "male and female relationships" should be construed in the wide sense—to include male and female relationships of a homosexual nature'.[20]

Another significant event of 1975 was CAMP's organising of two seminars on female homosexuality, funded by a $4000 grant from the National Advisory Committee for International Women's Year. The first seminar was held at Sydney University on March 22 and 23, with the theme 'Conditioning processes in education and the mass media'; the second was held on May 31 and June 1, with the theme 'Conditioning processes in society and the family'.[21] CAMP produced 10 000 copies of two booklets containing the papers presented at the seminars. These they sent to all general and psychiatric hospitals in Australia, all faculties of Law and Medicine and departments of Sociology and Psychology, all Colleges of Advanced Education, the family law courts, psychiatrists whose names and addresses they found in the phone book, to most schools in NSW and Victoria, and selected schools in other states. (One Queensland school returned the booklets, saying they didn't want to receive any more 'pornography'.)[22]

CAMP's submission had originally proposed a series of six seminars, but their request for a further $4000 was refused. Whether or not the Advisory Committee was influenced by the objections of the NSW Council of Churches is not recorded. After the first seminar, the Council expressed the view that CAMP's purpose was to undermine 'traditional attitudes to sexuality in Australian society, including even acceptance by society of marriages and adoptions by people of the same sex living together'. The Council was of the opinion that CAMP's seminars were outside the scope of educational grants for International Women's Year, and said that it regarded such a grant as 'an act of discrimination against traditional and Christian morality as held by most Australians'. The secretary of the Council, the Reverend Bernard Judd, said: 'The Council is not, of course, in favour of any kind of discrimination, but it regards CAMP as existing to change community attitudes rather than reflect them', and: 'The attitude of CAMP towards Australian [sic] sexuality is really that of anarchy.' He did not reply to an invitation to attend the second seminar.[23]

The year 1976 saw the first attempt to destructure and collectivise the work of the organisation. At the annual general meeting in February 1976, the members voted to amend the Constitution. The aim of the amendment was 'to encourage more participation in the activities of CAMP by not having a formal structure which daunts people into believing there is nothing for them to do', as the leaflet handed out at the meeting explained it. This aim was to be effected by replacing the two 'co-presidents' with two ordinary 'elected members' of the executive. The offices of treasurer and secretary were retained (as in all organisations, they had definite functions to perform), as was the notion of an 'executive', although all members of CAMP were entitled and actively encouraged to attend executive meetings. At the first general meeting after the AGM, the executive coopted five more members, in a further attempt to broaden the support and share out the workload which inevitably fell on the shoulders of the executive. (As things turned out, this and subsequent attempts to work in alternative ways were naive, particularly given the power which devolved on the secretary as the executive officer with the most responsibilities.)

At that same meeting motions were passed which enabled CAMP NSW to become, for the purposes of administration and continuity, an incorporated public association known as 'CAMP Lobby Ltd'. This provided CAMP with the status of a legal entity which could borrow money, receive government grants, obtain tax concessions, and accept bequests. It also meant that individual members acting on behalf of CAMP could not be sued. Earlier CAMP had been registered with the Chief Secretary's Office as a non-profit organisation. This registration was necessary before CAMP could be listed in the phone book under the heading 'Organisations—Charitable', and hence easily accessible to anyone using the phone book to find CAMP. But the possibility of a government grant to help set up permanent headquarters necessitated a more formal structuring of CAMP's legal status (although that possibility receded into the remote future with the demise of the Australian Labor Government at the end of 1975). The irony of attempting, on the one hand, to destructure the organisation within, while at the same time conforming to state bureaucratic requirements, did not occur to CAMP's members at the time. The contradiction was to be resolved later, at the end of 1978.

One of the major events of 1976 for CAMP was a Homosexual Solidarity Weekend, held in May to commemorate the death of George Duncan on 10 May 1972. The general feeling about the weekend was one of discouragement. The police were uncooperative. Having approved the march, they insisted the route be changed without having informed the organisers until it was time to move off. Hence fewer people saw it on the way through Woolloomooloo— 'Perhaps a few baffled people waiting for their bus' (CAMP NSW, 1976)—than if the marchers had been permitted to take the original route up William Street.[24]

However, others of CAMP's activities during that year promised more hopeful results (at least at the time). On 5 August a deputation went on behalf of CAMP to see the new State Attorney General, Frank Walker. The discussion made it clear that changes to the sexual offences legislation were very likely, but that unity among the various homosexual groups would help the change along. As a move towards unity, CAMP convened a meeting of the Homosexual Rights Coalition, which comprised Acceptance (the Catholic homosexual group), CAMP, Gay Liberation, Lesbian Feminists, Metropolitan Community Church (an interdenominational religious group), and the Socialist Homosexuals. During August and September, there were a further two meetings with the Attorney General. The Coalition was presenting two demands: changes in the law, and the establishment of a parliamentary committee of enquiry on homosexuality.[25]

On September 20, another deputation from CAMP met the then newly elected premier, Neville Wran. In their report of that meeting, CAMP's representatives said that they had pointed out that the draft Anti-Discrimination Bill did not give protection from discrimination to homosexuals. Mr Wran expressed surprise at this—he had been under the impression that homosexuals would be covered by the term 'sex'. On being informed that this was not so, the Premier asked for CAMP's suggestions. (A submission was subsequently sent arguing for inclusion in the Bill of the term 'sexual orientation'.) The delegation also brought up the issue of law change. They reported that the Premier 'assured us of his support in this area and said that the newly appointed Criminal Law Review Division would be taking up homosexual law reform as a matter of urgency'. Finally, the Premier 'expressed his concern that we have adequate resources to carry out our work'. CAMP's task was now to put specific proposals to the NSW Government.[26]

Those same social forces which so depressed the members of CAMP during their Homosexual Solidarity Weekend seem to have proved too much for the Premier of NSW too. In the light of the events surrounding the introduction of the 'sexual assault' legislation, and of the fate of the Petersen amendment during 1981, the 1976 'assurance' takes on a certain irony. Nevertheless, it is possible that CAMP's delegations to the Premier and the Attorney General had had some effect. The first draft of the Anti-Discrimination Bill, tabled at its first reading on 11 November 1976, contained no reference to homosexuality. The fully drafted Bill, which was tabled for the second reading on 23 November, included homosexuality, along with age, mental and physical disability, and religious and political conviction, as possible future grounds of unlawful discrimination. Whether or not CAMP's arguments helped in effecting this change is an interesting speculation.

Another of the major events of 1975 was the Tribunal on Homosexuals and Discrimination, held at the University of NSW on November 27 and 28. It was organised by CAMP's Actions Group which first came together in June 1975, to prepare the submission for the Royal Commission of Enquiry into Human Relationships. On completion of that submission, the members of the group decided to stay together as a cohesive group designed to initiate and carry out political actions. The case for a tribunal, rather than yet another conference, workshop or seminar, was argued by Peter de Waal, chief instigator and organiser of the project. He said that he felt that the usual kind of gathering was confined to homosexuals themselves, and hence failed to educate 'straight society' about homosexual oppression. A tribunal, where witnesses gave evidence to a disinterested panel (people who have no personal interests tied up in the outcome of the hearing), was more likely to reach beyond the already convinced. The tribunal was intended to be part of CAMP's education program directed towards the NSW Government to convince the legislators that the rights of homosexuals should be included in the proposed Anti-Discrimination legislation.[27]

On the Saturday, the four tribunalists—Dr Jim Cairns, Barry Egan, Senator Arthur Gietzelt, and Bridget Gilling, vice-president of the NSW Council of Social Services, with Helen Coonan and Jane Matthews as counsel assisting—heard 46 cases of discrimination against homosexuals. Some of these were personal histories, like those of Peter Bonsall-Boone and Mike Clohesy. Others were examples of general social discrimination, such as the laws against male homosexual acts, and (to quote the tribunalists' report) 'police, media, churches, the medical profession, service industries, government departments, private employers, etc.' In their report which the tribunalists presented on the Sunday, they argued that homosexuality was a taboo subject, and that homosexuals were subjected to discrimination and persecution when they transgressed that taboo: 'In every case brought to our notice, it was public knowledge that invoked retribution to homosexuals ... the whole weight of society is applied to homosexuals when their sexuality is known or acknowledged.' The tribunalists did not intend this statement as a reinforcement of the taboo, that is, they were not recommending that homosexuals remain 'closeted' if they wanted to avoid the worst effects of social disapproval. They were merely remarking on the very real pressures to remain silent. They concluded with a number of recommendations which pointed to the need for a wider dissemination of information and educational programs to overcome prejudices and misunderstandings about homosexuality.

The continuing need for such recommendations was very much in evidence on the weekend of the tribunal. Despite press releases and phone calls to various media outlets, press coverage was almost non-existent, although, as Peter de Waal has suggested, that may have been because the Australian dollar was devalued at the same time, and the press was mainly interested in discussing that. But whatever the reasons, the main purpose in holding the tribunal, public education, was defeated.

In contrast to the three preceding years, 1977 saw a tapering off in CAMP's political activities—it was a 'quiet year', as the 'Report to the Nation: '77' put it. The public speaker program continued, although at a somewhat diminished rate, and submissions continued to be presented to a number of governmental inquiries. On 24 June another delegation met with the Premier, and their original impression of Mr Wran, as 'a very sensitive, warm and caring man', was confirmed. (Now they are heartily wishing they could eat their words, not only because of the fate of the Petersen amendment, but also in the light of the behaviour of the police during the June and August demonstrations in 1978.) Mr Wran was very 'disturbed and angry', according to the members of the delegation, about the increase in arrests and the 'agent provocateur' tactics police used against male homosexuals. They also mentioned to the Premier that the film 'Pedophile', which was being shown to the public by the Education Unit of the Police Department, conveyed the message that all male homosexuals were child molesters. (The film was withdrawn by the police in 1980, on the recommendation of the Anti-Discrimination Board.)

But the second Tribunal on Homosexuals and Discrimination, which was planned for July 1977, on the topic 'Homosexuals and Children', did not happen. The general feeling among the activists from CAMP that year was one of discouragement and disillusionment. In part that was due to the decreased opportunities for civil rights action which followed the sacking of the federal Labor Government, and the winding down of the projects (and the optimism) which that government had initiated.

The feeling was also partly a reaction to the demonstration of political influence by conservative church groups, which followed on the Victimless Crimes seminar in February. According to the National Times,[28] the churches were slow to react to the introduction of the Anti-Discrimination Bill in the NSW Parliament. Even the inclusion of homosexuality in the Bill before the second reading in the Legislative Assembly failed to galvanise the conservative lobby groups into action at the time. However, it was likely that the Liberal–Country Party Opposition were saving their objections for the debate in the Legislative Council where they were in the majority. In fact, the Opposition did move a number of amendments in the Upper House, which were eventually incorporated into the Act.

Whatever the reasons for the delayed reaction on the part of the Parliamentary Opposition, the church lobby was spurred into action by what happened during the NSW Government's Seminar on Victimless Crime, which included prostitution, public drunkenness, and drug-taking, as well as homosexuality. At the seminar, Dean Shilton, of the Sydney Anglican Diocese and the Festival of Light, and Dr Ronald Conway, a Melbourne psychiatrist, received a hostile reception from most of the audience of 800. (The latter had fallen into disfavour with the audience despite his support for homosexual law reform, when he gave his expert opinion that the only good environment for the rearing of children was the conventional two-parent family.)

It was at this point, according to the director of information for the Anglican Diocese of Sydney, who was interviewed for the *National Times* article, that church leaders and politicians from both parties realised how strong the 'homosexual lobby' was. As a result of that seminar, moral arbiters from the Anglican Diocese, the Salvation Army, the NSW Council of Churches, and the Catholic Church, came together 'to lay the broad groundwork for a counter-attack' against what they perceived as 'government-sponsored decadence', namely the Anti-Discrimination Bill. When Cardinal Freeman and Archbishop Loane returned from overseas at the beginning of March, they both contacted Mr Wran to voice their objections to the Bill in no uncertain terms. Cardinal Freeman requested 'a total and explicit exception of educational institutions from the operations of this bill'. Archbishop Loane described the Bill as 'ambiguous on the question as to whether it discriminates against the right of voluntary association by like-minded people to pursue aims and ideals which they hold in common. It does discriminate against their freedom of action in seeking to establish and implement those ideals'.

These high-level objections were followed by a flood of telegrams from parishioners who had been advised of the 'threat to Christian parenthood' in Sunday sermons and parochial newsletters. One example of such advice was to be found in the Penshurst Marist Newsletter:

> If the Anti-Discrimination Bill becomes law, we would have to close down as a Christian school. I'm sure you wouldn't like your child to be influenced by either a prostitute or a homosexual but without discrimination people in either of these categories cannot be barred from employment for this reason in our schools.

As a result of the church campaign, 1000 telegrams poured into the Opposition offices in the Legislative Council. Mr Wran's office received over 400, and a similar number went to Mr Paul Landa, the Government leader in the Upper House. Even so, Mr Wran was not inclined to take the protests seriously, since they were based on a drastic misunderstanding of the purpose and content of the Bill. However, he was also faced with opposition within his own party, particularly from conservative Catholics in marginal seats, and with an Opposition-dominated Upper House.

The conservative attack was not specifically directed against the inclusion of homosexuality in the Bill (and there had never been any suggestion that prostitution should be included as a ground of unlawful discrimination). The purpose of the attack was to ensure the exclusion of educational and religious institutions from the scope of the Act. On 23 March the Opposition in the Upper House successfully moved an amendment exempting educational institutions from the Act. On 20 April 1981 a further amendment to the Anti-Discrimination Act precluded educational authorities from discriminating on the ground of a person's sex, but continued to exempt 'a private educational authority'.

The discouragement felt by the members of CAMP was not because of the bowdlerisation of the Anti-Discrimination Bill—it promised very little for homosexuals anyway, only a research report which was not released until five years later. As Mike Clohesy put it, the real setback for the 'social change movement' was 'the assertion of power by the churches'. He continued:

> The conservative campaign showed our movement to be apolitical, unmobilised and disorganised. We weren't able to call on masses of people for support; links with other parts of the social change movement were not sufficiently strong.

The picture was not all gloomy—at least the churches' campaign was motivated by their perception of the strength of the homosexual movement. CAMP's most pressing need (as always) was for more people to become involved in the work of the Actions Group (a plea which brought no appreciable response).

But the main reason for the diminution of CAMP's political activities during 1977 was the preoccupation on the part of the activists with conflicts within CAMP itself. The main disagreement involved, on the one hand, CAMP's function as primarily a political one, and, on the other, the increasing tendency to see CAMP as primarily concerned with the welfare of homosexuals themselves, in a mission of service to the (male) 'gay community', which had been growing in numbers and visibility with the proliferation of commercial interests in the male homosexual subculture. Both tendencies had been present in CAMP from the beginning, but had become increasingly incompatible. The eventual outcome of this incompatibility saw the culmination, at the end of 1978, of that depoliticisation which had been foreshadowed by Lex, Sue and Gaby in their letters of resignation, and marked the end of CAMP as a primarily activist organisation.

Since the psychiatric/psychological/psychoanalytic professions were a prime target of attack by the gay movement in the early 1970s, it is ironic that the therapeutic approach to homosexuality should have resurfaced within CAMP itself, with its emphasis on counselling, and the eventual insistence that CAMP was primarily a welfare organisation. For the movement's original criticism had been directed not only at the use of such 'treatments' as aversion therapy, psychosurgery, and chemical 'castration', but also at the general underlying assumption that homosexuality was a 'disorder', no matter how gently it was 'treated'.

But that is not to suggest that CAMP should never have become involved in counselling. Many homosexuals *are* severely wounded by the contradiction between their sexual desires and what is generally believed to be 'good, right and proper'. Entangled in this dilemma with no way of escape, many people manifest the contradiction in 'personality disorders' and despair. But to structure CAMP around the most immediate and pressing problem—individual distress— masked the need for an overall analysis which might have raised doubts about the pre-eminent position of counselling. After all, the gay liberationist analysis had already rejected explanations of the 'homosexual problem' in terms of individual pathology, in favour of explanations in terms of a fear and loathing of homosexuality. Although there was a need to help and support those homosexuals who were damaged by their status as social outcasts, that need was peripheral to the main task of gay liberation—criticism of the existing social order. Without that perspective, the 'problem' once again became that of the non-coping individual.

Counselling had not always been accorded the same emphasis at every stage of CAMP's history. It was an important motivation for John Ware in setting up CAMP Inc. initially. He was aware that the group, as the first homosexual organisation in Australia to go public, would attract many people whose coping mechanisms had failed. He wanted CAMP Inc. to be able to provide for their needs too, and not just for the undemanding needs of those who had already come to terms with their homosexuality. Hence John's wish to live on the premises and be available 24 hours a day. Hence, too, one of the original aims of CAMP Inc.—to search out members of the 'helping professions' who were non-judgmental about homosexuality. Some time in 1972 John succeeded in finding psychologists who fulfilled that criterion. Together they formed the Homosexual Guidance Service (HGS). As well as holding weekly discussion groups, the psychologists who helped out with HGS (not all of whom were homosexual) accepted referrals of people who contacted CAMP with crises of one kind or another, even sometimes in the early hours of the morning.[29] HGS wound up its operations some time in 1974.

In the meantime, the counselling function had been taken over by Phone-A-Friend. The people who volunteered for PAF duty received no special training at first—they were not expected to give personal counselling, but to refer callers needing that to HGS, special counsellors, professionals or the supervisors.[30] Since, however, those who answered the phone would sometimes be called upon to take on a counselling role with callers, 'it was decided that counsellors would have to have qualities that would enable them to respond with flexibility and to withhold their own value systems as much as possible'. There was to be 'some sort of selection process', which was intended 'to weed out people whose response would be contrary to the intentions of CAMP or incompatible with the philosophy of Phone-A-Friend'.[31]

Almost immediately, this scheme created new problems, two of which were pointed out by Sue Wills in her letter of resignation in 1974. The first concerned the elitist implications of having self-appointed (not membership-elected) supervisors, who had the final say in who was and was not suitable for PAF duty. The second was, once again, the implication that those who rang PAF were 'somehow or other in need of help'. This gave rise to further elitist implications, namely that those who belonged to the PAF collective were 'experts' in relation to their callers. This attitude, whether deliberate or otherwise, came dangerously close, Sue said, to perpetuating conservative views of what homosexuals are like.

These criticisms, however, appeared to have little effect. In the next four years, the main problem within CAMP itself was seen by the activists as an organisational one, and not a consequence of the conservative implications of PAF. There were a number of attempts to restructure (or *destructure*) CAMP along less hierarchical lines. But the dilemma between the tried and true methods of organisational efficiency, and the untrodden path of collectivism, was by no means resolved. It was to come to a head in 1978.

In July of that year Robyn Kennedy resigned from the position of secretary. She gave the reasons for her resignation in a letter which was printed in the July *CAMP NSW Newsletter*. She said that CAMP, which set itself up as an alternative group in society, should ensure that it did in fact provide an alternative, by working 'in an alternative way—one that shares power, knowledge and skills evenly and not hierarchically, i.e. a collective'. Unfortunately she had discovered that far from that being the case, most of the work and responsibility fell on the secretary's shoulders, despite the clearly limited duties as set out in the constitution. While this meant that the secretary's workload was far greater than it need be, that was not her chief complaint, but rather that so much time and energy was wasted in trying to convince people of what should be accepted as a basic principle of this kind of working group.

The inclusion of Robyn's letter in the *Newsletter* created something of a stir because it was done without the knowledge of the rest of the executive, who were antagonistic to the ideas expressed in it. In the fracas that followed, those who were committed to working in alternative ways (labelled 'doctrinaire extremists' by their opponents) handed in their resignations at a meeting in July. Some months later, together with others who had resigned earlier for similar reasons, they formed the Gay Task Force, which for some time continued the political work they had previously performed within CAMP. But CAMP did not lose all its 'extremists' at that July meeting. At the AGM on 25 September 1978 four motions were proposed, which once again were intended to transform CAMP into a collective endeavour. But all four were lost.[32]

On 14 October 1978 the Federation for Lesbian and Male Homosexual Rights (Gayfed) was formed. This coalition of all the homosexual groups in NSW was the brain child of a woman who had made a number of attempts to set up social clubs and commercial venues for male and female homosexuals. Since CAMP's beginning in 1970 the number of commercial establishments for gay men, and of homosexual social clubs, had proliferated. In the light of the police behaviour in the Cross at the end of the Gay Mardi Gras on 24–25 June 1978, this woman became convinced of the need to demonstrate this numerical strength of the gay community, and for an institutional base from which to organise. But the events which followed the gay march through the city on July 14, protesting at the arrests and the behaviour of the Darlinghurst police at the June Mardi Gras, made her wary of throwing in her lot with any of the gay groups which identified themselves as overtly political. On that occasion, the march itself was without incident. But during what was intended to be a peaceful (if noisy) sit-in outside Darlinghurst police station, some people stormed the police station, threw flour-bombs, and provoked the police, four bus-loads of whom had been waiting around corners in side streets, into making further arrests. She blamed 'extremists' for this provocative behaviour. What she did not appear to know was that this provocation of the police was widely condemned by all those on the march, including those political activists whose election to the executive of Gayfed she later objected to so strongly. Indeed, those same activists were convinced that that behaviour was the work of police agitators (ably assisted by the Spartacist League).[33] For example, one photograph taken during the fracas showed four men pounding on the door of the police station. None of the gay activists, who had been working in the movement for years, had seen the men before. Nor did they ever see them again. Moreoever, in the discussions leading up to the decision to hold the march, everyone had agreed that the use of such tactics was pointless, and likely to do the cause more harm than good.[34]

Nevertheless, at least at the time the November *Newsletter* came out, the newly revamped CAMP executive was not fully aware of the ramifications of these events. The *Newsletter* reported that the aim of Gayfed was to bring together all NSW-based groups, ranging 'over the whole spectrum of gay societies from welfare, to political to a strong representation of Sydney's long-established social groups'. A month later, in December, CAMP had withdrawn from Gayfed, because the elections for the steering committee had resulted in an executive 'heavily weighted to the more politically aware groups, leaving the purely social and closeted groups unrepresented', as the editorial in the December issue of the *Newsletter* put it. The editorialist expressed the opinion that this domination of Gayfed by the activists would mean the withdrawal from the Federation of the majority of social groups. He continued:

> This would be a disaster. Federation's stated aim was to unite the Sydney Homosexual Community . . . Because no one from the purely social, and especially the big social groups, was elected to the executive, the working body of the Federation is effectively in the hands of one particular grouping within Federation.

But on a superficial head count, this disquiet at the predicted 'domination' by the 'more politically aware groups', would appear to be unjustified. Only three of the seven positions were filled by members of activist groups, namely Gay Task Force, Gay Trade Unionist Group, and the Lesbian Feminist Action Front. Moreover, the election of activists to the executive was not part of an orchestrated plot to 'take over' Gayfed for the 'Revolution'. The fact is that those who had been active in the movement for some time were more articulate and better prepared, because they were more familiar with the issues, than those who had not. It was the activists' capabilities, rather than their political affiliations, which got them elected.[35] But, of course, it was those very capabilities which made them so threatening to those homosexuals who saw no need to 'rock the boat'.

This taking up of the cudgels in defence of the social groups and the 'closeted' was yet one more step in CAMP's retreat from the political fray. In a final attempt to reverse that trend, those 'politically aware' people who remained in CAMP called an Extraordinary General

Meeting for 22 January 1979, to present a motion calling on CAMP to rejoin Gayfed.[36] Arguments for and against the motion were printed in the January issue of the *Newsletter*. Chris Wright, who was one of the eleven signatories to the petition calling for the meeting, argued that the decision to withdraw from Gayfed was taken without the involvement of the majority of members. He also said that allegations which were being made that that meeting which had elected the executive was 'stacked' were unjust.

The letter which put forward the arguments against the motion was signed by twelve members of CAMP, including the Gayfed organiser and two of her offsiders. None of these three had been members of CAMP before the Gayfed issue arose. The letter began by criticising what the writers called CAMP's 'extremist stance' over 'the past three or so years', which, they asserted, had earned CAMP a reputation for 'encouraging violence in the streets'. They went on to say that previous executives had run CAMP to the detriment of the drop-in centre and Phone-A-Friend, had alienated many members, and had prevented other people from joining. They admitted that 'CAMP must be able to lobby governments and political parties, criticise events and practices in society, offer suggestions and make demands'. But they didn't want this 'dressed up in such radical terminology that the public rejects what we say', and hence 'alienates the good public opinion the homosexual movement has already achieved' (although they failed to mention that that 'good public opinion'—if such it was—had been achieved by the work of those same 'extremists' whose presence in CAMP and Gayfed the writers now so strongly resented). They said also that Gayfed had been set up to counteract the actions of these people (the 'extremists'), and that if those 'extremists' had been genuinely committed to the aims of Gayfed, they would not have stood for office. (Yet, at the time, even CAMP had been under the impression that Gayfed was intended for *all* gay groups, whatever their position on the political spectrum.) The writers concluded by saying that the social groups (and CAMP) had withdrawn from Gayfed in order to avoid having to work with 'the kind of person to whom they objected'.

The irony of those accusations was that the 'extremists' were far from the advocates of violent revolution they were made out to be. On the contrary, they had worked wholly within a conventional political framework, using conventional methods of lobbying, presenting submissions, and disseminating information. That such reputable modes of political action should be characterised thus was indicative of how far CAMP had moved to the conservative end of the political spectrum.

At the Extraordinary General Meeting, the motion to rejoin

31

Gayfed was lost. With that vote the involvement of CAMP NSW with the gay movement was at an end.

That was not quite the way CAMP's new executive saw the situation. The editorial in the 19 February 1979 issue of the *Newsletter* saw it in terms of different 'stages' of the movement, with the inaugural meeting of a new body, the Council of Gay Groups (COGG) on January 14, as 'heralding Stage III of the gay liberation movement'. That stage involved the 'difficult task' of 'finding some way in which homosexual people who cannot afford for any reason to identify themselves publicly, can contribute to the homosexual civil rights movement'. The first stage had involved people working 'underground', through personal contacts alone, to help others come to terms with their homosexuality 'in a hostile world'. The second was ushered in by the Stonewall Riot in 1969. This second stage was characterised by gay 'movements' which were 'loud and noisy, often unkempt and never the most efficient organisations'. In the opinion of the editorialist, 'CAMP NSW itself was one of these noisy offspring of the late 60s, early 70s, when protest was violent, public and fashionable'. In contrast, 'Stage III' was to be conciliatory on all fronts. It was to reassure 'the thousands of gays living in the suburbs (and out in the sticks)', that they did not need to 'come out' in order to be involved in the 'gay civil rights movement'. At the same time, it was to disclose to the 'heterosexual community' the existence of those 'thousands' of gays, as well as reassuring that 'community' that gays were not threatening.

It did not occur to the new executive (neither then nor since) that these two aims were in stark contradiction to one another. If the numerical strength of the 'gay community' was to be demonstrated to all and sundry, then it was *not* possible for the apolitical majority to remain 'in the closet'. Neither did it occur to them that social disapproval of homosexuality was sufficient to ensure that the 'heterosexual community' regarded overt homosexuals, no matter how well-behaved and polite, as at the very least tiresome, at worst, as a serious threat to that 'community's' cherished belief in 'the Family as the Basic Unit of Society'.

To point out this contradiction is not to deny that the consequences for many people of 'coming out' would be personally disastrous ('public opinion' is not all good); nor to assert that everyone should 'come out' regardless of the consequences. Nor does it mean that every homosexual ought to see his or her sexual orientation and behaviour in political terms, that is, as a challenge to heterosexual hegemony; nor that a political stance is necessarily superior to any alternative interpretation of an individual's life history. It *does* mean, however, that the contradiction must be resolved in one way or another. And the way in which CAMP subsequently resolved that contradiction was to turn the main emphasis of the organisation away from the political arena of public education, lobbying government, and generally working for social change, and to direct it inwards to the (male) 'gay community' itself, ministering to its needs in ways which reproduced established institutions exactly. As Bob Hay put it in the *Newsletter* for 28 July 1980 (which briefly acknowledged CAMP's beginning ten years earlier, without mentioning John Ware or Christabel Poll or their 'coming out'): 'We have come full circle in ten years and rejoined the ["wider", not "gay"] community we once left in protest.'

CAMP's establishment image is now beyond reproach (apart from that little matter of 'public opinion'). At the present time, CAMP is Australia's first gay charity. The original application for registration as a charity had been refused by the Department of Services in May 1977. CAMP queried the Department's 'uncharitable attitude', and resubmitted the application. It was finally approved on 3 November 1978. The application had originally been intended by those 'extremists' who first made the submission as a challenge to the bureaucracy, to 'raise the consciousness of yet another government department'. In doing so, they were prepared to submit themselves personally to the procedures required of those who propose to set up a charity, including a police investigation. But once the application had been approved, the possibility of any further challenge was at an end, and CAMP became just one more state-approved institution.

But the turnaround in the policies CAMP has pursued since the end of 1978 was more deliberate than simply falling in with the demands of the bureaucracy. On many occasions since then, the *Newsletter* contained references to 'political heavies' and their distressing tendency to 'go too far' before their activities were curbed by the election of an executive who were prepared to find CAMP a role less offensive to 'public opinion'. That role has become that of looking after the welfare of the (male) gay community, while leaving 'straight society' to its own devices. And that welfare involves, first and foremost, counselling distressed homosexuals, of whom there would appear to be a great number, since this is now CAMP's primary function. So important did this function become that in 1981 the name was changed from 'CAMP Lobby Ltd' to 'The Gay Counselling Service of NSW'. The reason given for this change was that the name 'CAMP' 'causes confusion in the gay community' because it 'carries all the political over-tones of our past—our history hangs heavily around our necks'.

The welfare of (male) homosexuals also involved fostering a sense of community by keeping close ties with the social groups, the bars, and all the other places where male homosexuals might be expected to congregate. Such places supply opportunities for social contacts with other homosexuals, contacts which are difficult to make in the every-day world of the automatic assumption that everyone is hetero-sexual. It is this potential which constitutes not only an incipient (male) 'gay community', but also the possibility of a mass constituen-cy from which to organise politically. Some of the bar managements have allowed political leaflets to be handed out on the premises, and the managements of the commercial gay male venues have recently become involved in the yearly Gay Mardi Gras, a demonstration of gay pride and solidarity and, in its first two years at least, a commemoration of the Stonewall Riot.

At the 1980 Mardi Gras there were murmurings of discontent on the part of the bar managements and their patrons at the political overtones of the occasion. The date was changed, eventually to March, so that the celebration could be held in warmer weather; in this way it was effectively divorced from its political origins. Hence at least one endeavour to politicise the 'mass base' ended in a depoliticisa-tion of the liberationist message. And it is with this tendency on the part of the 'gay community' to contract to the lowest com-mon denominator of political awareness that CAMP has now most strongly identified.

A further example of CAMP's decreasing interest in a wider political perspective is the decision not to reaffiliate with the Move-ment Against Uranium Mining (MAUM) in 1979 because 'MAUM did not seem to include anything specifically gay'. CAMP did, however, reaffiliate with the Mental Health Association (MHA). The reasons given for this decision were to maintain contact with other welfare groups and to keep CAMP's service under the attention of other agencies.[37] Not only did the executive not explain what was 'specifically gay' about welfare organisations, but neither did they appear to be aware of the unfortunate consequences of associating CAMP with the 'mental health' professions, whose reason for exist-ence lies in the purported *absence* of 'mental health' in their clientele. It cannot be suggested that the executive of CAMP intended to imply that its members suffered from a lack of 'mental health', although the current emphasis on counselling implies that the problems are pre-dominantly personal ones. But the association of a homosexual organisation with a 'mental health' organisation carries the implication that homosexuality is still a 'mental illness'. Such a solecism is the price paid for the abandonment of a political perspective.

Depending on the criteria used to make the judgement, CAMP NSW can be seen as either a success or a failure. On conventional criteria, it must be regarded as a success. It is Australia's longest-lived homosexual organisation, having been continuously in existence since 1970 (despite the current membership's repudiation of their history). It has achieved social recognition, and can justifiably be said to represent the interests of large numbers of homosexual men. But in terms of gay liberation,[38] it eventually failed by giving up any attempt to bring about social change and settling for social recognition and conformity with conventional standards.

And perhaps that was inevitable, given the contradictions faced by any group which proposes alternatives to the status quo. As Robyn Kennedy pointed out in her letter of resignation in 1978, despite a number of attempts to do otherwise, CAMP consistently adhered to conventional modes of organising, and using conventional methods to achieve radical aims involves a dilemma which is compounded by the likelihood that unconventional methods don't work either.

There is a kind of inevitability about CAMP's progressive return to the bosom of society, which cannot be explained by reference to the machinations of misguided or mischievous individuals. There were, after all, machinations on both sides, but every attempt by radicals to reverse the conservative trend failed. The suspicion arises that a social critique based on (male) homosexuality as a material basis of oppression is limited, that once it has demonstrated that discrimination exists and is unjustifiable, it has gone as far as it can go. By asking such a question it is not intended to imply that the gay liberation enterprise was ill-conceived from the outset. On the contrary, unless the anachronistic rubbish had been cleared away, it would not be possible to ask the kinds of questions we are asking now. But the 'clearing away' was taken further by gay liberation and lesbian-feminism that it was by CAMP.

2

SYDNEY
GAY
LIBERATION

THE history of CAMP was not the whole of the history of the gay movement. Indeed, in the early days there were those who argued that CAMP did not even belong to the movement. At least some of CAMP's critics saw its role as at best peripheral to the real issues of gay liberation, at worst, as a pandering to the very social forces responsible for the oppression of homosexuals. Either way, CAMP's link with the gay movement was regarded as tenuous. It was this kind of criticism which lay behind the antagonism between CAMP and Sydney Gay Liberation (SGL), although it was not confined to that context, nor did it completely divorce the two organisations, which shifted in and out of an uneasy alliance during the whole of the time SGL existed as an identifiable group.

However, the earliest of the criticisms did not emanate from SGL, but from a group calling themselves 'The Gay Liberation Front—a group of male and female radical homosexuals and bisexuals'. This group produced a roneoed handout, entitled 'Gay Is Good'. The title was taken from a paper by Martha Shelley, an American gay activist (Jay and Young, 1972), although the handout did not reproduce

Shelley's work. It began by expressing agreement with a statement attributed to David Cooper (author of *Death of the Family* and various other radical and anti-psychiatry manifestoes), to the effect that revolutionaries must be prepared to meet violence. As the authors of the 'Gay Is Good' handout put it:

> That statement has relevance not only to the struggles of those who are suffering sexual oppression, but also the entire struggle against the oppressive culture (moral codes, values, ethics and standards of behaviour) that goes with it ... What we demand is a radical transformation of society by violent revolution.

(Despite the brave rhetoric, this advocacy of 'violence in the streets' was subsequently shown to be due more to a propensity for whistling in the dark than to a plan for concerted action.) The authors went on to pour scorn on campaigns against the laws penalising male homosexual acts:

> We don't give a stuff about legalising homosexuality because the social institutions (e.g. organised religion) which perpetuate intolerance of us will still exist ... Working for homosexual law reform legitimises the status quo by allowing that the state or anybody has the right to be in any way concerned with our sex life.

The main target of their anger (apart from the 'oppressive culture') was CAMP Inc.:

> The Gay Liberation Front doesn't recognise CAMP Inc. as being a viable body capable of meaningful action. The aims, organisation and methods and apparent philosophical basis for CAMP Inc. are completely contained within the system as it exists. They have no social programme beyond the immediate realisation of their own insular ends. They don't see attitudes that exist towards homosexuals as being an evil symptom of an evil society. To them it is just a fault to be corrected.[1]

The group which called itself Sydney Gay Liberation held views largely in accord with these sentiments, although their expression of them, at least in their published work, was somewhat more temperate in language, probably because of the need to maintain some links, however uneasy, with CAMP. SGL had a much shorter history than that of CAMP—from the beginning of 1972, when it first defined itself as an identifiable group, to the beginning of 1974, when it ceased to exist in any organised form. It started out as a 'consciousness-raising cell' within CAMP in the latter half of 1971. Dennis Altman described the need for such a function within CAMP, in a letter printed in the August 1971 issue of *CAMP Ink*. He said:

> It is my belief that for the moment the main focus of CAMP Inc. needs to be on its membership itself. John [Ware] said at the last meeting that he

believes we need some consciousness-raising, that is some explanation of the homosexual experience, both individual and social. I agree strongly. Until we have come to terms with ourselves, we cannot ask society to change its attitudes.

By January 1972, the group was identifying itself as 'Gay Liberation', although still within the ambit of CAMP's function as an umbrella organisation. Their first autonomous 'coming out' was at the Sex Lib Forum at Sydney University on 19 January. At the Forum it was announced by Dennis thus (in response to cheers from the audience at his mention of gay liberation):

> As they have now identified themselves by the process of exhibitionism which, as we all know, is the hallmark of homosexuals, you will of course be aware that Gay Liberation has come out not only in Sydney but also in Australia.[2]

But by July of that year, when the first issue of the *Sydney Gay Liberation Newsletter* appeared, SGL had separated from CAMP, and had its headquarters at 67 Glebe Point Road, largely because the mutual (if muted) antagonism between the two groups had made it difficult to continue operating under the same roof. Admittedly, CAMP and SGL did continue to show a united front on a number of occasions. During 1972, for example, they combined to form a joint contingent at the Women's Day march in March; in July, members of CAMP joined SGL's protest at the banning of the ABC's TDT segment on gay liberation, and SGL joined in with CAMP's demonstration during Sex Lib week; and in November, SGL supported CAMP's protest outside St Clement's Church, Mosman, at the sacking of Peter Bonsall-Boone. In 1973 both groups, along with Women's Liberation, protested at the 'Psychiatry and Liberation' Conference at Prince Henry Hospital. Despite the split it was obvious that the interests and activities of the two groups overlapped.

In October 1972, CAMP made two suggestions for a closer working relationship. John Ware, who was still editor of *CAMP Ink*, suggested that SGL might produce a gay liberation issue of the journal; and Lex Watson and Sue Wills suggested that SGL might like to provide a representative on CAMP's executive.[3] Neither suggestion was taken up, however. One reason why the first did not eventuate was straightforward—SGL members were flat out producing their own publications. The reason for SGL's failure to respond to the second proposal was less obvious, although it was probably partly due to a reluctance on the part of the gay liberationists to involve themselves in what they saw as hierarchical structures ('the executive'), and partly to organisational problems within SGL itself.

Whatever the reasons, the relationship between the two groups during 1973 continued to be ad hoc and sporadic. SGL was involved with Phone-A-Friend at the beginning,[4] although that involvement was brief—when SGL moved into 33a Glebe Point Road in August 1973, they set up their own phone service. SGL had also briefly shared the premises at 10 David Street with CAMP early in 1973; and CAMP was eventually to move into 33a Glebe Point Road at the end of the year, when SGL was struggling to continue as a group and having difficulty keeping the centre going.

Nevertheless, despite these attempts to work together, the antagonism between the two groups was clear enough. And despite common interests and joint activities, the two were never to reamalgamate, even after the demise of SGL as a structured group. What was not so clear, however, was the basis of that antagonism. There was certainly a feeling among gay liberationists that CAMP was 'reformist', even 'conservative', and SGL was 'radical'. But what this meant in practice was not evident at first sight, since both groups at times engaged in similar, even identical, activities. The difference was partly one of style. CAMP Inc.'s initial reluctance to adopt unquestioningly the methods of the American movement was interpreted by gay liberationists as a reluctance to engage in the more radical forms of political activism. Gay liberationists preferred to shock 'the straights' into an awareness of their existence, to 'zap' the public rather than to engage in rational discourse.

To a certain extent, the two different ways of approaching the issue of homosexual liberation rested on two different reactions to the fact of homosexual oppression. CAMP Inc.'s conciliatory posture in relation to 'the wider society' was in sharp contrast to the anger of the gay liberationists, who wanted to challenge, not placate, a social order which had wreaked such havoc in the lives of homosexuals:

> Homosexuals who have been oppressed by physical violence and ideological and psychological attacks at every level of social interaction, are at last becoming angry. To you, our gay sisters and brothers, we say that you are oppressed; we intend to show you examples of the hatred and fear with which straight society relegates us to the position and treatment of sub-humans, and to explain their basis.

> Look out, straights! here comes the Gay Liberation Front. . . We are the extrusions of your unconscious mind—your worst fears made flesh. . . We want you to be uneasy, to be a little less comfortable in your straight roles.[5]

But more importantly, the antagonism between the two groups rested on a difference in their analyses of the reasons why homosexuals were oppressed. CAMP's analysis was implicit rather than spelled out in detail, and had to be inferred from statements about aims and policies. It was not surprising, then, that it did not go beyond a vaguely formulated feeling that there was 'something wrong' with society. In the busy efficiency of getting things done, CAMP failed to provide an adequate political rationale for their activities. This inadequacy sometimes led to errors of strategy—for example, the continuing reliance on conventional organisational procedures, and the importance placed on counselling—which compounded to produce CAMP's present orientation.

In contrast, gay liberation's chief concern was the development of an analysis of the political implications of homosexuality, that is, of the connections between homosexuality and social relations of power. (Whether or not they succeeded in this task is another question altogether. At least they tried.) Starting from personal experiences of oppression, gay liberationists argued that the suppression of homosexuality served certain functions in the maintenance of an oppressive social order, and that therefore the struggle against that suppression, exemplified in 'coming out' and 'gay pride', was inherently revolutionary—'by being who we are, we are in fact revolutionary'[6] The first step in the struggle was to turn the 'problem of homosexuality' on its head. From being a problem which 'society' had with the pathological, sinful or criminal individual, homosexuality in the gay liberationist account became a problem which homosexual individuals had with the 'oppressive society'. Up to this point, CAMP participated in the gay liberation enterprise, and played its part in the redefinition process. But CAMP played no part in the theoretical enterprise of investigating the reasons for homosexual oppression (although from 1975 onwards at least, CAMP's activists did attempt to introduce such an analysis into their practice—their eventual fate is detailed in chapter 1).

It was for this reason that gay liberationists were unable to rest content with small-l 'liberal tolerance'—'what people do in the privacy of their own homes is their own business'. In part the gay liberationist unease with this stance stemmed from the fact that it ignored the whole history of homosexual persecution—as one gay liberationist put it: 'It's too late for tolerance.' But more importantly, it left no room for questions about the origins of homosexual oppression, since it defined the social condemnation of homosexuals as a manifestation of personal prejudice, and its rectification as a matter of individual goodwill.

The best known of the gay liberationist accounts was Dennis Altman's book, *Homosexual: Oppression and Liberation*. Although the best known—because it was produced commercially, (fairly) widely publicised, and available in bookshops—its ideas were less influential than might have been expected, given how eagerly its release in

Australia was awaited. That may have been because of the complexity of the argument (he was accused by one critic of being 'too erudite'), along with his reliance on Freudian libidinal theory as interpreted by Herbert Marcuse. Freud had argued that 'civilisation' (what we call 'society') depended for its continuing existence on the sublimation of erotic feelings between men, that is, on the transformation of the overtly erotic into other kinds of relationships between men—what Lionel Tiger called 'male-bonding'. ,('Civilisation' in Freud's account was exclusively male.) If this was so, then, Marcuse argued, male homosexuality posed an intrinsic threat to 'civilisation', because it undermined the barriers which functioned to divert the erotic into other more productive channels. (Marcuse did not think this was a bad thing. Since he agreed with the Marxist critique of capitalist 'civilisation', he was in favour of the male homosexual potential for subverting that particular social order.)

Dennis did not wholly agree with the Marcusan analysis. For one thing, it concentrated on male homosexuality and ignored lesbianism, and hence failed to consider the subversive potential posed by homosexuals of both sexes to procreative sexuality. Moreover, Dennis argued, it is not necessarily homosexuality per se which had revolutionary implications, since it was as much a repression of one side of our original bisexual disposition (according to Freud) as was heterosexuality. It was revolutionary only to the extent that it exposed the one-sidedness of the conservative belief in the 'naturalness' of heterosexuality, and pointed the way to a return to bisexuality. 'It may be the historic function of the homosexual,' he wrote, 'to overcome this particular form of repression [of the bisexual potential], and bring to its logical conclusion the Freudian belief in our inherent bisexuality.'

He was not recommending that every homosexual should immediately go out and 'practise' the other side of his or her bisexual 'potential'. His own disastrous attempts to establish sexual relationships with women were too recent (as he described in the book) for him to suggest any such thing. He explicitly denied that he was 'advocating bi-sexuality as an ideal', or that he was saying that 'you should rush off and have sex with someone to prove something'. Moreover, he himself regarded his homosexuality as 'an integral part of my self-identity'.[7]

But if he was not recommending that, then what *were* the implications of his analysis for immediate tactics? What *were* gay liberationists to do if the revolution was bisexual? To that question there seemed to be no answer. The only possible response was to reject Dennis's account, or at least the 'bisexuality' aspects of it, since to accept it weakened the case for 'gay pride'. As one writer put it:

> The issue of our supposed bisexual potential is really a red herring ... [Gay Liberation]'s strategy and priorities are in question over this issue ... The aim of sexual freedom for all will not be realised ... [until gay liberation] has first formed a new identity that is proud, non-apologetic, aggressive and cohesive ... There is no substitute for homosexuals working for their own liberation, without it there will simply be no revolution.[8]

This writer was not arguing specifically against Dennis, but against what he called the 'human–sexual' argument, the weakness of which was that 'it neglects the here-and-now by glossing over the real differences in people's sexual practices'. Nevertheless, it is possible that objections such as these lay behind the reluctance to accept Dennis's analysis unreservedly. Apart from Dennis's argument, the 'bisexuality' theme was a popular theoretical catch-all in the early days of gay liberation. Martha Shelley's 'Gay Is Good' asserted that both heterosexuals and homosexuals were deprived of their inherent bisexual potential by the rigidity of gender-role conditioning—'you cut off your homosexuality—and we cut off our heterosexuality'. The theme was repeated in SGL's first handout: 'We base our analysis on the idea ... of wo/man's basic polymorphous sexuality, and in particular of our basic bisexuality. WE ARE ALL STRAIGHT, WE ARE ALL GAY.'

The most influential document to appear during the early days of gay liberation was 'A Gay Liberation Manifesto'. Produced originally by the London Gay Liberation Front, it was reproduced by SGL, by Melbourne Gay Liberation (without any prior consultation with Sydney), and throughout the gay movement in New Zealand and the United Kingdom.[9] It did not have the same popularity in the United States, possibly because it incorporated a Marxist analysis (of a kind). This perspective Dennis deliberately excluded from his own account for a number of reasons, not the least of which was the antagonism with which both communist regimes, and Left organisations in capitalist countries, had always regarded homosexuality: 'Experience with both Old and New Lefts have tended to make many gays feel they need to be anarchists; any regime, no matter what its ideology, will tend to persecute them.'

However, as things turned out, it was the Marxist analysis which provided the most adequate account of sexual relations of power. The Manifesto was one of the earliest of these accounts. According to this document, the revolutionary implications of 'gay pride' lay in the threat it posed to 'our society's most basic institution—the Patriarchal Family'. (Dennis was inclined to see it the other way around—both the breakdown in the nuclear family and the rise of the gay and women's movements were 'related to the impact of technology and resultant social and cultural change'.) However that may be, the

Manifesto went on to argue that 'gay pride's' threat to the family was based on the threat it posed to 'sexism', that is, to 'constructed patterns of "masculine" and "feminine" . . . the two stereotyped roles into which everyone is supposed to fit'. It was 'sexism', according to the account in the Manifesto, which ensured that (nearly) everyone ended up heterosexual and married. It was not, of course, always successful—'if it were, there would be no gay people for a start'. It was the need to maintain 'sexism', it was argued, which was behind the oppression of homosexuals, because they were living examples that the differences between the sexes were not natural and universal.

But, the Manifesto continued, not only did sexism ensure the continuation of the nuclear family—the nuclear family ensured the continuation of sexism, in a mutually reinforcing cycle, as the family reproduced sex roles in each succeeding generation. Sexism was not just an accident, but an essential part of 'our present society', and the elimination of sexism demanded a total restructuring of that society. For the differences between the sexes were a result of, and functioned to reinforce, the male-dominated society which had given rise to the 'patriarchal family'. This form of the family played an essential part in the maintenance of 'the present system of work and production'. The 'small family unit of two parents and their children' functioned to provide a private sphere of nurturance and support for the male breadwinner so that he could continue to work in the alienating environment of the production process. The 'captive wife', isolated in the private home, also contributed to the proper functioning of the economic system, by consuming manufactured goods at a far higher rate than was necessary for the satisfaction of 'genuine' human needs. (For a commentary on the sexist nature of this analysis, see chapter 3.)

Analyses such as the above entailed a number of strategies for the abolition of the 'sexist, male supremacist system' (as the Manifesto put it). Because of the theoretical link made by gay liberation between the oppression of women and the oppression of male homosexuals, the most immediately obvious strategy was to work with Women's Liberation to 'advance the day of our common liberation'. But although SGL, CAMP and Women's Liberation did appear together on a number of occasions, this strategy eventually failed. (Some reasons for that failure are suggested in chapter 3.)

But the most pressing task for gay liberationists was to divest themselves of their continuing implication in their own oppression, to 'free our heads'. A number of examples of this 'self-oppression' were given in the Manifesto:

> Self-oppression is achieved when the gay person has adopted and
> internalised straight people's definition of what is 'good' and 'bad'. Or

doing what you most need and want to do, but with a sense of shame and loathing, or in a state of dissociation, pretending it isn't happening, going on the beat not because you enjoy it, but because you are afraid of anything less anonymous. Self-oppression is saying: 'I accept what I am is second-best and rather pathetic'. Self-oppression is any other kind of apology: 'We've been living together for ten years and all our married friends know about us and think we're just the same as them'. Why? You are not.

Self-oppression is the dolly lesbian who says: 'I can't stand those butch types who look like truck drivers'; the virile gay man who shakes his head at the thought of 'those poor pathetic queens'. This is self-oppression because it's just another way of saying: 'I'm a nice normal gay, just like an attractive heterosexual'. The ultimate in self-oppression is to avoid confronting straight society, and thereby provoking further hostility. Self-oppression is saying and believing: 'I am not oppressed'.

Dennis Altman suggested a number of other examples: the hostility which many homosexuals felt towards a gay movement which threatened to upset their lives by bringing the issue of homosexuality into the arena of public debate; the tendency of male homosexuals to 'objectify' each other, that is, to avoid relating on any level but the physical, and to evaluate each other in terms of desirable physical characteristics such as youth and beauty; the 'passing for straight' which went beyond the need for self-preservation and the protection of families and careers, which was based on self-deception and self-denial, and which was the result of succumbing to a crippling, irrational fear; and finally, huddling together in the 'pseudo-community' of the commercial 'bar scene', which served to isolate and contain homosexuals as effectively as any suburban 'closet'.

Given this initial impetus towards collective self-knowledge, an obvious organisational tactic was the 'consciousness-raising' (CR) group (a device adopted from Women's Liberation). But that was not the only reason for the emphasis on CR groups—as self-confessed radicals, gay liberationists distrusted conventional organisational structures, which they believed led to hierarchical divisions of power and responsibility. In an attempt to avoid that eventuality, SGL organised around small groups: CR groups, action groups for specific tasks, and special-interest groups, along with a regular general meeting where issues were discussed and activities were proposed and decided on. From the beginning, everyone was expected to become involved in the general business of the organisation, such as answering the ubiquitous correspondence, helping with the production of the *Newsletter*, organising working bees, taking turns on the phone, and generally initiating and carrying out whatever needed to be done.

Not that this loose organisational structure was entirely successful in avoiding the problem of the concentration of responsibility in the hands of the few. The workload still tended to fall on the shoulders of the most willing and enthusiastic members. In an article in the second issue of the *Newsletter*, for example, John Lee criticised the membership for acquiescing in 'the perpetuation of a system of de facto leaders', by allowing SGL to 'depend on a few people to meet any agreed ends'. Not only did this have 'destructive emotional effects' on those who were forced to adopt leadership roles, he argued—he himself had found that he was 'relating to the "non-initiators" in veiled authoritarian terms (sometimes not too veiled either)'. But it was also counter-productive for one of the main aims of the group as a whole, which was to work in alternative, anti-authoritarian ways. He went on to say:

> I came to Gay Lib *assuming* like everyone else that we were by our very nature anti-authoritarian, we didn't want appointed leaders (cf CAMP), that our developments would arise 'spontaneously'. Concomitant with this belief was my assumption that most people in the group were responsible for where they were consciously at . . . Oh, what naive idealism on my part.

It was no use paying lip-service to anti-authoritarian ideals, he continued, unless something concrete was done to make those ideals work in practice. The argument that leaders inevitably arise in any group was defeatist, because the ending of homosexual oppression was dependent on 'taking responsibility for our own lives'. As a first step in handing back responsibility to the members, John announced that he was withdrawing for the time being.[10] In the short term, it appeared that this criticism had had the desired effect. Things continued to get done, and in the next month at least, no new leaders emerged to take the places vacated by John and the other 'initiators'.[11]

The acquisition of self-knowledge and the clarifying of organisational problems were not the only preoccupations of SGL. A third task was to 'provide a basis for a coherent attack on institutionalised oppression' (to quote John Lee again). This involved a number of public activities, some of which have already been mentioned in connection with the joint CAMP–SGL actions. SGL's first action (mentioned above) was to make their presence felt at the Sex Lib Forum at Sydney University on 19 January 1972. At the Forum, SGL presented their views on sexual liberation in a leaflet which said in part:

> Gay Liberation is an attempt by gay men and women to free ourselves as individuals from our own hang-ups and to bring to an end the direct oppression from our society: the beatings and the murders, the police harassment and imprisonment, the job discrimination. Gay Liberation

challenges not only traditional sex roles, where it is linked with Women's Lib, but together with other liberation movements of students, radicals, hippies and blacks, it refuses to accept the traditional standards of establishment capitalism . . . Gay Liberation wants to get away from possessiveness, elitism, inflexible roles and personal inequality. We want to define a new pluralistic, role-free social structure for ourselves. It must contain both the freedom and physical space for people to live alone, live together for a while or a long time, either as couples or in large numbers. Liberation for gay people is defining for ourselves how and with whom we live, instead of measuring our relationships in comparison with straight values. We must be free to live our own lives in our own way.

SGL's first demonstration was held in July, outside the offices of the ABC. On 2 July, 'This Day Tonight' had filmed a sequence on gay liberation at the launching of Dennis Altman's book, and the sequence had been banned, sight unseen, by the General Manager of the ABC. The launching and its aftermath were described in the *SGL Newsletter* thus:

And then Dennis released his book, we said let's go to the launching in that brilliant gender confusion drag. Only the Austrine Party and Angus and Robertson didn't understand and said do you fags have much trouble buying your makeup. So we laughed a little nervously and said well gosh we don't normally wear it, we're sending up stereotyped sex roles and showing how everyone can be beautiful in makeup and drag and all. So 'This Day Tonight' said great, get these gay lib people on camera and we'll have a great show, maybe not for the whole family but for our Austrine Party liberals and small-p poofters. Except they never showed the film on the box and we said look how oppressed we queens are in this rotten country. The ABC's a shit and let's demonstrate and tell them so.[12]

At the demonstration, SGL argued that the banning of the gay liberation segment was a reinforcement of that ignorance which perpetuated prejudice against homosexuals, and the harassment, violence and humiliation which that prejudice generated.

The ban remained, but the demonstration received fairly wide coverage. As one of the participants reported it in the *Newsletter*:

Coverage that night was great, the ABC reporting with the same blandness that they would report a semi-trailer running into a butcher shop along Parramatta Road. TCN9's 'A Current Affair' was the best of all with interviews from passers-by and Mike Willesee's usual impartial innuendo. TEN 10 was downright cynical but at least we made it. (Which means they shouldn't have any qualms about screening us in future.)"

Sydney Gay Liberation was not the only gay liberation group in Sydney—there was also a group at each of the three universities. On 8 August the group at the University of NSW held a street theatre

46

demonstration against the use of aversion therapy. It began in the Roundhouse at lunchtime with a dramatisation of electric shock therapy administered by 'The Man from McConaghy', who was finally vanquished by the 'Good Gay Lib Fairy'. The demonstration then moved to the library lawn where the performance was repeated, and the students were told about the use of aversion therapy, the implication of the university in that practice, and the negative way homosexuality was treated in courses.

One of the activities in which SGL joined with CAMP was the demonstration in November in protest at the sacking of Peter Bonsall-Boone. The account of the demonstration which John Lee gave in the *SGL Newsletter* illustrated the different styles of the two groups. Whereas the account in *CAMP Ink* simply described the demonstration and concentrated on the positive fact that it had been held at all, John's account reflected the bitterness at the social ostracism of homosexuals that permeated the gay liberation approach. He said:

> It was all fairly low key—deliberately so . . . it was argued beforehand that if the protest had been very zappy, the 'christians' of Mosman would have felt completely vindicated. 'See what they are like' . . . I doubt that we need have worried. The look of disgust that passed across many a parishioner's face entering the church as we politely attempted to hand them leaflets explaining our protest (which they duly refused) indicated that *the very fact that we were homosexual* made us in their eyes members of the shit-heap of humanity. One woman parishioner, with child who was upset by all the goings-on: 'Don't be upset . . . don't look at them, dear, they're unnatural'!

By the end of 1972 it had become clear that SGL's organisational problems had not gone away. In November, a position paper was prepared by the Publications Group for a 'gay caucus', called 'Towards a Workable Sydney Gay Liberation'. The paper put forward a number of suggestions to improve matters: that the 'gay caucuses' should continue fortnightly as the general gathering of SGL members, and should include a discussion paper around a specific topic as well as providing a forum for collective decision-making; that the Publications Group should be responsible for printing and distributing the papers, along with their current task of producing the *Newsletter* and other sundry publications; that a specific task group should be formed to deal with administrative matters and the running of the Centre rather than relying on the general meetings and the roster system; and that the principle of small groups as the 'primary units' of SGL should be reasserted.

But these suggestions were to have no permanent effect. Some discussions were held on: psychiatry, the law, anti-homosexual values, the gay movement in Australia, the connections between gay liberation, Black Power, and Women's Liberation. But they soon petered out. And the 'initiators' remained few, despite an influx of new people at the end of 1972 and the beginning of 1973. The Publications Group was almost non-existent by December (although its demise was not permanent). And the problem of running the Centre soon became academic anyway, because SGL had to move out of 67 Glebe Point Road at the beginning of 1973, and was not to have another centre until they moved into 33a Glebe Point Road in August.

Nevertheless, things continued to get done. In December, a Gay Liberation Weekend was held at Minto. It would appear to have been an exhilarating experience, at least for the men. In the words of one of the participants:

> Two years ago, the idea of eighty [male?] homosexuals gathering together for a weekend in the country would have meant only one thing: a non-stop drunken orgy with guilt-ridden sex. But last weekend, we all came together to discuss and talk about ourselves and society freely and sensibly. It was like an extended Thursday night meeting, only much better.

Another participant called the weekend 'a great milestone' in his life, because he had 'learned in a few hours that it is possible to love a group of people with a depth and power previously beyond my conception'. He concluded:

> Gay Liberation must remain a working and viable group, we must support it in every way we possibly can. We must be totally committed to this. Every homosexual who is able to must stand up and be counted. We shall not live our lives in closets.[13]

And despite the problems, 1973 was SGL's most successful year in terms of activities and visibility. Those activities included: a staged public display of affection between men by the members of the 'Zap Group' on the underground trains of the City Circle one Saturday morning in January; orientation week activities at all three universities; leafleting bars to protest at specific incidents, and to make the gay liberation presence felt; holding monthly dances; and handing out leaflets at a school.

In the last case, the Zap Group prepared and distributed a leaflet called 'Are You a Poofter?'. The purpose behind this action was twofold: to present school students with the idea that homosexuality was a valid alternative sexual preference, and to inform homosexual students about SGL; and secondly, to provoke a public reaction and media coverage in order to publicise the existence and aims of gay liberation (on the premise that the only bad publicity is no publicity). As Terry Bell explained it in his comments on the leaflet:

> to date, when Gay Lib sought publicity it spoke for itself about itself—in the eyes of straights, pooftas screaming their tits off about their dirty habits. We felt that by zapping a sufficiently sensitive straight institution, we could provoke a number of straights into doing the screaming for us.[14]

The ploy worked. The mother of one of the students who received a leaflet complained to the Department of Education, the police, and the media; and the Zap Group's action received coverage in the *Daily Mirror* and on TDT. However, some SGL members were not at all happy with what could be seen as a cynical exploitation of school students for gay liberation's own purposes. In response to this criticism, Terry admitted its cogency, but pointed out that 'SGL's opposition to the oppressive conditioning of students is sincere', and that the leaflet was a genuine attempt 'to reassure any students who may have felt attracted to members of their own sex, that such feelings were not aberrant'. Whether or not this disclaimer allayed the disquiet was not recorded.

In May, SGL and the gay lib groups at the University of NSW and Sydney University, and Sydney University's Campus CAMP, joined Women's Liberation in boycotting the May Day march, in protest at the May Day Committee's holding a 'Ms May Day' competition as a fund-raising event. (Despite the pseudo-feminist 'Ms', the competition was as sexist as any 'beauty queen' contest where women are judged for their value as desirable sex objects for men.) At the rally in the Domain after the march, two gay liberationists were refused permission by officials to address the crowd from the platform. But a group of feminists, who approached the officials with the same request, refused to be dismissed, even by police, and demanded to speak. In the face of the crowd's support for the women's right to speak, the officials removed the microphones from the platform. This action did not deter Gillian Leahy from reading out a statement explaining Women's Liberation's opposition to the competition. When she had finished, other speakers from the crowd also addressed the audience, including Craig Johnston who spoke on behalf of gay liberation.[15] Subsequently, the Committee agreed to drop the term 'Ms May Day' in favour of 'Most Popular May Day Candidate'. As Craig pointed out, the Sydney Trade Union Club always won anyway, because it always raised the most money.

The gay liberation group at Macquarie University was provided with two opportunities during 1973 for 'coming out' and educating the campus about homosexual oppression. The first of these incidents happened in March, and followed on the election for the president of the Students' Representative Council. The gay liberation candidate, Jeff Hayler, won the election, narrowly defeating his closest rival by one vote. The next issue of *Arena*, the student newspaper, carried a vitriolic denunciation of Jeff, chiefly on the grounds of his professed homosexuality. This article was unsigned, but the editor of *Arena* was that same rival, who was subsequently forced by the outraged reaction at his misuse of the position to acknowledge his authorship publicly and to resign.

The second opportunity occurred with the expulsion of Jeremy Fisher, the group's treasurer, from the Robert Menzies residential college. While Jeremy was away in hospital, the Master of the College, the Reverend Dr Alan Cole, discovered while he was packing Jeremy's belongings that he was treasurer of Macquarie University Gay Liberation. When Jeremy returned, Dr Cole asked him if he was merely an altruistic crusader, or if he had a deeper, more personal reason for his involvement with gay liberation. When Jeremy told him that the latter was the case, Dr Cole insisted, as a condition of his re-entry to the College, that Jeremy lead a celibate life and seek help to have his 'perversion' 'cured'. Jeremy refused, and was expelled. As a consequence, the student representative on the University Council, the governing body of the university, proposed a motion that the College be disaffiliated, because it was infringing one of the university by-laws which stated that 'A college shall not impose any religious test as a condition of membership of the college'. (Dr Cole's reasons for expelling Jeremy was that his homosexual behaviour was contrary to God's law.) The Builders Labourers' Federation voted for a work ban on the still uncompleted College. And Gay Liberation held a demonstration to coincide with the University Council meeting at which the censure motion was put. Jeremy was not reinstated, but by that time he had no desire to return to the College anyway.

In August, SGL 'zapped' the 'Psychiatry and Liberation' conference at Prince Henry Hospital. In January, SGL had received a letter from Dr McConaghy inviting members to send a speaker to the conference. However, along with CAMP and Women's Liberation, they had resolved not to take part 'in a conference, the terms and structure of which had been determined by shrinks who are members of a social institution—psychiatry—which has been and remains a major force in the oppression of homosexuals and women'. In a joint reply, the three groups pointed out that they would take part in the conference only on condition that they were involved in the planning stages, and that the conference was open to everyone. They received no reply. When the time for the conference came around, some members of SGL decided at a moment's notice that some further

50

protest, apart from a boycott, needed to be made. In the tea-break before the session on 'Homosexual Movements', they distributed throughout the hall copies of the 'Intellectual Poofter Bashers' issue of *CAMP Ink*, and a leaflet explaining why gay liberationists had refused to participate in the debate:

> We're just not prepared to come along and 'rationally' debate our position with our oppressors. No, we're fed up with that. We're sick of being reasonable anymore when the oppressive horrors of aversion therapy, psychosurgery and neo-Freudian bullshit psychotherapy continue to fuck us over . . . For you are all guilty as oppressors—even if you disapprove/feel repugnance at aversion therapy or psychosurgery . . . Your profession INVENTED the idea that homosexuality is some form of mental illness and there is nothing to suggest that that idea is radically being challenged within your profession.

And nothing in Dr McConaghy's talk challenged the 'homosexuality = mental illness' equation either. According to John Lee's account of the session in the August *Newsletter*, the main theme of that talk was a parallel Dr McConaghy drew between himself and Galileo, both of whom, he asserted, were champions of scientific truth against the forces of darkness and ignorance—in Galileo's case,those forces were represented by the sixteenth-century Catholic Church; in his own case, by the irrational hordes of liberationists of all kinds. John's account continued:

> We began to argue with him from the back of the theatre . . . He alternated between answering and continuing his incredible speech. We flew black and pink balloons all over the auditorium. His speech went on: we had 'no right to speak for other homosexuals—why weren't there any of his former patients amongst us?' (We screamed that there were, but he wouldn't listen) . . . We were 'not only arrogant but also very irrational, and yes, even disturbed'. So we let him have it with the eggs we'd grabbed on the way to the conference. One dozen nice fresh eggs splattered on the walls around him (only one.of us managed a direct hit). Turmoil had broken out, some members of the audience having by this stage been drawn into the shouting match. We were rapidly ejected by the back door. (No cops, it wouldn't have fitted in with the heroic struggle of the liberal humanists.)[16]

During 1973, an attempt was made to set up a national newspaper along the lines of the Canadian paper, *Body Politic*, which was to be called *Radical Homosexual*. The impetus for the project came from SGL, but the intention was to produce the paper in Melbourne, because rents were lower, and because the Melbourne people who had expressed interest in the project appeared to have already acquired much of the necessary expertise. In late March a group of Sydney people came together to form the nucleus of a collective which was intended to work full-time on the production of the paper. In May a fund-raising dance was held at Paddington Town Hall. Armed with an initial capital of $700 the Sydney collective arrived in Melbourne. But the project failed. The reasons why it did so are unclear. In his account of the venture, John Lee refused to give specific details, on the grounds that it would be 'irrelevant' and 'boring', and that, as a participant, he would only give a biased account. Instead, he referred in general terms to 'the alienation, suspicion and lack of trust that appears to plague virtually the whole gay liberation movement', and the continuing need for 'a lot more consciousness-raising, a lot more close examining of what we are really on about'. The money was returned to the donors, and the collective disbanded.[17]

While they had been away in Melbourne, those who stayed behind were busily organising Gay Pride Week, to be held from 8–15 September. The events of that week were to prove the highlight of SGL's career. The first event was a 'Speak Out' on Saturday, 8 September. Its intended purpose was described by Terry Bell, one of the chief organisers of the Week, thus:

> Our gay brothers and sisters will be telling each other about their oppression: this is still one of the greatest problems we face, seeing oppression as something we suffer individually, with no consciousness of the agonies of our sisters and brothers, and thus no powerful motivation to fight together with the assurance of unity . . . this reluctance [to 'speak out'] is founded in the feeling that when we are persecuted . . . we stand alone. Which is a feeling that can only prolong the oppression of gays at all levels . . . It is only our isolation from each other that is ultimately holding us down. And so, it is not others who must be prepared to stand with us, it is ourselves. We are kindred of oppression, and should realise this, offering our individual experience and resources in the struggle for liberation . . . We must be proud, we must be angry, to throw off the self-image that straight society has fucked us with.[18]

The feeling expressed in that article was to be intensified by the events of the march on 15 September, at the end of the Week. What happened on that march was reported both in the conventional media and the student press.[19] All the accounts were agreed on the following: that the demonstration numbered over 200, that it started at the Town Hall just after 10.00 am on Saturday morning and proceeded to Martin Plaza to lay a wreath on the Cenotaph, that there a violent confrontation occurred between police and demonstrators and a number of demonstrators were arrested, and that it finished with a rally in Hyde Park. There the agreement ended. According to the account in *Honi Soit*, the Sydney University student newspaper, the police had tried to prevent the march leaving Town Hall, and when the marchers arrived at Martin Plaza they were confronted with '8 paddy wagons, 4 busloads of police cadets and 2 black mariahs [sic]'. According to the account in *Arena*, the Macquarie University student paper, the police attacked the marchers before they left Town Hall—'they kicked one or two of us then'. The violence continued at Market Street corner—'they were bashing up a cameraman there'. At Martin Plaza, 'four or five [police] leapt onto [one man] . . . A burly sergeant knocked over a little girl . . . Six of them . . . punched [a man] to the ground. Pulled his hair, kicked him'. Fourteen people were arrested in Martin Plaza, and three more outside Phillip Street Police Station. The conventional press described the events somewhat differently. The *Sun* reported a ' "Gay Lib" Brawl at Cenotaph', referred to a 'mock wreath' which the demonstrators intended to lay on the Cenotaph, described the melee in Martin Plaza as 'a series of scuffles', and accused the demonstrators of shouting 'indecent words' outside the police station. The *Sunday Mirror* reported that the demonstrators 'jeered at police', 'used megaphones to express contempt of the police', and finally 'dispersed after a rowdy anti-police meeting in Hyde Park'.

But the catharsis of Gay Pride Week could neither solve the perennial organisational problems nor heal the splits between the divergent interests and needs and the differing views of what gay liberation was about. Once again, on 20 October, an all-day meeting was held in yet another attempt to come to grips with the issues. Once again, a number of suggestions were made with the aim of revitalising the organisation. One of the suggestions was to do away with the 'lived-in Centre' which had served a coordinating function for SGL since their move into 33a Glebe Point Road. It was felt that this arrangement had placed an undue burden on those who lived on the premises, as well as creating the impression that the residents *were* 'the movement'. At the meeting, it was decided to disband SGL as a single organisation, and replace it with a 'services group' called Gay Liberation Front, whose tasks would include maintaining the Centre and providing a contact point for a number of special-interest groups. These groups would collectively comprise Gay Liberation Front, and for that purpose would meet together once a month; but they would be autonomous, in the sense that GLF would exercise no authority over them, and that they would determine their own activities and structures, and arrange their own funding and media access. Some of these groups were already in existence: the Gay Teachers' Group, the groups on the three university campuses, a Police Persecution and Psychiatric Persecution Group, and Lesbian Liberation. The old Publications Group became the GLF Newsletter Group which was to concentrate solely on producing the newsletter.[20]

Another of the groups was the Gay Political Action Group, whose first exercise was to take a leaf out of CAMP's book and field a candidate for the NSW State election on 17 November. The candidate was Martin Smith, standing for the seat of Waverley. Like David Widdup before him, Martin was not intending to wrest the seat from the sitting member, in this case, Syd Einfeld, at that time Deputy Leader of the NSW ALP Opposition. The purpose of the campaign was threefold: 'to force politicians to pay attention to the [Liberal State] government's treatment of homosexuals, through media coverage to educate the public, and a consciousness-raising device to activate the gay community (in and out of Gay Lib and CAMP circles).' The first and third aims met with a marked lack of success, according to the summing up in the December *Newsletter*. None of the politicians mentioned the matter publicly, despite the Action Group's leafleting of the policy speech meetings of all the major parties. And the 'gay community' displayed no signs that its collective imagination was captured by the exercise. But the second aim of reaching the general public had some effect, at least in terms of media coverage.

This was one of the last activities to take place under the auspices of SGL. The setting up of a loose umbrella organisation to coordinate disparate groups did not resolve the organisational problems. Indeed, without some kind of central coordination, organisation proved impossible, and gay liberation as a coherent entity faded away in Sydney during 1974. As a debate, however, gay liberation raged on into this decade, when it appears finally to have become dissipated in a welter of theoretical esoterica, phallic erotica, and participation in those same 'reformist' practices so anathematised by the early gay liberationists, namely election campaigns.

3

LESBIANS AND THE GAY MOVEMENT

THE last two chapters contained a fairly standard history of the gay movement. That history recorded events and debates which were consciously devised by the participants with the purpose of furthering the aims of the movement, and would be recognisable to anyone who was involved in them. But there is another 'history' of the gay movement, a suppressed history, which, while it was recognised at the time, was *not* the result of deliberate action on the part of gay liberationists, but which proceeded with a momentum which no strategies on the part of perceptive and concerned individuals could halt or allay. That history is a history of the exclusion of lesbians from the movement.

At first lesbians greeted gay liberation with enthusiasm. Women's Liberation had been a disappointment for lesbians. In those early days, feminists' primary concern with lesbianism was how to convince 'the media', and hence the general public, that they were *not* 'a bunch of lesbians'. As a consequence, the lesbians in Women's Liberation were subjected to strong pressures to remain 'in the closet', and to set aside their own interests in favour of 'heterosexual' issues such as childcare, abortion, etc. Gay liberation promised a supportive environment within which lesbians could work towards overcoming their specific oppression as 'homosexuals'. That they had thereby committed a 'category-mistake'[1] in assuming that the term 'homosexual' could be applied equally to women and to men, soon became evident (see chapter 4).

Not that the lesbians involved saw the problem in terms of such a dry philosophical concept as a 'category-mistake'. Their immediate reaction was to accuse the men of 'sexism' (Bebbington & Lyons, 1975). And to the extent that 'sexism' can be defined with reference to negative attitudes and behaviour on the part of men towards women, amounting at times to outright misogyny,[2] it was an ever-present threat to the harmony of relationships between lesbians and gay men. Gregg Blachford (1981: 188), who was a member of Sydney Gay Liberation in the old days, gave some examples of this misogyny in action. He said that, within the (male) 'homosexual subculture',

> women are often referred to by their sexual organs; 'fish' is a common term for a woman and 'cunty' is used as an adjective referring to something that possesses the qualities of a woman. The derogatory term 'fag hag' is used to describe a woman who enjoys the company of gay men. Besides these peculiarly gay male expressions, most references to women are similar to the way heterosexual men can be seen to respond to women: 'cow', 'old woman', 'slag', 'tart', 'cheap', 'scrubber'.

In the face of experiences like these, many lesbians left the gay movement in anger and disgust.

But behaviour like the above was not, and never had been, a dominant theme in relationships between lesbians and gay men, and not only because such behaviour was so obviously reprehensible. There had always been a great deal of goodwill on both sides, and for many years there were a number of more or less persistent attempts, by gay men as well as by lesbians, to make the movement relevant to lesbians. But none of those attempts was successful.

From the beginning the gay movement was dominated by men and male interests, and it never managed to incorporate lesbianism into its strivings for 'liberation'. The process of exclusion increased in momentum over the years of the gay movement's existence, until finally, the 'gay community' (that result of so many years of 'fighting oppression') was exclusively the domain of men. As Bob Hay, secretary of the Gay Counselling Service of NSW, put it in an editorial in the January 1982 issue of *Gay Counselling News*: 'the ear I have to the ground tells me that in 1982 we gay men will call ourselves gay and by that mean men only.'

The earliest of the attempts to include lesbians in the gay movement was made by John Ware and Chris Poll when they set up CAMP Inc. as an organisation to include both sexes. This policy they saw as a new development in the way homosexuals organised, because, John was reported to say in the *Australian* in 1970, earlier groups had confined their membership to one sex or the other.[3]

But the contradictions were present even then. One of those contradictions, the one most pertinent within the 'reformist' context of CAMP's political activities, was the emphasis on law reform. Chris Poll herself placed this issue at the forefront of gay liberation. She devoted over half of an article (1970) to arguments for law reform, although, as she eventually pointed out, it had no relevance to lesbians. She went on to discuss, very briefly, some reasons for the failure of the English and Australian law to penalise lesbian sexuality, and for the failure of 'society' in general to acknowledge the existence of lesbianism. But despite this early awareness of the differing interests of lesbians and gay men, law reform remained a dominant theme of the movement, while the social exclusion of lesbianism was reproduced within the movement itself.

I am not suggesting that the gay movement ought not to have concentrated so much energy on the devising of campaigns demanding the repeal of anti-male homosexual laws. Quite the contrary. Given the reactionary composition of the NSW legislature it was hardly surprising that so much effort had to be expended on that particular fight. Nor am I arguing that the gay movement's preoccupation with law reform was anybody's 'fault', or that anybody could have done other than what they in fact did. I am simply pointing out that the fight for law reform was a struggle between competing *male* interests, and hence of no interest to lesbians.

But the emphasis on law reform was only one manifestation, although the most obvious one, of the reproduction of male dominance within the movement. Other more subtle and less readily identifiable indications also manifested themselves from the beginning. The kinds of mechanisms which operated to suppress lesbian interests, sometimes despite the best of intentions, can be exemplified by the story of the first attempt within CAMP to set up a separate time and space for a women's meeting from which men were deliberately and explicitly excluded. The woman who told me the story, whom I shall call 'Madeleine', was the woman who was responsible for organising this first tentative foray into 'lesbian separatism'.

57

The context within which 'Madeleine' made her attempt to provide a space and time for women can be illustrated by an argument which appeared in a short-lived column in *CAMP Ink*. (The column did not appear after the third issue.) It was called 'Josephine' and was purportedly written by a lesbian, as comment and advice 'for the ladies'. (I am not entirely sure who did write it, but it was suggested to me that it was written by David Widdup, who subsequently went on to bigger and better things with his 'Minnie Drear' column in later issues of *CAMP Ink*.) The 'Josephine' column in issue number three involved a diatribe against a recent issue of *The Ladder*, the journal of the American lesbian organisation, Daughters of Bilitis. The cause of 'Josephine's' complaint was that the journal was 'geared almost [*sic*] exclusively to lesbian interests', and purveyed 'a single sex strategy' which 'Josephine' doubted would 'contribute much to the wider movement'. She (if 'she' it was) went on to deplore 'the focus on "the women's viewpoint"', and concluded with the assertion that 'crouching in the ghetto of "womanhood" won't . . . achieve anything'. An addendum to the column was a short letter supposedly from a lesbian who signed herself 'Sappho', asking 'Josephine' if 'she' would join in 'a separate wing of the movement for us' (i.e. women). 'Josephine's' reply is worth quoting in full as an example of the kinds of sanctions applied against any attempt, no matter how minimal or apologetic, to assert some autonomy for women:

> Dear Sappho,
>
> No, I would not be in it, and I hope you'll decide against it too, as we need some assertive types like you obviously are. 'Men' can be tiresome; so can 'women'. Single sex organisations promote even more the defensive ghetto mentality that I for one object to in homosexuals, male or female. It makes for sad and limited people. Why limit yourself, when there are nice people everywhere, some of whom have vaginas and some penises.[4]

It was pressures such as these which 'Madeleine' had to contend with in setting up those Saturday afternoon get-togethers for women in the CAMP clubrooms. She herself does not remember how long those gatherings continued, but the first meeting was in June 1971,[5] and they were still happening in November of the same year.[6] During those few months 'Madeleine' was presented with many difficulties, not all of which, it must be admitted, stemmed from CAMP's lack of awareness of, and provision for, women's needs. Those difficulties, whatever their origin, were eventually to prove insuperable, and she finally had to give up the organising of the women's Saturday afternoons. She had initially taken on the onerous task because she could see how important it was for women to relate to each other without interference from the all-pervasive male presence. She could see that women were alienated at dances, talked over at meetings, and even on occasion ignored, patronised, ridiculed and rejected by men whose homosexuality went hand in hand with misogyny.

The following example was typical of the early CAMP's insensitivity to lesbian interests. 'Madeleine' had put up a notice in the clubrooms advertising that the Saturday afternoons were for 'Women only'. She was told to take the notice down. When I asked John Ware about this recently, he said that the notice had infringed one of the rules of CAMP, which stated that any group which formed within CAMP must be open to all members. He said that he had been sympathetic to the women's need to get together without men, but had felt that it had to be done in such a way that the fact that men were excluded was not made too obvious. However, it occurred to nobody at the time that this was an act of suppression, no matter how well-intentioned, which served to drive the women's demands underground and render them surreptitious and furtive.

At the same time this resistance to the setting up of an autonomous women's group within CAMP went hand in hand with at least some awareness that CAMP was failing to provide adequately for its lesbian members. At first this realisation was expressed as a failure on the part of *lesbians* to involve themselves fully in CAMP's activities. This was the gist of two editorials in *CAMP Ink*.[7] The first article admitted that the journal contained very little material relating to lesbians, but saw the solution to lie with 'the ladies' themselves. The second article gently chided lesbians for behaving like 'second-class members of CAMP Inc.', and suggested that they 'endeavour to participate more actively'. But gradually the emphasis shifted. Some eighteen months later David Widdup (1973?) was arguing that 'it is definitely the problem of men that women are oppressed in ... society', and that the limited participation of women in 'the homosexual movement' was the result of 'the fundamental issue of [the movement's] inability to involve women to the extent that men are involved'. He went on to argue that the oppression of male homosexuals stemmed form the same social source as the oppression of women, namely, 'the sexual structure of our society', and hence that 'homosexual liberation' was dependent on, and subsidiary to Women's Liberation. The obvious strategy was for 'the homosexual liberation movement ... [to] incorporate itself into the much wider movement of radical feminism'.[8]

It would appear that, for the time being at least, David's advice fell on deaf ears. When Sue Wills and Gaby resigned from the executive of CAMP in March 1974, one of their complaints concerned the continuing male domination of the organisation, and the active oppression of the women by many of the men. But things had, nevertheless, improved. Early in 1973 there were three lesbian groups in existence within CAMP. The CWA (which supposedly stood for 'Camp Women's Association', but which was also a mild send-up of the eminently respectable Country Women's Association) produced a fortnightly newsletter,[9] and were instrumental in challenging the first Women's Liberation Conference in Sydney, the Women's Commission, held in March 1973, on its failure to deal adequately with the issue of lesbianism (Antolovich, 1973). As a result of the debate (or fracas) at the Commission, two other groups for 'camp women' were formed. One was what Gaby called 'the reactivated Gay Women's Lib Group', whose purpose was 'to pressure Women's Lib to accept us (lesbians are women too) and from there to get women as a whole to face society with lesbian issues under the banner of Women'. The other was the Radical Lesbians Group which was primarily a consciousness-raising group.

Moreover, as with political awareness and activity in general, the feminist cause within CAMP went from strength to strength from 1974 to 1978 (at which time the 'political heavies' were finally outmanoeuvred and ousted), at least among those few members involved in political activism. In 1974 and 1975 there was an influx of women who had been strongly influenced by feminism and whose primary loyalties lay with the women's movement. Their presence, and the debates they brought with them concerning the primacy of women's liberation in the struggle against sexual oppression, provided a political context for CAMP's activism. They received support from those men who possessed an awareness of the interconnectedness of all forms of oppression, and who espoused feminism as the vanguard of a movement for broad social change. At the same time, the contradictions between the interests of women and those of men became submerged.

There were probably two main reasons for this appearance of compatibility between the interests of lesbians and those of gay men during this phase of CAMP's existence. In the first place, there was the busy activity of 'getting things done' within the reformist framework of lobbying established institutions for the rectification of discrimination against 'homosexuals'. As well, there was the constant pressure from those aspects of CAMP which tended to push the organisation in a conservative direction—Phone-A-Friend, and social activities like the coffee shop. This pressure stemmed from the view that political activity and analysis, whether feminist or reformist, was threatening to the secure niche which CAMP had become for the majority of members, and was frightening away the potential mass constituency, usually seen as residing on the North Shore. In the face of such pressures, feminists and politically-aware gay men found common cause.

One of those pressures involved the Wednesday night 'coffee shop' for women only. The main argument against it at this point in CAMP's history was that it was 'sexist' because it 'excluded men', a coopted version of the feminist term, which ignored the reality of the subordination of women's interests to those of men, and assumed a spurious already-existent equality between the sexes. This accusation of 'excluding men' was a constant undercurrent throughout CAMP's history, from 'Madeleine's' enterprise in 1971, to 1979 when the 'exclusion of men from the Coffee Shop on Wednesday nights' was reluctantly allowed to 'continue' by the executive, with the rider that this permission was not given 'in any spirit of separatism'.[10] More recently, the exclusion of *women* from the category of 'gay' altogether (as witness Bob Hay's remark quoted earlier), meant that the question of the participation of lesbians in the Gay Counselling Service of NSW (CAMP's most recent persona) largely became a non-issue. Women still sporadically make attempts to work within the Gay Counselling Service. One woman wrote a feature article for *Gay Counselling News* (successor to the *CAMP NSW Newsletter*) in May 1982. In that article, which was the text of a talk she had given during a counsellor-training program, she offered a few comments on what she called 'gay male/female gender differences', and concluded with a plea for the recruiting of more women into the organisation. Plus ça change, plus c'est la même chose! (which is French for 'It's always the same old story').

The demise of CAMP's political activism was documented in chapter 7. With that demise went the last vestige of its involvement with feminist ideas.

But again, CAMP was not the whole of the gay movement. Sydney Gay Liberation seemed at first to have reached a better accommodation with feminist ideas in those early days before 1974 than had CAMP, at least on that level of polemics (as opposed to actual practice). There was, for example, the emphasis on the oppressive nature of 'the family' and 'traditional sex roles', the call for the abolition of 'sexism' and the 'male supremacist system', the expressed wish to work with women's liberation, and the adoption of the tactic of the consciousness-raising group. Nevertheless, SGL had the same problems accommodating to lesbian interests as did CAMP (although those problems did not centre around an emphasis on law reform, at least in the early days, because the 'radicals' in SGL saw it as 'reformist', that is, too limited in scope to be worthy of the time and energy of revolutionaries).

That SGL, too, was dominated by male interests might have been evident to a perceptive observer at the time, had such a hypothetical observer examined closely the analysis underpinning gay liberation rhetoric (although hindsight provides a clearer perception). The London Gay Liberation Manifesto, for example, analysed the contribution of women's unpaid domestic labour to the process of capitalist accumulation thus:

> our economic system could not function properly . . . [unless] people [bought] far more manufactured goods than they need. The housewife, obsessed with the ownership of as many material goods as possible, is the agent of this high level of spending. None of these goods will ever satisfy her, since there is always something better to be had.

That the 'sexism' of this comment, not to mention the trivialisation of women and their work, could pass unnoticed in one of the major texts of gay liberation, throws some doubt on the willingness of gay liberation men to push the questioning of male supremacist ideology very far. Their analysis of the situation of the male worker implied that he had to be coerced and pacified into carrying out *his* role in the system, whereas 'the housewife' was directly to blame for hers (although she *had* been duped 'by advertising and everything she reads'—which only demonstrated her weak-mindedness). Further, it did not occur to the authors to consider the question of just *whose* income it was which enabled this 'high level of spending'. By definition it was not 'the housewife's' but her husband's, and the way she disposed of it was dependent on his say-so. If he withheld it (a not uncommon eventuality), then she and her children were destitute. But even if he were a good husband and provider to the best of his ability, if he were a production worker or unemployed, there was unlikely to *be* much money to spend.

But perhaps this weakness in the Manifesto account is not surprising, since the 'domestic labour' debate had not yet happened—the debate, that is, about the way in which the unpaid labour of women in the home contributes to the extraction of 'surplus value' from 'labour power' (people's ability to work). That debate itself reached no definite conclusions, but it did avoid the crassness of blaming women for a situation over which they had even less control than men.

On the other hand, the problems did not exist only on a theoretical level. In September 1972, Mim Loftus wrote an article for the *Sydney Gay Liberation Newsletter*, suggesting some reasons why 'women . . . have not been drawn to Gay Lib as active participators'. She started by saying that 'women (especially lesbians) are conditioned to stay in the background'. However, she did not rest content with this explanation, but went on to say that meetings were 'male-dominated/ orientated' and invalidated women's experiences. At the same time she also rejected separatism, a 'split into MALE and FEMALE groups', such as had happened in England and the US, as a solution to women's 'secondary' status within Gay Lib, and called for all members to 'recognise our common oppression as homosexuals in a repressive society and fight together'. A note from the newsletter collective at the end of the article said that the situation had changed since the article was written, and that women were now taking a more active role.

But this happy state of affairs was short-lived, and women continued to find gay liberation alienating. In an article in the December issue of the newsletter, Pam Stein, one of the original members of SGL, placed the blame squarely on the shoulders of the men. 'Men,' she said,

> after reading this article you may realise ... why the women in Gay Lib feel threatened and fucking mad ... When the men in Gay Liberation put us down by ignoring us, by saying we are aggressive when we are being assertive, when they refuse for the reason of masculine arrogance to participate in our movement, and also when they are [too] bloody lazy to look for themselves and come to the women to lean on and ask us what they can do. Brothers, if you can't see for yourselves or even take the time to look for yourselves why women are angry, then Gay Liberation is worth nothing in our eyes. (Stein, 1972:   )

Pam told me recently that her anger at the time stemmed from what she saw as the fact that the men were prepared to use the women's energy, imagination and political astuteness to further their own interests, while refusing (as she thought then) to acknowledge that women's needs were different. She said that she was now of the opinion that they were not able to understand what was going on, and that it had been pointless for the women to try to find common cause with gay men who merely assumed without question that their own interests were those of lesbians too.

Much the same point of view was expressed by Laurie Bebbington and Margaret Lyons in their 1975 paper, when they said: 'Lesbians in homosexual movements have carried our gay "brothers" on our backs for too long.' They stated that lesbians would not continue to work with gay men unless the men mended their 'sexist' ways. 'Sexism' they defined with reference to the sexes' differential access to power. In 'patriarchal society' women were powerless, both 'culturally and socio-economically', while men enjoyed 'automatic power benefits'. Homosexual men, they argued, also had access to the benefits of being male in patriarchal society. After all, they could 'pass as straight', while lesbians could never 'hide [their] womanhood' in order to avoid 'the prejudice and oppression of being female and therefore second-rate'. The writers characterised the benefits of being male as 'male cultural values' whereby the male was regarded as the norm and to be female was merely to be 'non-male'. Within such a framework even male homosexuality, derided and penalised though it might be, enjoyed a social acceptance of a kind, an acceptance denied lesbianism because of the patriarchal requirement that women must derive their status from relationships from men. Indeed, the writers even suggested tentatively at one point that male homosexuality might be the 'ultimate manifestation' of patriarchal culture. At a later point they elucidated this statement with reference to the civilisations of Greece and Rome which, far from having been destroyed by male homosexuality (as fundamentalist Christian opinion would have it), were in fact 'based on it'. They explained this by saying that 'a relationship between two superior beings (male) was the ideal—women were merely slaves or chattels'. They concluded by reiterating their demand that gay men 'seriously consider the questions lesbian-feminists are posing', and examine their behaviour in the light of the criticisms presented in their paper.

But to no avail. Exhortation is, anyway, useless as a strategy for challenging hegemonic patterns of behaviour; and while the women's accusations pricked the consciences of some gay men, others reacted with resentment and resistance. But even goodwill failed in the face of the all-pervasiveness of male supremacy. While the men, by and large, agreed that the gay movement had not succeeded in adapting itself to lesbian interests, and even to a certain extent accepted the 'sexist' label, they remained at a loss to know what to do (to put the best possible interpretation on their reactions). For example, Dennis Altman admitted the truth of the 'sexism' accusation (in a backhanded kind of way). 'Certainly most gay men are sexist,' he said. But, he went on to say, 'equally most gays, men *and* women, are almost certainly racist'. He said that he objected very strongly to what he called 'the new myth' that 'the women are more "advanced" than the men', and the 'new guilt trip some gay women are seeking to lay on the men'.[11]

This idea that the women in gay liberation were more 'advanced' than the men (if that is what the women were saying), and the concomitant idea that it was Women's Liberation which ought to be in the forefront of the sexual revolution, was, not surprisingly, unacceptable to gay men convinced of the need for an autonomous (male) gay movement. As Tim Carrigan expressed it in the paper he gave at the Third National Homosexual Conference in Adelaide in 1977: 'There has been a widespread tendency to accept [arguments like the above], more or less explicitly, and this reaction is a self-destructive and politically backward one.' He admitted that 'historically, the gay movement is not as advanced as the women's movement'. However, he pointed out, any suggestion that gay men should embrace as their primary goal the task of ridding themselves of their 'masculine traits' in order the better to serve the women's movement, could only lead to a denial of the oppression specific to 'our own position as homosexuals in this society'. For gay men to accept any argument that gay liberation was subsidiary to the women's movement, he went on, was 'a more sophisticated form of self-oppression: we are guilty no longer because we believe that homosexuality is sinful or abnormal, but because we are sexist men. This leads only to moralism and political ineffectiveness'.

In another paper given at the same conference, John Lee asserted that 'fighting sexism, conceived of in the simple formulation of men oppressing women, could never be the *primary* goal of a viable homosexual men's movement'. He went on to say that the problem, anyway, was not a simple choice between fighting sexism and fighting 'our own oppression', that in fact in fighting their own oppression homosexual men had the issue of sexism 'very much to the forefront'. Like Tim, John too saw the primary task of gay liberation as 'the struggle against our oppression as male homosexuals'. He voiced the opinion that 'we are beginning to reassert ourselves, not just as men. And as politicised homosexuals there is the renewed belief that we must work to relate to male homosexuals generally in order to make the struggle against oppression effective'. He did not, however, elucidate how male homosexuals relating to each other could advance the fight against sexism.

Not all gay liberationist men, however, resisted the idea that feminism should point the way forward for gay liberation. For a brief period, during 1974 and 1975, some gay men embraced a position called 'effeminism', which originated in New York and which received its clearest statement in the 'Effeminist Manifesto', the journal *Double-F*, and the poems of Kenneth Pitchford (Johnston, 1980).[12] One advocate of the 'effeminist' position summed up his stance thus:

> Ideologically, Feminism is the answer to my question 'Where to now?' once I had come out and understood certain premises of Gay Liberation ideology. My 'effeminist' reaction to Feminism is:
>
> 1.   To accept Feminist political, economic and cultural analyses.
> 2.   To understand my part as a WASP man in the oppression of women and to fight my maleness.
> 3.   To realise that the Feminist revolution is an all-embracing phenomenon without which there is no revolution but a series of male coups . . .
> 4.   To desist from defining for any woman her revolution. (Hawksins, 1975)

Others were more tentative, while still recognising the relevance of the 'effeminist' perspective. Johnston and Hurley, in their 1975 paper presented at the same conference as the paper quoted above, stated unequivocally that 'a clear line of support (by gay liberation) for that revolutionary feminism which seeks to completely end sex roles is imperative ... [because] it is the distinction between masculine and feminine which explains the oppression of male homosexuals'. They acknowledged that the 'effeminists' insistence on the 'primacy of the woman question', and their relating of the feminist analysis 'to our own lives', was a valuable political contribution to gay liberation. But they saw it as limited in its relevance to the extent that it uncritically accepted the basic premises of 'American radical feminism', and remained at the level of the 'personal solutions' of 'individual guilt' and 'stereotypic "effeminacy" in mannerisms'. The latter they saw as no more than 'anti-women mimicry and self-mockery'.

More recently, in 1980, Craig summed up the contribution of 'effeminism' to gay liberation thus: 'effeminist ideas added to the radical homosexual understanding of homosexuals' oppression and were the first major differentiation inside Gay Liberation between the reform-minded majority and a minority who wanted to develop a revolutionary perspective' (Johnston, 1980). This 'differentiation' had been spelled out in more detail in the 1975 paper. On one side was a reformist 'gay liberation politics' which directed its political activities towards the demand for 'gay rights' which, the authors argued, were solely '*male* rights' as long as the basic structures of capitalist patriarchy remained unchanged. On the other was the revolutionary stance which asserted that the subversive potential of 'homosexuality' (non-gender-specific) lay 'in the extent to which we separate sexuality from power'. As should be clear from earlier chapters, I do not agree that the advent of 'effeminism' was the occasion of the first reformist–radical split in the movement. Neither was it the first time feminism had influenced gay liberation.

Nevertheless, despite this recent acknowledgement of the positive contribution of 'effeminism' to gay liberation, the dominant tendency of the movement was to reject any analysis which suggested that gay liberation was subordinate to the women's movement. And it is difficult to see how gay men could have reacted in any other way, given the basic strategic requirement of radical feminism (American or otherwise), namely the exclusion of men from the sites of the struggle for women's liberation. In the light of that requirement, no man could adopt feminism as his primary personal/political commitment, and the price of any attempt to do so was self-abnegation, hovering on the periphery of a movement he was not allowed to join. (This conse-quence was clearly perceived by those gay men who firmly resisted the enticements of 'effeminism'.) That is not to say that feminism is of no relevance to men, nor that men cannot incorporate feminist insights into their lives and politics. They can and they do. But at the time when both gay liberation and feminism were breaking new ground, feminists had to work out (and on) the nature and extent of women's oppression without interference from men, no matter how well-intentioned. The time for that requirement is by no means past, but now that so much of feminism is a matter of public debate, it is accessible to all.

But while it may not have been in the interests of gay men to embrace feminism as their primary commitment, neither was it in the interests of feminism to be coopted into the service of (male) homosexual liberation. Again Hurley and Johnston provided an example of the consequences for feminist theory of such cooption. The aspect of 'revolutionary feminism' which they decided was of most benefit for their own lives was its critique of 'sex roles'. This critique, they said, exposed the 'sex ranking' inherent in the masculine/feminine dichotomy: that men had power over women. The subordination of women was necessary, they argued, for the main-tenance of the 'capitalist nuclear family' which served a number of functions for the capitalist mode of production. The function which was of particular relevance to the oppression of male homosexuals was what they called 'the production of discipline', that is, the 'disciplining of children ideologically and psychologically so they become docile workers or petty tyrants'. The suppression of male homosexuality was necessary for the continuation of the 'capitalist nuclear family' and hence capitalism, because, they asserted, 'the subversive potential of our [gay male] sexuality' tended to undermine the discipline required for a docile labour force. In an aside, they remarked: 'fucking a lot and feeling like work don't mix, let's face it' (Hurley and Johnston, 1975: 55).

Leaving aside any question of the correctness or otherwise of the theoretical stance adopted by these authors, it was this conviction on the part of gay men that their sexual activities were somehow intrinsically 'subversive' of the patriarchal social order, which more than anything else alienated lesbians from the gay movement. It is true that this thesis was not stated without reservations of some sort—the above authors referred to a 'potential' rather than an actual subver-siveness. Some such qualification had always been necessary given the intransigently conservative attitudes and behaviour of many homosexual men. Nonetheless, the conviction remained. For women, the idea that the untrammelled exercise of male sexuality, with its valorisation of the phallus, its 'fucking a lot', and 'sexual freedom' (and whatever that meant it did not include long-term monogamous relationships), could have any positive consequences for their own lives, was beyond the bounds of credibility.

The antagonism lesbians felt towards gay male sexuality was dramatically demonstrated at the Fourth National Homosexual Conference held in Sydney at Paddington Town Hall in 1978. In the foyer of the town hall was a display of lesbian and gay male art. Some of the men's work depicted gay male sexual fantasies which objectified men in the same way women are depicted in 'girly' and pornographic magazines. The most offensive (to the women) of these pieces was a depiction of a number of scenes of sadomasochistic sex between men. This piece was destroyed by some women. Some of the men argued that the piece was a *commentary* on this form of sexual expression, and was in fact intended as a criticism of it. The piece was not advocating sadomasochism, as the women believed—the explicitness was intended to shock, not entice. If that was indeed the artist's intention, then the fact that the women had missed the point may have been partly a consequence of the contradiction inherent in any artistic enterprise which attempts to provide a critical commentary on hegemonic modes of expression (modes which institutionalise and make meaningful a social order of domination/subordination), while using identical images to those which function to reinforce the dominant modes.

Undoubtedly the destruction of that piece of work was an outrageous act on the women's part, and aroused a great deal of controversy. The general consensus at the conference, among lesbians as well as gay men, was that such destruction was 'going too far'. By and large, lesbians in the gay movement tended to keep their own counsel about their reactions to gay male sex, either because of a reluctance to appear as moralistic wowsers, or because they felt it was none of their business anyway. Rarely was their distaste expressed so forcefully. Nonetheless the antagonism was there, an antagonism based on radically different sexualities, and hence perceptions of the kinds of strategies most likely to advance the process of sexual liberation, or alternatively retard that process.

A story from the early days of gay liberation illustrates this antagonism and the mutual incomprehension it gave rise to. The woman who told me the story said that during one of SGL's first consciousness-raising sessions, the women present had had no difficulty talking about their personal experiences—as feminists, and perhaps even more to the point, as women, they were quite used to the exercise. The men, however, were at first more reticent. At one point one young man finally summoned up all his courage and started talking about a personal experience which was obviously of great importance to him at the time. That experience involved 'glory holes'.[13] On being enlightened as to the nature and function of these, the women reacted with a unanimity and spontaneity which left no room for argument. Their reaction could be summed up in the phrase: 'Ugh, yuck!' (my informant said). To the 'poor boy' (as my informant described him) that reaction was no different in kind from the disapproving moralism he had been subjected to all his life because of his homosexuality.

It was a standard response on the part of gay men to regard as 'moralistic' these reactions on the part of lesbians to typical (although not universal) gay male sexual practices. For example, Gavin Harris, writing in *Gay Information* in 1980, put what he called 'anti-pornography lesbian-feminists' into the same category of 'puritans' as the Festival of Light, because he perceived both groups disapproving of his new-found sexual freedom (Harris, 1980: 4–5, 12; Thompson, 1980). But to assert an identity of interests between lesbian-feminists and the righteous ravings of the rabid Right is to advance the cause of sexual liberation not a whit. At the risk of stating the obvious, it must be said that such an assertion is ridiculous. While lesbian-feminists (like many other women) might disapprove, more or less forcefully, of gay male sexual activities, they are unlikely to call upon the wrath of God or the repressive state apparatus to assist in the suppression or eradication of those activities. Lesbian aversion to gay male sex, whether based on repugnance, or on an intellectualised justification (for example, gay men treat each other like 'sex objects'), has rarely, if ever, implied that 'something ought to be done about it'.

But lesbians' reactions to gay male sex were not just moralistic. Nor were they a manifestation of 'sexual repression', a term which implied that women had somehow been browbeaten by a (postulated) 'socialisation process' into an inability to get any fun out of sex, and hence envied men who did. Their disagreement with gay men was about the political implications of the men's sexual activities, and not simply a conventional reaction towards 'promiscuity'. Rather it arose out of a conviction that the gay male championing of a multiplicity and variety of sex acts, with a multiplicity and variety of ('pretty' or 'well-hung') partners, served as no more than a device 'pour épater le bourgeois', or, as the early gay liberationists used to say, 'to shock the straights'. Moreover, lesbians remained unconvinced of the efficacy of male sexuality, of whatever orientation, as a strategy for advancing the process of sexual liberation. For gay male sex, and the gay liberation discourse based on it, remained phallocentric, in other words, dominated by male interests. Gay men were inclined to the view that their personal non-involvement in sexual relations with women automatically absolved them of any implication in the sexual exploitation of women. And while that might have been true up to a point, that same non-involvement gave rise to a certain blindness where women's sexuality was concerned, and reinforced patterns of exploitative sexuality which were no different in kind from those which had always functioned 'to keep women in their place'.

The model of 'sexual freedom' espoused by gay liberation was and remained intransigently masculine—fucking for fucking's sake, erotic stimulation confined to the genitals and a few selected erogenous zones, anonymous sex at the beats, bars, clubs and bath houses, and more recently the fetishised role play of 'clones' (the 'new' understated masculinity), machismo (the old overstated variety), sadomasochism, leather and chains, and Nazi paraphernalia. Not that all these forms were explicitly embraced by gay liberation. But the most recent forms can be seen as direct descendants of the original gay liberationist avowal of the liberating potentiality of sex with no commitment to the partner beyond the act itself. For lesbians (like other women) to adopt such a stance would be at best pointless. At worst, it would ensure that lesbians behaved sexually towards each other in ways which were no different from the ways in which masculinity dictated men treat women.

At this point it must be said that not all lesbians reacted negatively to gay male sex. Some reacted with envy of the sexual athleticism of gay men, who could experience 'the joys of sex' without the burdensome demands of 'a relationship'. At the same time, there were some gay men who preferred the typical (although not universal) pattern of lesbian relationships, which were long-term, committed and sexually faithful. Nevertheless, it was the masculine pattern of 'sexual freedom' (a concept which implied, first and foremost, an ever-changing supply of sexual partners) which predominated.

At the present time any question about the relationship between lesbians and the gay movement is a dead issue. Women and men continue to work together in the various groups, activities, etc. which are all that remain of a continuing gay movement. These groups, etc. are short-lived and/or task-oriented, forming, dissolving and re-forming according to the demands of the moment. The most sporadic are the discussion groups which periodically take up issues involved in a theory of sexuality, give them yet another airing, and then fold from lack of further insight into the problems. The academically inclined journal *Gay Information*, struggles valiantly along despite a permanent financial crisis, as does the radio program, 'Gaywaves'. And the Sydney Gay Writers' Collective periodically produces a publication, the latest of which is the Bradstock et al. volume (1983). The annual homosexual conferences continue to stagger along from year to year, and a Gays and Socialism conference happens now and again.

But as a coherent entity, the gay movement is no more. To a

certain extent the demise of gay lib is a measure of its success, a success which is manifested in a public opinion which is now more accepting of and knowledgeable about a 'homosexual lifestyle'. The chief beneficiaries of the movement's activities are the (male) 'gay community' and the social clubs, for whom political agitation is a bore or anathema. But then it is difficult to see what they could agitate about. For ultimately gay liberation failed to provide an adequate critique of the relationships of power embedded in sexuality (not that anyone else succeeded either), beyond a series of more or less bald and simplistic variations on the theme that 'the family' was somehow to blame for the oppression of homosexual men. The path of liberation, therefore, necessitated the avoidance of the kind of sexual relationships which gay lib defined as intrinsic to 'the family'—long-term, committed and monogamous (labelled 'possessive' by gay lib), in favour of brief encounters with strangers or acquaintances. (Interestingly this ideological stance went hand in hand with a taboo against fucking friends.)

The ease with which this path was trod appeared to arouse no suspicions among gay men. After all, no political activist expects the revolution to be easy. But if all gay liberationists had to do to bring about the millenium was to continue doing what they had always done with the addition of a modicum of honesty ('coming out'), then they didn't need to change anything in their own personal practice (as opposed to the perennial issues of law reform and public opinion, issues which demand change on the part of someone else). The continuation of the sexual status quo, at least as far as gay lib's own practice was concerned, was hardly likely to ensure the decline and fall of the Western nuclear family as we know it.

I realise that the above sounds very harsh. It is not intended to be so—who am I to judge, after all? I cannot see how gay liberation could have developed in any way other than it did. That the process did not bring about the goals which were deliberately intended by the participants is hardly anyone's 'fault'. It *did* expose the issues, and if that was more by inadvertance than conscious design, then perhaps that is an inextricable aspect of any moves for social change.

II
THE SOCIAL MANAGEMENT OF HOMOSEXUALITY

4

THE
MEDICAL
MODEL

IT was the medical profession, in the guise of its raffish poor relations in the field of 'mental health'—psychiatry, psychoanalysis,
clinical psychology, and 'helping' therapies of various kinds—
which took over primary responsibility for the social management of
'unacceptable' sexual behaviours from the churches and the law. Both
of the latter remained involved with 'the problem', despite the contradictions produced by continuing to define (male) 'homosexual' behaviour as sin/crime, for which the individual could be held morally
responsible, *and* as the symptom of an illness over which the sufferer
had no control. Both these institutions have made some attempt to
deal with this contradiction: the churches by making a distinction
between 'homosexual condition' and 'homosexual behaviour', and
holding the individual responsible only for the latter; the law by
sometimes using the psychiatric, etc., professions as an alternative line
of defence to the penal system. Nevertheless, these were merely minor
accommodations to the increasing predominance of the 'medical
model', and did not resolve the contradiction between blaming (male)
'homosexuals' for their behaviour, while acknowledging that it

resulted from a condition over which they had no control. The obvious resolution would have been to acknowledge the hegemony of what has come to be known as the 'medical model', that is, the incorporation of 'homosexuality' into the domain of medical science as an object of investigation and as an 'illness' to be cured. This the churches and the law appeared reluctant to do. For, on another level, all three discourses—medical science, Christian morality and the criminal law—were in complete accord. All three were explicitly concerned with the 'eradication' of (male) 'homosexuality' (or the behaviour, at least)—by cure, condemnation or criminal sanctions.

A major theme of the ADB's report was the assumption that the social management of (male) 'homosexuality' involved various forms of social control. This was based on the prior assumption that structures of social control, beyond those devised to penalise (and curb) offences against the person—rape, murder, assault, thefts of an individual's personal property, etc.—function to serve ruling interests. This is an insight from gay liberation, an insight arising out of the personal/political strategies of 'coming out' and 'gay pride', which demonstrated the irrationality inherent in discourses devised for the 'eradication' of (male) 'homosexuality'.

The gay liberation analysis, however, was not able to elucidate the ways in which the 'suppression' of (male) 'homosexuality' functioned to reinforce ruling interests. At first, gay liberation asserted that (male) 'homosexuality' (and sometimes lesbianism too) was intrinsically subversive of the status quo because it undermined (in a manner never adequately specified) the 'basic unit of society', the family. But this remained no more than an assertion, and could not be substantiated on closer investigation. Moreover, by situating the phenomenon of (male) 'homosexuality' within an historical context, and demonstrating that mechanisms of 'suppression', far from eradicating 'undersirable' (to whom?) behaviour, actually succeeded in constituting the (male) 'homosexual' as a new historical subject, gay liberation undermined its own claims to being in the forefront of the sexual revolution. For within the terms of a theoretical discourse derived from the premise that historical subjects are constituted in accordance with ruling-class interests, whatever contradictions are generated thereby, the constitution of the (male) 'homosexual', derided, vilified and persecuted though he might have been, must have served some functions by no means inimical to the status quo.

That this is so is suggested by the direction in which the gay movement has developed. Far from providing the revolutionary potential which the early gay liberationists had hoped for from their constituency, it has evolved, as we have seen, into a (male) 'gay community', embracing every conceivable form of sexual fetishism (every form, that is, that excludes women), but which nevertheless has 'rights' codified by the state (since the 1982 amendment to the Anti-Discrimination Act which makes discrimination on the grounds of 'homosexuality' unlawful). Persecution, from poofter-bashing and police harassment to criminal sanctions, has not diminished, but the (male) 'homosexual' now enjoys a status recognised by commercial interests and 'the wider society' alike. (Lesbians can tag along too, as the possessors of a 'valid alternative sexual preference', if they care to so define themselves.)

This accommodation to the status quo on the part of the (male) 'gay community' was recognised early in gay liberation by lesbian-feminists who discovered that gay men were no more likely than 'straight' men to respond to the interests of women, and had devised their own way of belittling and denigrating women (see chapter 3). Lacking heterosexual desire, that prime motivating force for relationships between the sexes, those homosexual men, untrammelled by any other need to relate to women—for example friendship, familial ties, political allegiances—gave every appearance of having achieved in microcosm the patriarch's dream: a world without women.

Nevertheless, whatever further contradictions the gay liberation discourse has given rise to, their critique of the 'medical model' remains cogent, and has already been incorporated into the 'mental health' professions. One consequence of this is that the time for the predominance of the 'medical model' of (male) 'homosexuality' has passed. (Male) 'homosexuality' per se can no longer be categorised as a 'mental disorder'. (There were anyway, always 'mental health' professionals, including Freud, who found themselves unable to define it as such.)

Defining homosexuality

The task of defining homosexuality is not as simple a matter as it might appear at first sight. To give the dictionary definition, without further comment, is uninformative, since to do so is to ignore the controversies which still surround homosexuality, and which give the concept its social meaning. People are probably aware that the word 'homosexuality' refers to 'having a sexual propensity for someone of one's own sex',[1] and that 'homo' is derived from the Greek word for 'same' and not the Latin word for 'man'.

Definitions of homosexuality vary according to context. Within a fundamentalist Christian framework, for example, homosexuality is a 'sin', a violation of God's law. Within the framework of the criminal law, male homosexual activity is a crime. Within the medical model, homosexuality has been variously defined as a symptom of degeneracy, a constitutional abnormality, a biological anomaly, a mental illness, and a personality disorder. Within the 'homophile'[2] movements and organisations of the last 100 years or so, whose reason for existence was to counter the negative definitions of the Christian churches, the law of the state, and the more extreme versions of the medical model, homosexuals were ordinary citizens, notwithstanding their more or less unfortunate tendency, with the same human rights as other 'normal' citizens. Within the context of the recent gay liberation movements of the last eleven or twelve years, homosexuality is asserted to be 'a normal variant of human sexuality, and a challenge to the hegemony of heterosexuality and the family'.

Varying and contradictory though they may be, all these different views about homosexuality share a common tendency to define the word with reference to men only. The omission of lesbianism from discussions of 'homosexuality' is not invariable—it *is* possible to use the term 'homosexuals' to refer to both lesbians and homosexual men (and that is the sense in which the term was used wherever it appeared in the report). But time and time again during the course of the ADB's research, we found that the general terms, 'homosexuality' and 'homosexuals' did not in fact include lesbians in their reference, although that omission was rarely explicitly stated. This was nowhere more evident than in the case of the criminal law. The English legislation of 1885 prohibited 'any male person' from committing 'any act of gross indecency with another male person'. There was no mention of the unlawfulness of such conduct between 'female persons'. There *was* an attempt in the English Parliament in 1921 to introduce a clause prohibiting 'acts of gross indecency' between 'female persons', but it was rejected by the House of Lords. Section 81A of the *NSW Crimes Act* 1900 refers to 'whosoever, being a male person' commits 'any act of indecency with another male person'. There is no reference to 'female persons' committing 'acts of indecency', nor has there ever been any attempt in Australia to introduce criminal penalties for consensual lesbian behaviour. The Christian condemnation of homosexuality would no doubt also include lesbianism, were the omission to be brought to their attention. But the overwhelming concern of the Christian moralists is with male homosexual behaviour, a concern which is only partly the result of the inclusion of that behaviour within the scope of the criminal law.

Perhaps the most peculiar aspect of the omission of lesbianism from the category of 'homosexuality' is the failure to acknowledge that this has in fact occurred. One example from psychiatry is a volume edited by Dr Hendrik M. Ruitenbeek, called *Homosexuality: A Changing Picture*. None of the contributions in this volume mentions lesbianism. That they are in fact restricted to a discussion of male homosexuality can be indirectly inferred from the editor's introduction, where 'the homosexual' is referred to as 'he'. But no direct reference is made to this restriction. Such examples could be multiplied indefinitely. Although some recent volumes do treat homosexuality as a phenomenon which occurs in both sexes (Bell and Weinberg, 1978; Masters and Johnson, 1979), they are by no means typical of books on homosexuality even now. As Jeffrey Weeks (1977:88) remarked, 'The aim was, it often seemed, not so much to trace the characteristics of lesbians as to establish that they existed at all.'

Explanations for this disproportionate amount of attention devoted to male homosexuality at the expense of lesbianism are few, the main reason being that by and large it is not perceived as a problem. This unproblematic status of lesbian invisibility is a manifestation of what would appear to be the irrelevance of lesbianism to matters of social concern in general. Unlike homosexual men, who are frequently subjected to legal penalties, physical violence and reactions of moral outrage, lesbians are, more often than not, treated to a 'conspiracy' of silence and ignorance above and beyond the general ignorance of homosexuality.

It is possible to speculate about the reasons for this. It may have had to do with the prevalent myth that women (or at least 'nice' women) lacked sexual feeling, a myth which has only recently come to be challenged by the work of such researchers as Masters and Johnson. If 'respectable' women were devoid of sexual desire, then whatever it was that went on between them, it could not be sexual. And in many cases, it may indeed not have been. Given the all-pervasiveness of myth, women themselves may often not have been aware of the implications of the feelings they expressed in 'romantic friendships'. Affectionate relationships between women were well within the feminine norm, and hence socially acceptable. But myths are not free-floating ideas which one can believe or not as one pleases —they are based in the exigencies of the real world. The belief that women lacked an autonomous sexuality was one manifestation of the denial to women of the prerequisite for autonomy, that is, earning their own living. It is true that women's access to employment has varied during the last 100 years, with two world wars, a major depression and alternating periods of prosperity and recession. Before World War I, the paucity of economic alternatives to marriage ensured that relationships between women which were independent of male economic support were rare. Even today, economic necessity, reinforced by the belief that marriage and motherhood is the only right and proper career for a woman, still guarantees that most women marry with the expectation that they and their children will be dependent on a male breadwinner. Constrained by such strong social expectations, it would not be surprising if fewer women than men became aware of homosexual feelings. Nor would it be surprising if lesbianism were less readily identified as a social problem, and hence received far less attention, than male homosexuality, given the efficiency of alternative means ensuring women's compliance with social norms.

Another of the unquestioned assumptions behind conventional definitions of homosexuality is the moral conviction that homosexuality is 'wrong'. (The homophile and gay liberation viewpoints are concerned to demonstrate that this conviction is false.) This is obvious in the case of certain Christian views, and of the criminal law, neither of which would be concerned with (male) homosexuality unless it were presumed to be 'immoral/criminal'. It is not so obvious in the case of the 'scientific' approach to the study of homosexuality, as in medicine, psychiatry, psychology, etc., which explicitly disavows the influence of which would be concerned with (male) homosexuality unless it were presumed to be 'immoral/criminal'. It is not so obvious in the case of the 'scientific' approach to the study of homosexuality, as in medicine, phenomena is warned to be aware of personal prejudices and value biases, and to guard against them during the research process. Unfortunately for this 'value-free' approach to the study of social phenomena, values are not the product of the idiosyncratic attitudes of any particular individual. On the contrary, individual attitudes reflect those shared social values which structure and make meaningful people's interpretations of the way the world is, and which remain beyond awareness to the extent that alternatives are (literally) 'unthinkable'. The attempt to exclude 'value judgments' from the research project has one of two consequences: either it achieves no more than to drive them underground, their presence all the more influential because unacknowledged, whence they emerge as 'facts' uncovered by the rigour of the research procedure; or their exclusion, if successful, leaves us with a dry catalogue of facts, figures and clinical details, which bear no relationship to the human experience they purport to describe. This is particularly the case in the investigation of socially unacceptable forms of behaviour such as homosexuality. Because of the censorship to which such forms are subjected, an 'objective observer' is less likely to uncover the experiential reality of a suppressed minority voice than is an empathic participant.

In the sexological literature of the late nineteenth and early twentieth century, homosexuality was regarded as a congenital defect, which was at best an 'inborn constitutional abnormality', at worst a serious symptom of a degenerate blood line. With the advent of the psychoanalytic perspective the version of the 'medical model' which defined homosexuality as a biological defect fell into disfavour. It was not discarded altogether (indeed, it seems to be enjoying a revival in popularity at the present time). Psychoanalysis had not demonstrated the falsity of biological explanations, but provided an alternative, and more widely accepted, explanation in terms of a 'personality disorder' resulting from a failure in the socialisation process. More recently, this type of explanation has come to be questioned within the psychiatric and psychological professions, partly in response to the critique of the 'medical model' by the gay liberation movement. Both this more recent psychiatric–psychological approach, and the gay liberationist perspective, define homosexuality as a normal variant of sexual behaviour and no more symptomatic of personal pathology than socially disapproved forms of *heterosexual* behaviour, for example prostitution, promiscuity, adultery, fornication.

The nineteenth-century background

In order to grasp the significance of changing definitions of homosexuality, it is necessary to place the phenomenon within an historical context, rather than resting on the current prevalent practice of defining homosexuality as an isolated problem of individual pathology. As Jeffrey Weeks (1977:2) pointed out in his history of homosexuality:

> attitudes to homosexuality are inextricably linked to wider questions: of the function of the family, the evolution of gender roles, and of attitudes to sexuality generally . . . 'official' and popular responses to homosexuality and the homosexual can be taken as crucial indicators of wider notions of sexuality.

As already pointed out, this historical process of definition and redefinition, which was played out chiefly within the 'official' institutions of the criminal law and 'medical science' (psychiatry and sexology), focused attention predominantly on male homosexuality (exclusively, in the case of the law). Within the sexological literature, lesbianism was sometimes mentioned—it was variously called 'sapphism',[3] 'tribadism'[4] or 'female inversion'. But references to it usually deplored the paucity of information, either without attempting to remedy that deficiency, or meeting with a marked lack of success when such attempts were made. Havelock Ellis made a valiant effort in *Sexual Inversion* to devote as much attention to lesbianism as to male homosexuality (for personal reasons—his wife Edith was a lesbian). But his attempt too was defeated. On the whole, then, references to 'homosexuality' (or 'inversion') in what follows are to *male* homosexuality, as was the case in the original contexts.

It is not generally known that the medical approach to homosexuality, which defines it as a pathological condition to be investigated, treated and (it was hoped) cured by medical science, is of fairly recent historical origin. It is only since the second half of the nineteenth century that the medical profession has addressed itself to the 'problem' of homosexuality and the homosexual. Before the incorporation of what we now call homosexuality into the domain of medical science, the issue was a moral one of sinful behaviour—'the Abominable Vice of Buggery'—which could be indulged in by any sinner lapsed from grace, but was not a defining characteristic of a certain kind of individual. One aspect of that incorporation was the devising of a new terminology. The word 'homosexuality' was not coined until 1869, and did not gain currency in England until the 1890s. Before that time the preferred terms were 'inversion' and 'invert'.[5] These were also an invention of medical science, as part of the attempt to divorce the 'scientific' investigation of the phenomenon from the moralistic overtones of such terms as 'sodomy' and 'pederasty'.

It is even less well known that the first deliberate legislative enactment in English legal history against male homosexual behaviour is of even more recent origin. The Labouchère Amendment, section 11 of the English Criminal Law Amendment Act was passed in 1885. (This section is the precursor to sections 81A and 81B of the NSW Crimes Act, sections which were introduced in NSW only in 1955.) The Labouchère Amendment stated:

> Any male person who, in public or in private commits, or is a party to the commission of, or procures or attempts to procure the commission by any male person of any act of gross indecency with another male person, shall be guilty of a misdemeanour, and being convicted thereof shall be liable at the discretion of the court to be imprisoned for any term not exceeding two years, with or without hard labour. (Weeks, 1977: 14)

Male homosexual 'soliciting', that is, male prostitution, became a criminal offence only in 1898 in England, when it was brought within the terms of the Vagrancy Act.

Before 1885, all enactments were based on a statute established in 1533, during the reign of Henry VIII. This statute was not a deliberate attempt on the part of Henry and his ministers to stamp out the 'abominable vice', but rather one part of the process of reducing the jurisdiction of the ecclesiastical courts by withdrawing from them the right to try certain offences. As H. Montgomery Hyde (1970: 50–2) pointed out, the Preamble to the Act of 1533 clearly stated that the secular law had up to that time provided no appropriate and adequate penalties for the 'detestable and abominable Vice':

> Forasmuch as there is not yet sufficient and condign [i.e. worthy] punishment appointed and limited by the due course of the law of this Realm, for the detestable and abominable Vice of Buggery committed with mankind or beast . . .

While 'sodomy/buggery' has been subject to various more or less severe penalties, including the death penalty, throughout 2000 years of Judaeo-Christian civilisation, during the latter half of the nineteenth century in England, a change occurred in the judicial reaction to the phenomenon. As late as 1826, Sir Robert Peel had re-enacted the death penalty for 'sodomy/buggery', and provided for easier convictions by removing the requirement to prove 'emission of seed', thus asserting that proof of 'penetration only' was sufficient to establish that the offence had occurred (Weeks, 1977:13; Hyde, 1970:106–9). As Jeffrey Weeks pointed out, this reassertion of the death penalty for the 'unnatural offence' was particularly startling at a time when the death penalty was abolished for over 100 other offences. By 1836, the death penalty had been tacitly abandoned, and was officially abolished in England and Wales in 1861. But this was not a prelude to an easing of the law—the lesser penalties made for easier convictions. The culmination of this process of change in the English law during the nineteenth century, the 1885 Labouchère amendment, widened the scope of the law's interference to include *any* behaviour between men which might be regarded as 'gross indecency', and explicitly stated that it was irrelevant whether that behaviour occurred 'in public or in private'. It was this phrase which aroused the most concern among the opponents of the amendment, which was immediately dubbed 'the blackmailers' charter'.

But not only did the late nineteenth century in England see a change in judicial penalties for 'unnatural offences', there was also a change in the interpretation of what constituted an 'unnatural offence'. Before 1885, the intervention of the law was confined to 'sodomy/ buggery'. That offence referred not only to the act of anal penetration of one male by another, but also to bestiality, and to heterosexual anal intercourse, although convictions for the latter were rare. (They are still rare. In NSW at the present time, charges for heterosexual buggery are laid only when a man has raped or sexually assaulted a woman as well.) Under the statute of Henry VIII, women could also be put to death for bestiality, and for participating in heterosexual 'sodomy/buggery'. After 1885, men could be convicted of *any* act which the courts ruled might constitute 'gross indecency', but the specific details of which were not spelled out in the legislation (as they are not in the 'act of indecency between male persons' provision of section 81A of the Crimes Act).

It is interesting to speculate to what extent the widening of the scope of the English law was a reflection of the inordinate concern displayed by the late-Victorian and Edwardian age in the 'perversions', the varied categories of which proliferated in the sexological literature of the time. Michel Foucault (1976: 60) provides us with a list of other 'petty perversions', which escaped the attention of the law, but which took on a solidity and permanence as their 'strange baptismal names' multiplied in the classifications of the nineteenth-century psychiatrists: for example, 'exhibitionists', 'fetichists', 'zoophiles', 'zooerasts', 'auto-monosexualists'. The explicit psychiatric purpose behind this multiplicity of names of 'perversions' was to identify them in order to eradicate ('cure') them. But by naming them and exhaustively describing their aetiology, symptoms and effects, the profession created a whole new field of 'scientific' investigation of behaviours which were previously unheard of.

This intense curiosity about the 'perversions' was a late stage in a process of redefining sexuality and its relation to 'society' which had been going on for three centuries. For the Victorians, the 'perversions' were a sign that the race was declining. (The sexual repression/ obsession which has come to be associated with the reign of Queen Victoria was not confined to England. As Foucault, a Frenchman, remarked in the first paragraph of his *History of Sexuality:* 'The imperial prude is emblazoned on our sexuality.') To halt the decline, it was necessary to search out and eradicate every last vestige of non-procreative sexuality. Male homosexuality, as the most serious threat to the purity of the race, was too important to be left to the vagaries of the scientific endeavour (at least in England). At the same time as the medical experts were identifying 'inversion' as a discrete phenomenon and giving concrete definition to a category of individuals who not only committed 'sodomy/buggery', but who were prone to other 'gross indecencies' too by reason of their innate disposition, the English law was widening its scope. The increasingly coherent and precise medical definition of the phenomenon identified the problem, and the criminal law attempted to eradicate, however ineffectually, that obvious anomaly to 'the laws of nature'.

Both Havelock Ellis and Michel Foucault date the appearance of the modern concept of (male) 'homosexuality' from the appearance of an article by Dr Karl Westphal in 1870. Westphal himself did not use the term—he referred instead to 'contrary sexual feeling'—and he confused transvestism (dressing as the opposite sex) with homosexuality (the distinction between the two is in fact a recent development in sexual theory). Ellis (1915:65) referred to him as 'an eminent professor of psychiatry at Berlin [who] may be said to be the first to put the study of sexual inversion on an assured scientific basis'. Westphal did have a precursor in Karl Heinrich Ulrichs, a lawyer who was himself a homosexual, whose numerous books and articles written over three decades from 1862 were an apologia for male homosexuality. He called homosexual men 'urnings', after a character in Plato's Symposium, Uranos, who gives a spirited defence of love between men. It was Ulrichs who coined the phrase (in Latin) 'a female mind in a male body' to describe the homosexual man. He argued that homosexuality was innate and no more pathological or reprehensible than colour-blindness or left-handedness.

But Ulrichs was a lone voice crying in the wilderness when he argued for the 'naturalness' of male homosexuality. By far the more prevalent view among the late-nineteenth-century medical profession was that homosexuality (including lesbianism) was a symptom of an inherited genetic defect. While no single term was used to refer to the phenomenon—other variations included 'inversion of the genital sense' and 'psychic hermaphroditism'—the preferred view of medical science was that homosexuality was one of the 'stigmata of degeneration', and hence of insanity (which was also regarded as a genetic defect). Towards the turn of the century, that view started to change. Although homosexuality remained an 'hereditary taint', it was no longer the serious symptom of psychopathology it had been earlier, and could even be compatible with psychic health (although what the 'taint' consisted of, if the patient was healthy, was not made clear).

The best-known and most influential of these theorists of the 'perversions' was Richard von Krafft-Ebing, a specialist in 'nervous diseases', the director of a mental asylum, and an acknowledged expert in forensic medicine. His weighty tome, *Psycopathia Sexualis*, first appeared in 1887, and went through twelve editions by the time he died in 1902. The numbers of case studies of 'paresthesias' or 'perversions of the sexual instinct', including male homosexuality and lesbianism, grew with each edition, as people suffering from the same or similar (or even completely different) conditions came to see him or wrote to him. (The sexual acts were all described in Latin, no doubt with the aim of preserving the innocence of those without a classical education.) In the earlier editions, he was unequivocal in attributing the perversions to a genetic flaw, which weakened the nervous system (at least in men) so that it was easily excited, and constantly demanded ever-increasing levels of stimulation. This led to excessive masturbation, which led to homosexuality, which in turn led to impotence, and the early grave of the neurasthenic. In 1901, however, the year before his death, Krafft-Ebing repudiated his 'degeneracy' theory, and admitted that homosexuality was not necessarily pathological (see Karlen, 1971).

These nineteenth-century advances in sexological science, with their identification and definition of 'inversion', took place for the most part in Germany and France. The English Victorians appeared to have no liking for such an enterprise (although doubtless the well-established psychiatric profession was conversant with the literature). The very mention of the 'vice not to be named among Christians' (as it was called during the Oscar Wilde trial—again in Latin) was enough to ensure that science took second place to moral outrage. In 1897 Havelock Ellis published his *Sexual Inversion*, in an attempt to draw the attention of the educated British public to the new 'scientific' approach to the issue. The next year, it was described in court as 'a certain lewd, wicked, bawdy and scandalous libel' (Weeks, 1977: 60; Hyde, 1970:156) and its first edition was recalled and destroyed because the executors of the estate of J.A. Symonds objected to his name appearing as co-author. It was finally published in the United States in 1914, with all references to J.A. Symonds deleted. It has never been published in England (Ellis, 1950: 295–313).

Nevertheless, while it cannot be demonstrated that the 'medical model' of 'inversion' had any influence on the motivations of the English legislators, the consequence of the 1885 attempt to suppress the 'unmentionable vice' was the same—to define its nature and publicise its existence. As D.J. West pointed out in his recent exhaustive overview of research into homosexuality (1977: 130): 'the really great scandals came after the passing of the Criminal Law Amendment Act of 1885, which permitted the prosecution of homosexual acts other than buggery'—the Oscar Wilde trials in 1895 being the most famous example. Given these consequences, the English law can be seen as one aspect of that process of redefinition and identification which was the domain of medical science elsewhere in Europe, as part of the process which Michel Foucault described thus:

> Sodomy—as specified in the old civil or canon law—was one kind of forbidden act, whose author had only a legal existence. The [male] homosexual of the nineteenth century has become a personage, with a past, a history and a childhood, a character, and life style . . . [male] homosexuality has arrived as one of the forms of sexuality once it has been transformed from the practice of sodomy into a kind of interior androgyny, a hermaphroditism of the soul. The sodomite was one who had lapsed from the state of grace; the [male] homosexual is now a species. (Foucault, 1976: 59, my translation)

Medical science did make some attempt to incorporate lesbianism into this process, although more as a logical requirement based on the supposition that a genetic quirk of nature must be of equal incidence in both sexes, than as phenomenon of interest in its own right. The

English law ignored its existence altogether. If the view of female sexuality held by William Acton, nineteenth-century physician and author of *The Functions and Disorders of the Reproductive Organs*, was at all prevalent among influential opinion makers of the time, then that omission is not surprising. This treatise, which went through six editions between 1857 and 1875, was primarily a dissertation on the evil consequences for men of 'sexual abuse' (masturbation) and 'marital excess', that is, 'sexual congress ... more frequently than once in seven or ten days'. On the whole, Acton showed a marked lack of interest in women. As Wayland Young, author of *Eros Denied*, expressed it: 'About men, Acton writes like a bluffy affectionate elder brother, warning, exhorting, even from time to time forgiving. About women he writes like a vet' (Young, 1969: 185–90). Acton asserted that the suggestion that women were capable of sexual feeling was 'a vile aspersion', and exhorted women to purity with injunctions like the following:

> As a general rule, a modest woman seldom requires any sexual gratification for herself. She submits to her husband's embraces, but principally to gratify him: and were it not for the desire of maternity, would far rather be relieved from his attentions. (Young, 1969)

Whether such strictures accorded with the true state of affairs, or whether they merely reflected wishful thinking or moral admonition on Acton's part, it was generally accepted that women did not need any sexual feeling in order to propagate the race. A man with a disinclination to heterosexual intercourse—that 'congenital invert' discovered by medical science, or that 'male person' prone to 'acts of gross indecency' identified in the 1885 legislation—might have difficulty in participating in the act of 'sexual congress'. But a woman's willing acquiescence was unnecessary, since she needed only to submit. Along with a disinclination to accept the existence of female sexuality—a disinclination which was not all-encompassing, since even Acton was prepared to accept the existence of 'courtesans' and 'mistresses'—there was the disinclination to accept that any erotic activity which took place in the absence of the male organ was 'sexual'. Whatever it was that 'female inverts' did together, once again it couldn't be sexual, since it lacked the definitive organ.

Henry Havelock Ellis

The work of Henry Havelock Ellis epitomises the dilemma of those liberal thinkers in the early years of this century who rejected the condemnatory attitude towards homosexuality of Christian religion and the criminal law, but whose only alternative framework was that of 'medical science', which defined the 'invert' as congenitally defective. Admittedly, by the time Ellis was writing, the degeneracy theory of homosexuality was on the wane, and Ellis himself took pains to counter the most extreme versions of the medical model. He was a humane polemicist with a firm belief in the ability of 'science' to expose ignorance and prejudice. As he himself expressed it:

> A few years ago . . . sexual inversion was scarcely even a name. It was a loathsome and nameless vice, only to be touched with a pair of tongs, rapidly and with precaution . . . As it now presents itself, it is a psychological and medicolegal problem so full of interest that we need not fear to face it, and so full of grave social actuality that we are bound to face it. (Ellis, 1915: 74)

Not that he himself approached the subject with the detachment of the disinterested observer. He was not homosexual, but his interest in 'inversion' was based on his perception of the disparity between his society's condemnation of homosexuality, and his own acquaintance with 'several persons for whom I felt respect and admiration' who were themselves homosexual, like J.A. Symonds and Edward Carpenter, 'not to mention Edith' (Ellis, 1950: 295). But ultimately he failed to resolve that contradiction. For while the concept of 'inborn constitutional abnormality' appears at first sight to provide a more rational approach than the labelling of homosexuality as 'vice' or 'insanity', yet that definition, too, cut the 'invert' off from full membership of the human race. Sinners can at least repent; the congenitally defective are beyond redemption.

Nevertheless, Ellis's book was an attempt to ameliorate the lot of the male homosexual. He argued at some length against the 1885 legislation. He was concerned about the provision within the Act for convicting men of 'acts of gross indecency' committed 'in private'. He pointed out that indecency is in the eye of the beholder; if there is no beholder, that is, when the act occurs in private, then there are no grounds on which to judge whether or not the act is indecent. Further, he argued that any attempt to penalise private behaviour brought the law into disrepute. It would become a 'legal farce', since very few convictions would be obtained because of the difficulty of acquiring evidence. Perhaps the most worrying aspect was the increased opportunity such a law gave for blackmail. He also pointed out the irrationality of legislative attempts to eradicate behaviour which, as he believed, was grounded in a congenital condition. Even were it possible to influence the behaviour, harsh legal penalties were not the most efficient method. He cited the example of France which did not have laws against male homosexual acts, and where public opinion was just as efficient as the law in keeping such behaviour in check, if not more so. Indeed, he felt that there might even be a direct correlation between punitive legislation and the public visibility of male homosexuality, since

> the chief effect [of harsh laws] seems to be that the attempt at suppression arouses the finer minds among sexual inverts to undertake the enthusiastic defence of homosexuality, while the coarser minds are stimulated to cynical bravado. (Ellis, 1915: 351)

Obviously Ellis was not criticising the endeavour per se to suppress male homosexuality, simply the efficiency of the method. However, he thoroughly disapproved of the law, and not only on the grounds of its inefficiency but also because it fulfilled none of the functions of good law, which he listed as the prevention of violence, the protection of the young, and the preservation of public order and decency.

His commitment to 'science' as the only rational way of understanding the phenomenon of 'inversion' led him to reject the extreme view that homosexuality was 'a functional sign of degeneration'. Although he had observed, he said, that the families of 'inverts' often contained a number of individuals who could be regarded as eccentric, yet eccentricity was not insanity. He drew a distinction between 'anomaly' (or 'abnormality') and 'disease', and argued that a phenomenon that fell outside the bounds of what was generally regarded as 'normal' could not for that reason alone be labelled pathological. 'The study of the abnormal is perfectly distinct from the morbid,' he stated at one point. He rejected the term 'degenerate' on the grounds that it was 'unscientific'. But its lack of scientific status, according to Ellis, was a consequence of its vagueness and lack of precise definition, rather than its reliance on a set of social evolutionist assumptions within which the dominant moral preoccupation of the times with 'the survival of the fittest' masqueraded as 'science'. This latter possibility could not have occurred to Ellis, since he shared those assumptions unquestioningly.

It was the unwarranted extension of Darwin's theory of the evolution of species into the sphere of human society which lay at the root of the liberal dilemma. On the one hand, Ellis (and others like him) needed to argue that homosexuality was not an acquired characteristic if they were to present a case against the moral condemnation of homosexuals, who could not be held to blame for something they had no control over. So Ellis argued that homosexuality was not acquired by 'association or suggestion'. If it were, he said, then it would be the sexual orientation of the majority of the population, since most of the time men associate with other men, and women with women. On the other hand, by arguing that homosexuality was inborn, Ellis was left with no alternative but the eugenicist framework which defined the health of the population by the 'survival' of its 'fittest' members. 'Survival' could only be assured by a continuing high birthrate among both the 'educated classes', the bourgeoisie who were industriously accumulating the wealth of the nation, and the 'labouring classes', a tractable, productive and reproductive working class. There was no such thing as a minor exception to this 'law of Nature'. Since Ellis himself subscribed to this view, his attempt to modify the 'degeneracy' theory succeeded in doing no more than modifying the harshness of some of the terminology. He inclined to the view, which he admitted was 'speculative', of an original 'latent organic bisexuality', which was probably influenced during foetal development by 'the stimulating and inhibiting play of internal secretions', that is, hormones. However, he was not neutral about the direction of this 'influence'. The preferred outcome was 'normality'—the masculine men and feminine women who were sexually attracted to the opposite sex. Any other outcome resulted in 'a person who is organically twisted'.

Hence, despite Ellis's sympathy with, and admiration for, the 'inverts' of his acquaintance, despite the distinction he drew between 'anomaly' and 'morbidity', he continued to confound 'Nature's design' with dominant social prescriptions of 'normality', and hence was unable to regard the 'invert' as anything other than deficient in the basic human endowment. He was uncertain whether or not this deficiency called for deliberate remedies. He and his wife Edith decided not to have children, although less because of her lesbianism than because of her 'inherited nervous instability' and his own 'nervous excess' (Ellis, 1950: 231). However, enforced eugenic measures might be unnecessary to ensure that 'inversion' was not passed on to succeeding generations. Homosexuals were, after all, less likely to marry and breed than were those whose heredity had endowed them with a sound sexual instinct. Indeed, homosexuality might be an integral part of Nature's grand design:

> The tendency to sexual inversion in eccentric and neurotic families seems merely to be nature's merciful way of winding up a concern [i.e. a particular family line] which, from her point of view, has ceased to be profitable. (Ellis, 1915: 335)

Ellis devoted one chapter in his book to lesbianism: 'Sexual Inversion in Women'. It contained only six case histories compared with 33 of men in the corresponding chapter 'Sexual Inversion in Men'. In the general sections of the book, 'inversion' almost invariably referred to men, although that was nowhere stated explicitly, but had to be inferred. For example, he wrote of 'love disappointment with a woman' as one of the precipitating factors in 'inversion' (unqualified), and of 'erections' and 'seminal emissions', without any other indication that the discussion no longer referred to both sexes. He also included an appendix on 'The School Friendships of Girls', which summarised a number of works describing schoolgirl 'crushes', 'flames' or 'raves', as they were variously called. The relevance of this to a theory of 'female inversion' which originated in an innate condition was not specified.

Freud and the psychoanalytic influence

The conviction that Havelock Ellis shared with most of the sexologists of the nineteenth century, that homosexuality was due to an 'inborn constitutional factor', was seriously challenged by psychoanalysis, which was the invention of one man, Sigmund Freud. By demonstrating that sexuality, whatever its eventual form, had already undergone numerous vicissitudes by the time it finally arrived at its adult outcome, Freud undermined the belief that biological factors determined the sexual preference of the adult. Instead, he argued, experiences during the earliest stages of childhood influenced the development of the sexual 'instincts', which originally (at birth) had no particular shape or direction. He did not argue that all forms of sexual expression were equally valid—the 'normal' outcome remained heterosexual intercourse in the service of the 'propagation of the species'. But his theory shifted the main focus of the 'medical model' of homosexuality (and the 'perversions') from the investigation of biology to the elucidation of the childhood family relations of homosexuals.

In *Three Essays on the Theory of Sexuality* (1905) and other works, Freud argued for two main ideas—that the sexual 'aberrations' were not different in kind from 'normal' sexuality, but variations of an initially undifferentiated sexual drive common to all human beings; and that this sex drive was not something which arose fully formed at puberty, but was in existence from the earliest stages of life, even in the newborn baby. Given the long series of developmental phases the sexual 'instincts' must pass through, it was not surprising that sexuality diverged and ramified into any of the number of possibilities which were present in potential from the beginning. Admittedly, Freud never doubted that 'one of the tasks implicit in [sexual] object-choice is that it should find its way to the opposite sex'. But the fact that it did so in the majority of cases was not due to any innate capacity for mutual attraction between the sexes, but rather to a variety of factors, one of which was the 'authoritative prohibition by society' against other ('aberrant') forms of sexual expression.

In the case of homosexuality, Freud argued against 'any attempt at separating off homosexuals from the rest of mankind as a group of a special character', since they were simply people who had continued along a path that everyone had travelled more or less briefly at some stage in their lives. He said that homosexuality could not, strictly speaking, be called a 'perversion', since it had a 'normal' sexual aim, the stimulation of the genitals to orgasm. He described it as an 'inversion' of the 'normal' sexual object choice (although he preferred to call it 'homosexuality' rather than use Havelock Ellis's favourite term). 'One must remember that normal sexuality too depends upon a restriction in the choice of object' (Freud, 1920: 151). Like Havelock Ellis, Freud too argued (rather more cogently) against 'degeneracy' theories. If homosexuality were a sign of innate 'nervous degeneracy', he said, then it would be accompanied by other abnormalities as well, to the point where it would seriously impair the individual's 'capacity for efficient functioning and survival'. Far from that being the case, homosexuality was frequently found in people who manifested no 'serious deviations', and often in people who were individuals of high intellect and 'ethical culture'. Moreover, homosexuality had been found in other cultures and historical periods, even among 'peoples of antiquity at the height of their civilization'. 'Degeneracy', therefore, was not a term of any clinical significance at all.

But neither did Freud find that the alternative explanations then available were any more adequate. On the one hand, he could not accept that homosexuality was innate in any sense which implied that individuals were born with their adult sexual object choice already fixed. On the other hand, neither could he accept that it was acquired in any simple cause-and-effect relation, since 'many people are subjected to the same sexual influences ... without becoming inverted or without remaining so permanently'. His own explanation, stated in the most general terms, was that 'a bisexual disposition is somehow concerned in inversion, though we do not know in what that disposition consists ... and ... we have to deal with disturbances that affect the sexual instinct in the course of its development'.

The kinds of 'disturbances' which could lead to a homosexual outcome in the adult varied. Freud was inclined to the view that there were different types of homosexuality (at least in men), which were probably due to different types of 'disturbance'. Nevertheless, he depicted one type of male homosexuality at some length in a paper on Leonardo da Vinci, and it is this account which has become the prototype for most subsequent theories of male homosexuality. In this paper, Freud suggested three main factors which could determine a male homosexual outcome: a mother who compensated for her own frustrations and 'penis envy' by an overintimate attachment to her son whose erotic feelings she awakened prematurely; an absent, harsh and/or indifferent father; and, later, a rivalry with other males—father and/or brothers—from which the boy withdrew by giving up all claims to sexual rights over females. It is not possible here to go into exhaustive details of how and why these factors were seen by Freud to be conducive to the making of the male homosexual. But one factor stood out above the others, and has come to be accepted among psychoanalysts as the primary 'cause' of homosexuality in men: the role of the mother. If the erotic bond between the mother and son was too strong, because it was reinforced by the mother's own dependency needs, and/or the father's weakness or absence, then the boy identified with his 'castrated' mother instead of with his father. Freud put the blame for this state of affairs squarely on the shoulders of the mother:

> Like all unsatisfied mothers, she [Leonardo's mother] took her little son in place of her husband, and by the too early maturing of his erotism robbed him of a part of his masculinity. (Freud, 1910)

In the case of the 'female homosexual', Freud was less sure about the factors determining the outcome, because she typically went through all the 'normal' vicissitudes of female development up to the point when she had to transfer her erotic feelings from her father to men in general. Moreover, the factors which eventually tipped the balance were also not different in kind from 'normal' development. This uncertainty on Freud's part was probably due to the fact that he only ever analysed one 'female homosexual', and even that analysis was not completed, because the girl (she was 17) left before it had run its course. However, on the basis of that analysis, and in the light of his general theory of female sexuality, Freud felt able to draw some tentative conclusions. If, when the time came for the girl to become interested in other men, her disappointment at her father's 'failure' to provide her with a 'penis substitute' (a baby) was too great, and/or the rivalry with her mother for her father's love too strong, then she renounced her father as a love object (and men in general) and identified with him instead.

In the case of both the male and the female homosexual, according to Freud, these 'disturbances' resulted in 'an inhibition in development'. The boy remained fixated on his mother rather than moving on to the next stage of identification with his father; and the girl regressed to an even earlier stage of mother-fixation. But in neither case did Freud regard homosexuality as 'psychosexual pathology' or even 'personality disorder'. In his famous letter to the American mother of a homosexual son, he reassured her:

> Homosexuality is assuredly no advantage, but it is nothing to be ashamed of, no vice, no degradation; it cannot be classified as an illness; we consider it to be a variation of the sexual function, produced by a certain arrest of sexual development. Many highly respected individuals have been homosexuals, several of the greatest men among them (Plato, Michelangelo, Leonardo da Vinci) . . . It is a great injustice to persecute homosexuality as a crime—and a cruelty . . . [If the woman's son were] unhappy, neurotic, torn by conflicts, inhibited in his social life, analysis may bring him harmony, peace of mind, full efficiency, whether he remains homosexual or gets changed. (Roazen, 1975)

It is this point of view which finally prevailed with the majority of members of the psychiatric and psychological professions (although, ironically, not among psychoanalysts) after decades of defining homosexuality as an 'illness', when, in 1974, the members of the American Psychiatric Association voted to delete 'homosexuality' and 'lesbianism' from the list of 'personality disorders' in the Association's Diagnostic and Statistical Manual.

In between this judgment of Freud's in the 1930s, and that recent reclassification (strictly speaking, *de*classification), Freud's followers took up and expanded upon what were no more than suggestive insights in his work, and ignored the tentative status of those ideas as their originator first expounded them. Oriented more towards 'cure' than comprehension, psychoanalytically influenced therapists asserted a Freudian dogma, with none of the intellectual caution displayed by the master:

> In general, to undertake to convert a fully developed homosexual into a heterosexual does not offer much more prospect of success than the reverse, except that for good practical reasons the latter is never attempted. (Freud, 1920)

Not all of the post-Freudian theorists of homosexuality were psychoanalysts. Many were members of other 'helping professions' (as they have come to be called), for example psychiatrists, psychologists, medical doctors. Nevertheless, it is the psychoanalytic view which has predominated.

In psychoanalytic theory, there were two aspects to explanations of homosexuality. One was the elucidation of certain disordered personality characteristics which were regarded as typical of homosexuals. The other involved the investigation of the aetiology ('causes') of homosexuality. The drive to establish that homosexuality involved a 'mental/personality disorder' owed very little to Freud's theory,

94

despite the lavish use of psychoanalytic terminology, or, alternatively, its extrapolation into commonsense concepts which had nothing to do with Freud's own theory. His concept of 'an inhibition in development', for example, did not have the same connotations as the commonsense term 'immaturity', a theme which runs through many subsequent authoritative pronouncements on the personality characteristics of homosexuals. The 'great men' mentioned in Freud's letter were also 'inhibited in development', but it would be ridiculous to call them 'immature'. A further concept which appears frequently in psychoanalytic treatises on homosexuality is that of 'narcissism'. This term means 'self-love', and in Freud's theory it was a necessary component of the process whereby the developing ego identified itself as separate from the world around it. If carried to the extreme, it could no doubt be called pathological, although it would seem that the pathology would be more likely to be manifested as catatonia (a complete withdrawal from interaction with the outside world), than as homosexuality. As the term 'narcissism' is used in post-Freudian accounts of homosexuality, it appears to mean no more than the dictionary definition of homosexuality, that is, love of someone of the same sex. But if Freud cannot be held responsible for some of the more bizarre pronouncements on the personality characteristics of homosexuals, he *can* be held responsible for subsequent theories of the causes of homosexuality, and the part played by the parents of homosexuals, particularly mothers. Primed with this insight from the master, psychoanalytic therapists 'discovered' smothering mothers and indifferent fathers by the score in the childhoods of male homosexuals.

One of the most influential works to put forward this point of view was a study published in 1962, called *Homosexuality: A Psychoanalytic Study*. Its principal author, Irving Bieber, who for many years was an acknowledged authority on male homosexuality, was among the most vocal opponents of the American Psychiatric Association's decision to remove homosexuality from its diagnostic list of mental disorders in 1974. The conclusions reached in this volume were based on data collected over ten years by a research committee of the Society of Medical Psychoanalysts. The information was not gathered directly from homosexual men themselves, but from 77 psychiatrists, all members of the Society, who filled in questionnaires about the case histories of 106 male homosexual and 100 male heterosexual patients.

According to Bieber and his co-authors, homosexuality in the male was due to the destructive influence of a 'close-binding intimate' mother, who overprotected, dominated and 'demasculinised' her son. She was typically frigid towards her husband, the psychiatrists reported to the researchers, while at the same time seductive towards her son. She was also inclined to dominate her husband and to treat him with contempt. The boy's father was detached from the family, if not openly hostile towards the son. Up to this point, these findings were in accordance with the Freudian schema. But the research team also claimed to have discovered another parental behaviour pattern which operated to produce homosexual sons. According to the researchers and their psychoanalyst informants, both parents combined to inhibit their son's heterosexual development, and to discourage him from engaging in assertive masculine behaviour. Evidently, because of the anxiety which masculine assertiveness evoked in both parents, they suppressed any manifestations of masculine behaviour and heterosexual interest their son might display, leaving him no choice but a homosexual orientation as an adult.

The researchers also claimed to have discovered certain personality traits which were typical of homosexual men. Male homosexuals, they stated, displayed an 'excessive' amount of interest in sexual gratification, engaging in sexual activity at an earlier age and more frequently than the heterosexual men. That this 'excessive' sexual activity could be due to the greater sexual availability of males than of females, rather than an intrinsic personality characteristic of homosexual men, did not appear to have occurred to the researchers. The psychoanalysts also made reference to the 'narcissism' of homosexual men, a trait which purportedly manifested itself in the exhibitionistic display of, and voyeuristic interest in, the genitals and buttocks. But there was no evidence supplied that the exhibitionism of homosexual men was more excessive than that of heterosexual men (called in common parlance 'flashing'), nor that homosexual men were more interested in the genitals and buttocks of other men, than heterosexual men were interested in the genitals and buttocks (not to mention breasts) of women. Homosexual men, their therapists asserted, lived their lives in fear of exposure and of attack by other males, but why this should be seen as a deficiency of character rather than as a rational assessment of the risks of being homosexual in a heterosexual world, was not stated.

It might be considered that, as an empirical study, this work could be relied on as an accurate picture of the male homosexual, and as a substantiation of the psychoanalytic account of the origins of male homosexuality. But the data which formed the basis of the study was the clinical practice of psychoanalysis itself, and hence was not an independent verification of that theory. Moreover, the therapists' claim to have discovered that the parents of a homosexual son suppressed his heterosexual assertiveness, is a strange one, not the least because it is difficult to see how a small boy could assert himself 'heterosexually'. Even if we assume that 'heterosexual' behaviour is behaviour which is conventionally regarded as appropriate for the male sex, the 'discovery' is still strange, because it implies that at some stage the boy *had* been assertive, but that by some means the parents had 'knocked it out of him'. But the general agreement within the profession was that potentially homosexual boys characteristically had a childhood history of preference for 'feminine' behaviour and activities, and no interest at any stage in 'masculine' pursuits. Hence, there would be nothing for parents who were fearful of 'masculine assertiveness' to react to. Nevertheless, this oddity remained unnoticed within the profession, and the 'homosexually-inducive family' entered the literature as one of the causes of male homosexuality.

Bieber himself displayed no interest in the phenomenon of lesbianism. However, one of his co-workers on the *Homosexuality* volume, Cornelia B. Wilbur, felt that the schema developed for the genesis of male homosexuality also applied to the genesis of lesbianism. The puzzle facing researchers into homosexuality, Wilbur explained, was how to account for homosexuality since heterosexuality was a 'biologic norm' (an assumption which, incidentally, flatly contradicted Freud's views on the matter). Wilbur went on to say:

> the capacity to adapt homosexually is, in a sense, a tribute to man's [*sic*] bio-social resources in the face of thwarted heterosexual goal achievement. Sexual gratification is not renounced; instead fears and inhibitions associated with heterosexuality are circumvented and sexual responsivity with pleasure and excitement to a member of the same sex develops as a pathological alternative. (Wilbur, 1965: 268)

She then went on to consider the question of what kinds of experiences could lead to 'such intense fears and inhibitions of heterosexuality that homosexuality can be the only outcome', and argued that the inhibitory process involved 'anti-heterosexuality' mechanisms at work within the parent–daughter relationship, as in the case of the parents of homosexual sons. Some of these mechanisms included 'distortions' of 'sexual training', whereby the girl received the idea that heterosexuality was disgusting or threatening. Her parents actively and explicitly warned her against, and punished her for, engaging in boy–girl relationships, while ignoring the existence of lesbianism and hence failing to warn her against *its* dangers. However, Wilbur admitted, there were many families in which girls experienced a taboo against heterosexuality (although Wilbur did not consider the implications of why that might be so). Hence, there must be some dynamic operating in those families which produced lesbian daughters. And that dynamic involved 'typical' personality traits on the part of the parents, just as it did in the case of families which produced homosexual sons.

The 'typical' mother of a lesbian daughter was domineering, and placed excessive restrictions on her daughter, who was always the loser in the constant struggles between them. The mother controlled her daughter by means of techniques of rejection, disparagement and guilt inducement. The daughter reacted with hostility and rebellion, caught in the ambivalent situation of longing for affection and approval from her mother, while at the time resenting her mother's overbearing behaviour. The 'typical' father was an unassertive individual who detached himself from the conflict between his wife and daughter. He was unable to offer his daughter any protection, and although he was basically kind, he was ineffectual and helpless in the face of his wife's manipulation of the family dynamics. (Is it any wonder that psychiatrists and psychologists who do not subscribe to this point of view have felt compelled to write books reassuring the parents of gay people that they were not, after all, to 'blame' (Silverstein, 1979; Hay & Goulden, 1982); or that CAMP NSW should have formed a group for 'Parents and Friends of Gays'?)

In another paper in the same volume with Wilbur's paper, a psychoanalyst, May E. Romm, offered an explanation for lesbianism which put the onus for her 'immature' sexual orientation on to the lesbian herself. The development of lesbianism, according to this schema, involved a failure on the part of the lesbian to come to terms with the universal female dilemma of 'penis envy'. Instead of transcending the girl child's conviction that women are devalued in comparison with men, a process which involved coming to terms with and accepting woman's traditional role of wife and mother, the lesbian had reacted with feelings of hostility and inferiority in relation to men. (That this might be regarded as a perfectly understandable reaction within a framework which defines the life of *every* woman as a search for substitutes for the organ they lack, did not occur to May E. Romm.) The lesbian, in compensation for her lack (which she shared with all women), 'may' take refuge in identifying with men, and playing a 'masculine' role with other women; or she 'may' develop an ultra-femininity which seeks a mother–father figure in her sexual partners. But, however she expressed her sexual preference, the lesbian remained 'immature', because 'one of the cardinal requisites for maturity is heterosexual mating and the creation of a family', said May E. Romm—a statement which owed more to moral admonition than to Freudian theory.

Another acknowledged expert on homosexuality, both male and female, was Charles W. Socarides, author of *The Overt Homosexual*, published in 1968. Like Bieber, Socarides thoroughly disapproved of the American Psychiatric Association's removing 'homosexuality' from the category of 'mental disorder'. He was also in complete agreement with Bieber's concept of the homosexually inducive family. But Socarides' main interest lay not in the family histories of homosexuals, but in 'typical' homosexual patterns of personality and behaviour. In the true post-Freudian tradition, he regarded homosexual men as as 'narcissistic', his reason being that they 'identify with the mother, taking themselves narcissistically as their sexual object. Consequently they search for a man resembling themselves whom they could love as their mother loves them'. He also asserted (unsurprisingly) that homosexual men displayed signs of 'immaturity', which was manifested as 'a low frustration tolerance' and 'ideas of grandeur existing along with a poor image of self'. As well, homosexual men were sadistic and masochistic at one and the same time, the masochism (erotic pleasure experienced through pain inflicted on oneself) being a reaction to, and a defence against, sadistic aggressive impulses towards both parents. Socarides even managed to make loneliness a personality trait. Homosexual men, he said, had forfeited any possibility of succeeding in interpersonal relationships. They could not relate to other men because they had failed to acquire a masculine identity; and they could not relate to women because they were incapable of seeing women as sex objects. The remaining alternative of homosexuality was 'an attempt to achieve human contact and to break through stark isolation ... The pathological quality of the homosexual's loneliness is in reality an acute tense depression mixed with mounting anxiety which threatens his psychological equilibrium if contact is not made quickly'.

Female homosexuality (he refused to use the term lesbianism, on the grounds that it was 'an attempt to romanticise it') was more 'complex'. (From Freud onwards, psychoanalysts have been in agreement that female sexuality in general was more 'complex' than that of the male.) He was of the opinion that there were more 'types' of female homosexual than of male homosexual, of which there were two: the 'active' and the 'passive'. At one point, he listed three, quoting Ernest Jones, including 'the familiar type of women who ceaselessly complain of the unfairness of women's lot and their unjust ill-treatment by men'. At another point, he listed nine, inserting in the middle of the list the irrelevant comment: 'In all homosexual women there is an intense unconscious aggressive murderous hatred of the mother and reproachful feelings towards the father'. Despite the 'complexity', Socarides managed to make a number of other generalisations about female homosexuals. They were equally as sadomasochistic as male homosexuals, although in women the sadistic urges were directed more against the mother than the father. They were also 'narcissistic', since 'one loves oneself in another person of the same sex in homosexuality'. And they were even more 'immature' than the male, since their 'fixation' on the mother necessitated a regression to an earlier stage of infantile existence than the father fixation of the male. Female homosexuals did, however, have one saving grace over the males:

> In contrast to the frequent interest of the male homosexual in young boys, the female homosexual is seldom attracted to young girls to the point of actual seduction. There are very few, if any, female pedophiliacs.
> (Socarides, 1968: 47)

Another so-called 'expert' is Frank G. Caprio, MD, author of *Female Homosexuality: A Psychodynamic Study of Lesbianism*. This volume was first published in 1954, but Caprio is still being quoted as an authority on homosexuality (for example, in the Personal Development course prepared for use in NSW schools). Why this should be so is by no means obvious. Unlike Socarides' work, which made extensive use of psychoanalytic theory, and hence spoke with the authority of a tradition which must be taken on trust by the ordinary reader, Caprio's book provided no more than a pseudo-psychoanalytic gloss to chatty little bits of conventional opinion. The book contained the obligatory reference to 'narcissism': 'lesbianism is a regression to narcissism'. For Caprio, the concept appeared to have something to do with 'man's [*sic*] desire to survive'. He admitted that everyone wanted to survive; but went on to insist that 'inverts have *unconsciously*, if not consciously, a neurotically *excessive* wish to *survive*'. The emphasis was supplied by Caprio himself and appeared to function as a substitute for evidence and rational argument.

He presented the reader with a disparate and unconnected series of 'contributing factors' to the development of lesbianism. The first mentioned was (unsurprisingly) the influence of the parents who 'unconsciously [or 'knowingly or unknowingly'—he didn't seem to be able to decide] contribute to the establishment of these fixations ... to one or both parents ..., which are often associated with incestuous fantasies, by fostering in their children feelings of rejection or neurotic dependence on them'. A second factor was that of 'psychic Traumas', some of which he listed as follows without specifying any order of priority: being accosted by an older male relative during adolescence; observing parental intercourse; being subjected by men to 'obscene language, selfishness, brutality, or a lack of adequate [sexual] technique'; being involved in seductive games with her father; and rape. A third factor involved what Caprio called 'environmental conditions', which he restricted to the discussion of 'certain occupations'. Whether the choice of particular occupations was a cause of lesbianism or an effect, is not clear from the text. But he warned young women against a 'slavelike devotion to a career which rules out the responsibilities of married life', and against sharing living quarters with other women.

A further factor which Caprio regarded as relevant for the genesis of lesbianism was the 'Feminist Movement' which had given women a greater sense of independence from men. While not denying that this movement had had a number of beneficial effects on the lives of women, Caprio expressed disquiet at the possibility that this emancipation might go too far. He quoted with approval a certain Dr Bauer, who said:

> Freedom for women means freedom to love. But we cannot go against Nature. Woman is intended for reproduction; she has been appointed to take an active part in the reproduction of the race by pregnancy and child birth. And while these laws of Nature remain every attempt at emancipation is futile.

Caprio appeared to perceive no incongruity between this fanciful and moralistic appeal to 'Nature', and the 'scientific' enterprise which he assured the reader he was engaged in. But this quotation clarifies the meaning of the term 'narcissism' as it is used by Caprio. Obviously he intended it to imply that lesbians were 'selfish' because they refused 'to take an active part in the reproduction of the race', and to sacrifice their own interests for the sake of husbands and children. He is, of course entitled to his opinion, but not to portray that opinion as unquestioned fact.

A more recent example of the influence of psychoanalysis on theorists of homosexuality, and one closer to home, is the paper which Ronald Conway presented to the NSW Bureau of Crime Statistics and Research seminar on Victimless Crimes in February, 1977. The paper concentrated on male homosexuality because, as Conway put it, 'almost twice as many homosexuals are male and . . . the law discriminates only against males'. He was highly critical of the legal situation, saying that the phrase 'the abominable crime of buggery' was 'surely the most offensive single formula existing in the criminal law'. He was also critical of general negative social reactions towards homosexuals, and argued that 'homosexuality between consenting adults presents no real threat to the life of the nation, the integrity of family life or indeed the most tender of religious consciences'.

He began the paper by pointing out that deviations from the sexual norm were deviations from 'the style of sexual attachments favoured in each human society', and not from some grand design of Nature. He went on to consider various factors which might be involved in the genesis of male homosexuality, the most important of which was the influence of the parents on the developing child: 'the basic Freudian insight into the principal cause of homosexuality in the *male* remains essentially unchallenged.' His paper did not address itself to the question of typical personality patterns of male homosexuals—three years after the American Psychiatric Association's decision to delete homosexuality from the category of mental disorder, it was no longer a valid exercise to assert that homosexuals had this or that character trait. Nevertheless, he felt that 'whatever might be said by gay liberation, homosexuality remains for most people a less satisfying and less naturally complete form of sexual expression'. He did not consider that homosexuals are not 'most people', and that for them homosexuality is the *only* satisfying and 'natural' form of sexual expression. He went on to state that 'great numbers of homosexuals would change their sexual orientation if they could', but failed to consider the possibility that these might be the very attitudes which constituted that 'self-hatred and despair' felt by so many homosexuals, which Conway himself so regretted further on in his paper. Conway's paper reflected some of the more recent positive changes in the approach of the helping professions towards homosexuality. However, he remained convinced that homosexuality could be 'cured' in some cases and hence implied that it could be an illness. He himself had used 'the psychedelic drug LSD 25', with at least as much 'success' as other therapies, although he felt that the 'success' rate would be lower if 'we were to take homosexuals off the street and try to treat them willy-nilly'. Hence, he continued to subscribe to the 'homosexuality as illness' thesis.

One final example of the way in which the psychoanalytic theory of homosexuality has been watered down for popular consumption, is a short section on 'homosexuality' in Derek Llewellyn-Jones's *Everywoman* (1978). This book, written by a well-known Sydney gynaecologists, has been a best seller in Australia and the UK and hence is a very influential work. In his brief account of lesbianism, Llewellyn-Jones expounded a popularised version of the psychoanalytic account of the genesis of homosexuality: 'Ultimately ... the sexual inclinations of the child are determined by the attitudes of the parents, and some parents unwittingly encourage homosexuality in their children'. This applied to both male and female homosexuality, and Llewellyn-Jones devoted as much space to males as to females in this short section. Why this should have been so in a treatise devoted to *female* sexuality he did not make clear, unless it was meant as a warning to his women readers about the way they were bringing up their sons: 'The mother who perpetually pampers her son [etc.] ... may turn him to homosexuality'. In the case of lesbianism, the possibility that it might be a valid sexual alternative was ruled out a priori, because men were to women 'the complementary sex' (presumably because each needed the other to complete her/his 'wholeness'). He concluded the section on a liberal (if condescending) note, however, by pointing out that 'many female homosexuals' lived 'full and contented lives' with another woman, and that those who didn't needed 'compassion and tolerance rather than derision and disapproval'.

It is treatises such as these which provided the definitive account of homosexuality until recently, when its validity was called into question by the American Psychiatric Association's decision that homosexuality was not a mental disorder. They have more than merely historical or academic interest—time and again in the course of our research we found them surfacing in everyday myths and stereotypes. Whatever might be the connection between the authoritative pronouncements of the 'experts' and popular mythology, variations on the above themes have filtered through into common knowledge. We have been told that homosexuals are childish, immature, exhibitionistic, insanely jealous, incapable of long-term relationships, sexually promiscuous, have uncontrollable sexual passions, and live lonely and frustrated lives because 'there will be no one to care for them in their old age'; that lesbians are masculine, violent and aggressive; that homosexual men are effeminate, weak and passive, and child molesters. The influence of such theories remains as justification for still prevalent anti-homosexual attitudes, but the task of uncovering certain personality defects which were purportedly typical of homosexuals is now problematic, since the helping professions have on the whole discarded such an enterprise. Whatever it was that psychoanalytically oriented therapists claimed to have discovered about homosexuals in clinical practice since Freud, those 'discoveries' were more likely due to that practice itself, rather than to any deficiency of human functioning intrinsic to homosexuality. Moreover, the abandonment of the search for signs of 'mental disorder' (because none were presumed to exist) has implications for the other aspect of the psychoanalytic theory—the part supposedly played by the parents of homosexuals. If there is now no longer any 'deficiency', there is no longer anything to explain.

But even before this latest challenge to the psychoanalytic theory of homosexuality, its validity was very much dependent on the acceptance of psychoanalysis as a whole. If it depicted homosexuals as less than fully-functioning adults, it must be remembered that Freud's depiction of *heterosexuality* did not present a favourable picture either. For example, Freud discussed the prevalence among men of what he called 'the tendency to debase sexual objects', that is, women. While only the most extreme form of this syndrome could be called a 'neurosis', yet the tendency, said Freud, appeared 'to be a universal affliction under civilisation and not a disorder confined to some individuals' (Freud, 1912). The reason behind this 'debasement', according to Freud's theory of the Oedipus complex, was the boy's realisation that women lacked the 'phallus', the symbol of human value:

> One thing that is left over in men from the influence of the Oedipus complex is a certain amount of disparagement in their attitude towards women, whom they regard as being castrated. (Freud, 1931: 376)

Freud's portrait of the normal feminine woman was even less flattering. Not only was she passive, repressed, hovering on the brink of neurosis and frigidity, in jealous rivalry with her daughters, and emotionally smothering her sons, she also possessed a weaker moral sense than a man. According to Freud,

> for women the level of what is ethically normal is different from what it is in men . . . they show less sense of justice than men . . . they are less ready to submit to the great exigencies of life . . . they are more often influenced in their judgements by feelings of affection and hostility. (Freud, 1937: 342)

Is it any wonder that some people become conscientious objectors in the war between the sexes? Even Freud felt the need to apologise to the 'ladies' for what could be interpreted as 'impoliteness': 'standing on the ground of bisexuality . . . we had only to say: "This doesn't apply to you. You're the exception: on this point you're more masculine than feminine"' (Freud, 1933: 166).

Hence the picture Freud painted of the normal heterosexual adult offered no more positive model of what might constitute the mature autonomous adult than the model which was usually applied to the analysis of the homosexuals. There is, of course, no obligation to accept the Freudian account at all. Nevertheless, to the extent that Freud's theory of homosexuality had any validity at all, it was valid only within his general theory of sexuality. To select certain aspects which reinforce one point of view, while selectively ignoring others, indicates an enterprise motivated more by prejudice than by scientific curiosity.

Recently the trend has been away from studies which 'demonstrate that homosexuality is a symptom of 'psychopathology'. But even when the psychoanalytic account was in its heyday there were studies which contradicted that account. For example, the findings reported in Kinsey's *Sexual Behavior in the Human Male* (1948) were a strong indication that to engage in homosexual behaviour was not an indication of severe personality disturbance. It was highly unlikely that over a third of the white adult male section of the American population—the 37 per cent of the adult male population uncovered by the Kinsey research who had had some homosexual experience as adults—were suffering from personality disorders.

Since the publication in 1957 of Evelyn Hooker's paper, *The Adjustment of the Overt Male Homosexual*, it is difficult to see how anyone could seriously entertain the 'psychopathology' hypothesis, without at least referring to this definitive work, and taking into account the challenge it posed to 'several widespread and emotional convictions' (as the executive editor of the *Journal of Projective Techniques* put it). Dr Hooker's interest in the issue of male homosexuality was first aroused when she came to know personally, through one of her students, a group of people who suggested that she do some research investigating 'people like them'. These men had read the clinical literature on male homosexuality, and had come to the conclusion that, as Dr Hooker put it, 'much of it was irrelevant to an understanding of their condition'. Hence, the first step in her investigation of 'male homosexuals and their worlds' involved a relationship of 'friend to friend', rather than the distancing one of research 'expert' to research subjects (Hooker, 1965: 92). This unconventional starting point influenced the subsequent direction of the research—it is difficult if not impossible to retain prejudices about 'pathology' or 'abnormality' if one likes and respects one's research subjects.

Hooker's findings indicated that 'homosexuality is not necessarily a symptom of pathology'. She 'very tentatively' suggested three implications for psychology of that hypothesis. The first was that 'homosexuality as an entity does not exist', that is, homosexual men displayed as many and as varied forms of behaviour, personality, adjustment, etc. as heterosexual men did. The second implication was that, although homosexuality 'may be a deviation in sexual pattern', as far as general psychological functioning was concerned, homosexual men were 'within the normal range'. The third suggested implication was that 'the role of particular forms of sexual desire and expression in personality structure and development may be less important than has frequently been assumed'. Even were it necessary to retain the assumption that homosexuality was a 'severe form of sexual maladjustment', it was not necessary to extrapolate from the 'maladjustment', in the sexual sphere to other aspects of personality or behaviour. But for many years, Dr Hooker's views took second place to those 'several widespread and emotional convictions'.

Psychology

The dominating influence of psychoanalysis on theories of homosexuality was also challenged by the discipline of psychology, which preferred a more pragmatic approach to the issue. Psychologists were wary of the 'grand theory' approach of psychoanalysis, whose validity was seen to depend on the judgments of individual therapists already convinced of its correctness, and whose findings could not be replicated by anyone who lacked the commitment to the psychoanalytic perspective. Instead, psychologists preferred to use objective testing procedures which were meant to obviate the individual biases of the researcher and of the subjects. These test procedures were applied to single or limited hypotheses, and the results quantified so that they could be replicated easily.

Unfortunately for drawing generalisations from the psychological data, there are a number of difficulties in making generalisations from one piece of psychological research to another. One of those difficulties concerns the variety of research instruments used. Some of the findings were based on biographical data elicited by means of questionnaires, open-ended interviews, or participant observation, data which depended on the conscious memory of the subjects being studied. Others were based on the results of 'projective tests', which involved giving the subjects pictures of non-specific situations, or random and ambiguous shapes (the most famous of these are the Rorschach 'ink-blots'), and asking them to devise a story around the picture, or to describe what they see in the shape. These tests were designed to give indirect indications of personality traits and motivations, by (supposedly) mapping the unconscious aspects of experience and character. Still other findings were based on questionnaires designed to elucidate clusters of personality traits. These differing research methods suggest extreme caution in comparing findings reached thus independently.

A further difficulty concerned the diverse nature of the subject populations studied. Among the earliest groups studied were psychiatric patients who were not necessarily in therapy because of their homosexuality, and the inmates of institutions such as hospitals, both general and psychiatric, and prisons. Obviously such populations were not representative of the general population of homosexuals, as they were not representative of the general population of heterosexuals. But even the later research which endeavoured to tap the general population of normal homosexuals was biased towards the college-educated and the upper socioeconomic levels, probably because most researchers were affiliated with tertiary educational institutions and had a readily available subject population among students. More recently, researchers recruited subjects from among the members of homosexual organisations and from social and friendship networks. It is likely that the more favourable (to homosexuals) research findings from these studies were due to the fact that people who had the supportive milieu provided by these organisations and networks did not suffer the isolation and deprivation, with their consequent 'personality disorders', of those homosexuals who had no one to turn to. This shift in the kinds of subject populations studied means that the earlier and later studies are not comparable.

Nevertheless, for the very reason that psychological research studies have produced such conflicting results, they have at least brought into question the findings of the psychoanalysts. One team of researchers did find themselves in agreement with Bieber's conclusion about the part played in the causes of male homosexuality by a 'close-binding intimate' mother and a 'detached' father. Snortum and his team (1969) studied 46 men who were being evaluated for separation from military service because of homosexual behaviour, and compared them with 21 enlisted men in training (assumed to be heterosexual). None of these men was in therapy. All were asked questions, to which they gave written answers, about their childhood family relationships. The researchers concluded from the results of this study that: 'It appears that the family dynamics for homosexual patients described by Bieber et al. were confirmed almost in toto.' Another researcher (Robertson, 1972), however, did not find evidence of 'an abnormally intense mother–child relationship' in the childhood experiences of the male homosexuals he studied. Robertson studied four groups of men: 'homosexual–normal', 'heterosexual–normal', 'homosexual–neurotic', and 'heterosexual–neurotic'. While his findings did indicate that the 'neurotic' men, both homosexual and heterosexual, could recall having been in an over-intense relationship with their mothers in childhood, the 'homosexual-normal' men displayed no consistent pattern of mother–child relationship. He concluded that 'the existence of a too powerful relationship between child and mother is not itself of primary importance' in the genesis of male homosexuality. This finding is in accordance with earlier conclusions drawn by Eva Bene (1965a). In her study, Bene found no evidence that the homosexual men had had closer or more intense relationships with their mothers than had the heterosexual men. However, they did appear to have had 'weak and ineffectual' fathers, and as Bene pointed out, 'if a man is weak, his wife does not have to be domineering to appear dominant'. If it was the case that homosexual men were more attached to their mothers than to their fathers, that was because they had such poor relationships with their fathers. Bene concluded by pointing out that the prevention of male homosexuality depends on the availability of 'father figures' for young boys. Siegelman (1974), however, found himself unable to draw any conclusions at all about a cause-and-effect relationship between parental behaviour and the sexual orientation of their children. He cited a number of researchers who had reached similar conclusions to his own. The findings of his study would seem to point to a lack of *any* association at all between family relations and homosexuality or heterosexuality.

Much the same state of affairs is apparent in the data on the early familial relationships of lesbians. In an overview of research based on biographical information, Mannion (1976) concluded that 'no consistent picture of the lesbian's family background emerges', although she went on to say that the tendency of the data pointed to the importance of the girl's relationship with her father. Lesbianism appeared to be a response to the father's failure to meet 'the affectional needs of his pre-lesbian daughter', or even, according to Bene (1965b), to a 'fear of the father'. However, the results of another study (Armon, 1960) suggested that lesbianism was a defence mechanism against feelings of hostility, fear and guilt in relation to women which originated in the early relationship with the *mother*. As in the case of male homosexuality, the research data on lesbianism provided no secure base from which to decide one way or another on the relative importance of the same or the opposite-sex parent in the genesis of lesbianism.

The data on the personality characteristics of homosexuals was as inconclusive and conflicting as the data on family relationships, although the tendency was away from the psychoanalytic (post-Freudian) view of homosexuality as psychopathology. It is true that at least one researcher (Loney, 1971) found that homosexual men scored higher than heterosexual men on a personality inventory designed to measure maladjustment. The group of 29 homosexual men was recruited through social networks, and matched with a similar group of heterosexual men. Loney stated, however, that it was not possible to say whether the source of the maladjustment was to be found in the homosexual orientation itself, or whether it was the result of 'society's strong proscriptions'. De Luca (1967) found that it was not possible to differentiate between the personality characteristics of homosexual and heterosexual men. This failure suggested that the homosexual men and the control groups of heterosexual men were not in fact significantly different in terms of the degree and kind of psychosexual conflict. Clark (1973) failed to find any correlation between degree of psychopathology and position on the Kinsey scale, that is, degree of homosexual behaviour. Clark studied seven matched groups of men, each group comprising twenty college-educated, socially functioning, non-patient adult males. These groups were chosen so that they varied from each other only in the degree of homosexuality admitted to by each man. In the results of the tests, the 'homosexual' groups did not vary significantly from the exclusively heterosexual group.

As in the case of homosexual men, the research into the personality characteristics of lesbians has, on the whole, failed to provide any evidence that lesbians display more personality defects than heterosexual women. Mannion (1976) concluded:

> In spite of some evidence to the contrary there seems to emerge a rather consistent profile of the lesbian as a woman who is independent, self-assertive, dominant, possessing an apparent ability to achieve a degree of satisfaction characteristic of the actualising adult.

To the extent that these qualities are seen as 'masculine' prerogatives and hence as inappropriate for women, lesbians could perhaps be characterised as 'abnormal'. However, that 'normal' women are not expected to possess the above qualities is more a comment on the limitations of conventional definitions of womanhood, than it is on the personal qualities of lesbians. (See also Freedman, 1971; Hammersmith and Weinberg, 1973; Hopkins, 1969; Myrick, 1974; Saghir and Robins, 1971; Siegelman, 1972; Thompson et al., 1971; Wilson and Greene, 1971.)

On the whole, then, the evidence from psychology on the causes of homosexuality and the personality characteristics of homosexuals is confused. Nevertheless, as already mentioned, there has been an ever-increasing trend away from the 'discoveries' of pathology.

A biological basis?

As the psychoanalytic account of homosexuality which explained its origins in terms of a failure of the socialisation process grew more influential, those explanations which defined homosexuality as innate, as due to an inborn hereditary defect, fell into disfavour. However, despite its popularity, the psychoanalytic explanation was not entirely adequate as an account of the causes of homosexuality. It could not explain, for example, why people who were subjected to the same childhood experiences, even to the extent of being brought up by the same parents, should have a different sexual orientation as adults. Freud himself was aware of the limitations of the psychoanalytic account. Since both homosexuals and heterosexuals experienced the vicissitudes of the Oedipus complex, and since even the 'normal' outcome of the process entailed enormous difficulties, Freud felt the need to postulate as well a stronger tendency within the original bisexual potential for a homosexual outcome than for a heterosexual one, a biological substratum which could influence the individual in a homosexual direction when combined with the appropriate socialisation experiences. Moreover, he was convinced that eventually it

109

would be possible to reduce psychoanalytic phenomena such as the unconscious, bisexuality, the death instinct, etc., to an unequivocally biological basis. In the meantime,

> it is not for psychoanalysis to solve the problem of homosexuality. It must rest content with disclosing the psychical mechanisms that resulted in determining the object choice, and with tracing back the paths from them to the instinctual dispositions. There its work ends, and it leaves the rest to biological research. (Freud, 1920: 171)

This biological research involves assuming that sexual desire is at least primarily, if not exclusively, determined by biological factors, a plausible enough assumption given the undoubted biological connection between heterosexual intercourse and reproduction. However, the assumption becomes less plausible on closer examination. Human individuals are rarely motivated to engage in sexual activity by a desire to reproduce. Sexual activity has its own intrinsic motivations which do not depend on an event which may or may not eventuate nine months later. The variety of sexual behaviours, even between heterosexual couples, are not necessarily conducive to reproduction, and often involve an active avoidance of conception. Moreover, to dismiss all non-heterosexual activity as 'unnatural perversions' is to settle the issue a priori, without considering the challenge the existence of such activities poses to the biological assumption that human sexual behaviour derives from some kind of instinct for reproduction.

Moreover, biological research into the origins of homosexuality also frequently involved assuming that homosexuals displayed characteristics which were presumed to be the prerogatives of the opposite sex: homosexual men were assumed to be 'feminine', and lesbians, 'masculine'. The earliest studies, inspired by the work of the late-nineteenth-century psychiatrist and criminologist, Cesare Lombroso, made crude measurements of physical characteristics and body types. Male homosexuality was supposedly associated with 'small stature, excess fat, wide hips, smooth skin, a feminine distribution of pubic hair, narrow shoulders, a boyish face, luxuriant hair [presumably confined to the head], a "too good-looking appearance", and an inability to whistle' (West, 1977: 74). This last had been suggested by Ulrichs, and, as Arno Karlen (1971: 190) put it, 'case histories taken all over Europe dutifully noted whether the subject could whistle'. Lesbians, by the same token, were investigated for 'mannish' characteristics and behaviour (including the ability to whistle). Among the characteristics which were regarded as male prerogatives was assertive sexuality. Since prostitutes and 'female criminals' were regarded as initiators of sexual activity, they were investigated for evidence of lesbianism. When the 'evidence' was found, it served to vindicate 'degeneracy' theories of homosexuality. However, with the decline of such theories, and the increasing sophistication of disciplines like cytogenetics (the study of chromosomes) and endocrinology (the study of hormones) not to mention the eventual failure to find any physical differences between homosexuals and heterosexuals, this kind of biological research fell into disfavour.

But the search for a biological basis continued. Since the 1940s and 1950s, when it became possible to identify and count the number of chromosomes in the human cell, a number of sex-chromosomal abnormalities have been discovered. Instead of the normal male sex chromosome XY pattern, some males were discovered to have one or more X chromosomes in an XXY or XXXY pattern; others were discovered to have an extra Y chromosome, in an XYY pattern; and some females, instead of the normal female sex chromosome XX pattern, were discovered to have an extra X, in an XXX pattern; others were found to be missing one X, in an XO pattern. Since the earliest and most basic level of sex differentiation occurs at this chromosomal level, it was hypothesised that such sex-chromosomal abnormalities might be implicated in the genesis of homosexuality. However, the hypothesis was unequivocally demonstrated to be false. There was no greater incidence of homosexuality among these people than within the general population; nor did sample groups of homosexuals display a higher incidence of these chromosomal defects than did the general population.

A further area of investigation for a biological substratum for homosexuality is the influence of hormones on sexual characteristics. As usual, most of the research interest had been confined to homosexual men. D.J. West (1977) cited one study which had examined *four* lesbians and found that their testosterone (an androgen) level was unusually high while their oestrogen levels were low. But four people hardly constitute an adequate sample, and West cited no follow-up research. In the case of homosexual men, some of the earliest studies (West, 1955) attempted to demonstrate that adult male homosexuals were deficient in androgens, on the assumption that, since male homosexuals were insufficiently 'masculine', they must suffer from an insufficiency of the 'masculine' hormones. These attempts were unsuccessful, largely, it was asserted, because of the crudity of both the hypothesis and the measurement techniques used.

Nevertheless, the search goes on. The latest in the long line of claimants for the distinction of having discovered that biological basis is the East German endocrinologist, Gunter Dörner, whose work has popularised in the program shown on ABC television, 'The Fight to be Male'. Dörner and his co-researchers (1975) asserted that their findings indicated that 'homosexual men possess a predominantly female-differentiated brain which may be activated to homosexual behaviour by normal or approximately normal androgen levels in adulthood'. In other words, their claim was that they had discovered the neuro-endocrinological basis for Ulrich's suggestion of over a century before that the male homosexual possesses a female mind (brain) in a male body (although they made no reference to Ulrich's writings). The starting point for the research with homosexual men was a series of observations Dörner had made of male rats which had been castrated at birth, thus stopping the flow of androgens to those centres of the brain which controlled the sexual behaviour of the adult rat, at the critical time when those centres were differentiated into typical male or female patterns. The rats, when dosed with androgens as adults, displayed 'predominantly female-like'—'homosexual'—behaviour, as Dörner and his colleagues expressed it. The reason suggested for this was that androgen deficiency at a crucial stage of sex-specific brain development, just after birth in rats, led to a 'predominantly female brain organisation'.

They went on to suggest that it was now 'theoretically' possible to institute 'a preventive therapy of sexual differentiation disturbances'. Since it is possible to determine both the sex of the foetus and the level of androgens produced by the foetus, from a sample of amniotic fluid, then male homosexuality could be prevented by injecting into the amniotic sac surrounding a male foetus deficient in androgens, sufficient androgens at the crucial stage to prevent his brain being 'feminised'. The fact that the 'simple and reliable method for prenatal diagnosis of genetic sex' involves puncturing with a hollow needle the abdomen and uterus of the pregnant woman—perhaps even *all* pregnant women if male homosexuality is to be eradicated—appears as a matter of small moment to these intrepid scientists. Nor were they deterred by the fact that amniocentesis, as this procedure is called, carries a high risk of miscarriage.

Dörner did not neglect 'female homosexuality', or rather, and more accurately, the occurrence of 'predominantly male sexual behaviour' in female rats, which had been given doses of androgen during the crucial developmental stage. The cure (at least for the rats) is anti-androgen injections at the right moment. The relevance of the problems of androgenised female rats to lesbianism was not specified (see Dörner, 1969).

One of Dörner's critics (Meyer-Bahlburg, 1977) pointed out that Dörner's unequivocal findings on male homosexuality were in direct contrast to every other study which has tried to link homosexuality with hormonal abnormalities, and were 'in urgent need of replication by independent laboratories'. Meyer-Bahlburg also questioned the relevance of studies of rats to human beings. He asked: 'Are so-called rat homosexuality and human homosexuality really homologous?' He found it unlikely, since human homosexuals are defined with reference to erotic attractions, sexual fantasies, and sexual experiences which have no analogue in the animal world; and 'male homosexuality' in rats is defined by increased readiness to display lordosis (the bending of the back so that the genital area is presented), and/or decreased readiness to engage in mounting and intromission. Moreover, the human phenomenon of habitual and preferential homosexual behaviour has never been observed in mammals other than humans. He might also have pointed out two well-established facts of animal behaviour which do not necessarily have any analogues in human behaviour or motivation. The first is the connection between levels of androgen and aggression; the second is the part the female sexual presenting position plays in communicating a submissive, non-threatening posture. The de-androgenised rats were less aggressive than normal male rats, and their presentation of the female sexual position was more likely to indicate their low status in the 'pecking order', than the rodent equivalent of homosexual desire. Until other endocrinologists take up and investigate these findings, the blatant anthropomorphising of Dörner and his associates suggests that we cannot accept their conclusions at their face value. Meyer-Bahlburg concluded: 'Whether or not and to what extent there is a neuroendocrine predisposition for sexual orientation in humans cannot be decided on the basis of the current evidence'.

'Curing' homosexuality

With the categorising of homosexuality as 'illness', it is not surprising that there have developed within the 'helping professions'—psychology, psychiatry, psychoanalysis, and psychotherapies of various other forms—a number of techniques for 'curing', 'treating' or 'helping' homosexuals. (Once again, most of these efforts have been directed towards men.) A brief review of the main kinds of psychotherapeutic methods used in the United States was given by Jerome D. Frank (1972) in a background paper presented to the National Institute of Mental Health Task Force on Homosexuality in 1969. Most of the reported studies Frank examined had used 'a more or less analytically oriented interview type of therapy', sometimes combined with group therapy. All the studies of this type, Frank said, 'assumed ... that certain childhood experiences lead to general passivity and timidity, coupled with fear of the female as a sex object'. The obvious therapeutic implication of this assumption was to reinforce 'the patient's aggressiveness and self-confidence as well as ... removing his inhibitions against the opposite sex'. On the whole, the analysts in these cases, according to Frank, more or less devalued the 'patient's' homosexuality, and encouraged 'heterosexual approaches'.

The second group of therapies was unequivocally directed towards eliminating homosexual desire. This group comprised the 'aversion therapies'. One type of aversion therapy 'consisted of repeatedly giving patients an emetic [a nausea-inducing drug] and showing them stimulating male photos at the height of their nausea' (Frank, 1972). This was sometimes coupled with a further procedure which involved giving the 'patients' testosterone, a male hormone the effect of which was presumably intended to increase sexual desire, and then showing them pictures of nude females. One case Frank mentioned involved playing a tape-recording while the 'patient' was feeling nauseous, 'which described vividly how disgusting and revolting homosexual practices are'. Another type involved showing the 'patient' slide pictures of nude men which he could turn off. If he failed to do so, he was given an electric shock, immediately after which he was shown a picture of a nude female 'to associate it with relief of anxiety'.

According to Lex Watson, in an article in a volume called *Mental Disorder or Madness?* (1979), the use of aversion therapy on male homosexuals 'has had a short and stormy history'. The first papers claiming some success were published in the 1960s, but by the middle of the next decade such claims had come to appear less feasible, and fewer therapists were offering to 'cure' male homosexuality by these means. The best known of the Australian aversion therapists who used these techniques on homosexual men was Dr Neil (or Nathaniel) McConaghy, Associate Professor of Psychiatry at the University of NSW, at Prince Henry Hosptial in Sydney. (He had never tried to 'cure' lesbianism because, as he said in an interview, 'we haven't developed techniques to measure sexual changes in women, largely because there were not enough women presenting themselves to justify it in terms of a research technique') (Wills, 1972). The emetic used by McConaghy was apomorphine. He described its use thus:

> With apomorphine aversion... the subject was initially given a subcutaneous injection of 1.5mg. of apomorphine. After about eight minutes, he began to feel nauseated. Severe nausea lasting ten minutes without vomiting was aimed for, and the dose was constantly adjusted throughout to maintain this response. One minute before the nausea came on, the patient slipped on a slide projector and viewed a slide of a nude or partly nude man. Before the nausea reached its maximum he turned off the projector. Twenty-eight treatments were administered at two-hour intervals over five days. (Agel, 1973; McConaghy, 1971)

At some stage, however, he abandoned the use of the emetic and concentrated solely on electric shocks, because it was 'shown in the early stages that it [apomorphine] is no more effective than the using of electric shocks'. The instrument to 'measure sexual changes' was a 'penile plethysmograph' which was attached to the 'patient's' penis to record volume changes in the penis and hence the level of sexual arousal (Wills, 1972?).

During the course of our research we came across a number of indications that other methods, too, had been used to deal with male homosexuality, either directly or indirectly (for example, because of the 'patient's' depression), such as hormonal therapy, psychosurgery, and electro-convulsive therapy (ECT). Frank (1972) mentioned briefly the 'adjunctive use' of hormones, but pointed out that the use of the male sex hormone was 'contraindicated' because it increased the sex drive while having no influence at all on whether that drive was directed towards men or women. Female sex hormones 'may occasionally help to dampen sexual preoccupation' (in men), but in one case mentioned by Frank it had had the opposite effect—'by making the patient impotent without decreasing his drive, it increased his homosexual preoccupations'. He did not mention that oestrogen treatment had a number of unpleasant and dangerous side-effects, including breast growth in men. Thrombophlebitis, pulmonary embolism, myocardial infarction and strokes are known to be more prevalent among men dosed with oestrogens, and there is also the possibility of an increased risk of cancer. Moreover, there is no hard and fast evidence that oestrogen is in fact a male sex drive suppressant.[6]

In 1973, John Ware, co-founder of CAMP, in response to media reports that male homosexuality was being 'treated' by the use of brain surgery, made a number of inquiries to find out where this was being done and by whom. He could get no information from the main teaching colleges and hospitals in and around Sydney, but through an article in the Australian he learned the name of a doctor who had testified in court that he had performed a brain operation on a homosexual man. He rang this doctor, a psychiatrist, and was told that he and his team were indeed performing psychosurgery. According to the psychiatrist, it was not being used to treat (male) homosexuality as such, but rather 'sexual immaturity', which included homosexuality. He said that he and his team did 90 per cent of all such operations in Australia, and so far had performed 150, of which 15 per cent were on (male) homosexuals. At the time he spoke to Ware, the surgeon on his team was performing three of these operations a week (Ware, 1973?).

Lex Watson (1979) discussed the work of the same psychiatrist. He claimed that this team was the only team in Australia which has performed psychosurgery specifically to change male homosexual orientation, although their published reports rarely mentioned homosexual behaviour. Rather, they referred to 'obsessive compulsive antisocial compulsive [sic] behaviour'. Watson included in his article the case of 'Bill', who had appeared twice before the courts charged with homosexual offences, the second time with adolescent boys (none of whom had complained about the activity). Before 'Bill' appeared in court the second time, he was given a cingulotractotomy[7] by this team, and on the strength of the psychiatrist's evidence that the operation had 'cured' him of his homosexual and paedophiliac tendencies, 'Bill' was given a five-year good behaviour bond. Three and a half years later, 'Bill' was again in court charged with offences involving a 10-year-old boy and a 7-year-old boy. Despite the psychiatrist's testimony that the operation had been successful—'Bill's problem now being one of alcoholism—he received a two-year prison sentence.

From submissions, the Phone-In[8] and other sources, the ADB came across a number of cases of people who had been subjected to psychiatric treatment in connection with their homosexuality. One man who contacted the ADB said that he had sought treatment for his homosexuality in 1968. He was given a course of aversion therapy in hospital, which comprised eight sessions a day for two weeks. The treatment consisted of viewing a set of homosexually erotic slides, for example two men having intercourse or performing fellatio. He was given an injection which caused nausea and which made him vomit violently while operating the slide projector. He said that when the course ended, he felt 'sexually washed out', but after three months he believed its effect had worn off completely. Some months later, he returned to the same hospital for another course of treatment, but again the treatment failed. He had his first homosexual experience a short time later, and felt slightly nauseous at the sight of the man's genitals, but all vestiges of the treatment had since disappeared. He described himself as having been an ideal candidate for aversion therapy: 'I really wanted to be cured, but it didn't work.' He said that he now accepted his sexual orientation, and was living in a long-term relationship with another man.

Another informant wrote to the ADB about his own experiences, which he situated within the context of the wider social condemnation of homosexuality:

> Some homosexuals tend to blame themselves for the way in which they are discriminated against. Psychiatrists take advantage of these people and the way they blame themselves by reinforcing their self-hate and 'curing' them. This only consists of fleecing them of their money.

116

This happened in my case. Even though other doctors told me I suffered no genuine psychiatric disorder, I still went to a psychiatrist and paid huge amounts for analysis and LSD. Also, I had been taught (implicitly) to despise the word 'homosexual' before I even knew what it meant. Imagine my feelings when I realized I was one. The way was clear for me, and others, to be taken advantage of. However, I was not the cause of my discrimination—society was. This also severely retarded the treatment of a physical condition that I had, viz. epilepsy, as I cannot take any psychiatric drugs with that condition.

This only proves that anything can become a sickness if one is taught to *think* of it as such, anyone can suffer *from* anything if they are made to suffer *for* it.

Also, related to this, when I went to North Ryde Psychiatric Centre to overcome the effects of a drug prescribed for my condition and found unsuitable, because I mentioned I was homosexual, I was bombarded with questions about the intimate details of my sex life which had nothing to do with my drug treatment (or any 'treatment' for that matter). Such questions were: 'How old were you when you first had sex with a man?' 'What did he do to you?' 'Have you ever had sex with a woman?' 'Was she a prostitute?' 'Why did your parents marry so late?'

No reason was given for these questions, they were not given voluntarily but under duress, I did not know what the information was to be used for or who else might have access to the information, I was shown no report and I was not given the option of having the information destroyed. I can't see my reason to question homosexuals just because they *are* homosexuals or to keep files or make reports on us.

Several of our Phone-In respondents complained that doctors and psychiatrists saw homosexuality as something to be cured, rather than as a form of sexuality as valid as heterosexuality:

* In 1968, when I was a teenager, my doctor asked me what my sexuality was. I said I didn't know. He offered me aversion therapy but I refused. In 1970 I sought help for long-term depression, and was told repeatedly that I was not homosexual and that I should try to be more rugged. I was treated with anti-depressant drugs. In 1974 I joined a psychiatric therapy group, which helped me because the other participants in the group emphasized that I should just be myself. The growth of the gay rights movement has also helped me as it has given me a feeling of support. In my opinion, the medical profession had not only refused to help me, they actually prolonged my period of depression.

* My brother arranged sessions with a psychiatrist for me after finding out I was homosexual. The psychiatrist wouldn't help me accept my homosexuality, and the sessions only made me depressed.

* In my experience G. Ps. are reluctant to discuss homosexuality, and tend to 'fob off' a complaint as due to 'homosexual nervousness'. One psychiatrist I was sent to said: 'You can't possibly be a homosexual as you have a hairy body'.

117

★ I got a broken jaw as a result of a poofter-bashing incident. I went to the casualty section of a Sydney hospital and explained the circumstances. I was given no support for the emotional strain of being poofter-bashed, and was misdiagnosed as having only a broken tooth. An X-ray by my G.P. the next day showed that my jaw was broken in 3 places and needed wiring. I believe that my homosexuality was a major reason for the poor treatment I got at the hospital.

Another case referred to us concerning aversion therapy occurred in 1969 or 1970. The patient was referred by another psychiatrist:

I was interviewed once [by X] for about a quarter of an hour. He suggested I come back and go into hospital for a week for the electric shocks and the nausea making drug as well—both. I'd have the shock therapy in the morning and in the afternoon I'd go up to the place and have the drug. On one occasion he was there, he was doing it, once. But the other times there were all different people for the shocks. I don't think they were doctors, students maybe, I'm not sure. That was really horrible, you know—they didn't speak to you or anything. Just brought you in and sat you down, they never showed any sort of . . . they never tried to be kind to you or anything like that.

I just had male slides, no female, dozens of them, all nude, and they were all hideous. I had the thing strapped around my penis, and electrodes on my hands. I had to choose a whole lot of slides and the ones that I chose were put into the projector and they automatically went on when I was having the shocks. I can't quite remember some of the things that went on because later . . . after I had the aversion therapy, I had a breakdown and I had shock treatment (ECT) and there are some things I can't remember.

I can remember that it was an incredibly traumatic experience. Before each session I felt terrible. I don't know why I kept going—I was frightened and anxious. The drugs went on for ages—an hour or an hour and a half, that was awful. I think that was worse than the shocks . . .

During the first interview he asked me whether I was an active or passive homosexual. During the therapy he increased the voltage, I'm sure, I could feel it. At one stage I was going to rip the whole thing off, it was incredible, it hurt so much, it really did. What stopped me, I don't know. At the time I really hoped it would work . . .

I think after the aversion therapy I found it harder to communicate with camp people, it's still a problem, I think. It was hard before, but after that, it was worse. I think after aversion therapy I really hated myself, I don't know why, I just did. (Wills, 1972?)

Another ex-patient explained the lack of success of aversion therapy thus:

I'll tell you why you get bloody increased homosexual behaviour during aversion therapy. You've just had a session, right, and you've got another bloody session to-morrow and you've got to get through the night alone.

118

So what do you do? You hit the beats. You need someone, anyone, to get you through those nights. (Wills, 1972?)

Recently a debate occurred in the professional journals on the ethical implications of the use of therapies such as those described above, to 'cure' homosexual men of their homosexual desire.[9] Most of the disputants held the view that homosexuality was not pathological, and that attempts to 'cure' it were unethical because such attempts were motivated by and served to reinforce anti-homosexual prejudice. The debate revolved around the question of the extent to which homosexual men could be said to be 'voluntarily' seeking treatment for their sexual orientation given the social condemnation of homosexuality. As Silverstein put it:

> To suggest that a person comes voluntarily to change his sexual orientation is to ignore the powerful environmental stress, oppression if you will, that has been telling him for years that he should change. To grow up in a family where the word 'homosexual' was whispered, to play in a playground and hear the words 'faggot' and 'queer', to go to church and hear of 'sin', and then to college and hear of 'illness', and finally to the counseling center that promises to 'cure', is hardly to create an environment of freedom and voluntary choice. The homosexual is expected to want to be changed and his application for treatment is implicitly praised as the first step toward 'normal' behavior.
>
> What brings them into the counseling center is guilt, shame, and the loneliness that comes from their secret. If you really wish to help them freely choose, I suggest you first desensitize them to their guilt. Allow them to dissolve the shame about their desires and actions and to feel comfortable with their sexuality. After that, let them choose, but not before. (Quoted in Davison, 1976: 160)

Needless to say, Irving Bieber and Neil McConaghy, two of the contributors to the debate, expressed disagreement with this point of view. Bieber (1976) stated without qualification that male homosexuality *was* pathological, and that 'promulgating the new myth that homosexuality is a normal variant of sexuality' did more harm than good to 'the (male) homosexuals themselves', because it 'robs' them of the opportunity to be cured. McConaghy (1977) rejected the idea that moral judgments were relevant at all, preferring instead what he regarded as the basic tenet of liberal humanism: whether or not certain behaviour leads to 'an increase or decrease in human happiness'. Since homosexual behaviour leads to unhappiness, at least in the case of the people who had come to him to be 'cured', it revealed 'a disquieting lack of concern for the patient' to refuse to treat him (or her? One of the case histories he used to demonstrate how unhappy homosexuals can be concerned a lesbian with strong religious convictions who lived with her very religious family in a country town). He did not say how treatments such as those described above contributed to the sum total of human happiness.

Another of the contributors (Halleck, 1976) agreed that the 'voluntary nature' of a request for therapeutic help to change sexual orientation was problematic. Halleck's solution, however, was not to reject out of hand 'patients' requests to 'cure' their homosexuality, but to emphasise the importance of giving the 'patient' the fullest possible information on every aspect of homosexuality. He did not commit himself on the question of whether or not he would proceed to treat homosexual men if they continued to demand to be 'cured' despite the information. In the final paper of the debate Feldman (1977) argued that, while the social distress of homosexuals was real enough, to deny the 'client' (Feldman's term) one of the options available, 'treatment' for homosexuality, was to limit the 'client's' range of possible choices.

Such a pluralist position, however, is dependent on 'other things being equal'. One of those other things is the question of whether or not sexual orientation can actually be changed by therapeutic methods. On this question there is little consensus among the helping professions. On the whole, the difference of opinion seems to divide into those who regard homosexuality as pathological and are convinced it can be 'cured' and those who regard it as a normal variant of sexuality and are convinced that it cannot; a middle ground, exemplified by Feldman's position, is taken by those who do not subscribe to the pathology view but who are inclined to believe that homosexuality can be at least influenced by therapeutic measures.

Another of those 'other things' which is far from equal is the social condemnation of homosexuality. Even were it undeniably possible to 'cure' homosexuality, the main dilemma would still remain. On the one hand, the therapist could acquiesce in a client's request to change his sexual orientation because of the distress his homosexuality caused him personally. On the other hand, by doing so that therapist would also be acquiescing in that condemnation, tacitly if not overtly, by defining the homosexuality as the prime cause of the client's problems. For it must be remembered that social condemnation is not simply externally imposed by social institutions such as the law, the Christian churches and prejudiced public attitudes, or even by loved ones' disapproval, but is also internalised as shame, guilt and self-hatred. To suggest, as a number of the contributors to the debate did, that a blanket refusal on the therapist's part to make any attempt at all to 'cure' a client's homosexuality, is 'coercive' because it closes off that particular alternative, is to ignore the coercion that drove the homosexual man to seek to visit himself of his 'undesirable desire' in the first place. For those therapists who are convinced that homosexuality is 'a normal variant', to acquiesce in any way in clients' demands to be 'cured' of what is not a disease is to run the grave risk of damaging still further those people who are already so severely damaged that they can seriously consider eliminating from their emotional lives their most intense emotional experiences. It is also to act as agents of social control, albeit in collaboration with the client, in the absence of any reasonable grounds (in particular demonstrated harm to others) for controlling the behaviour in question.

Contemporary views

On 15 December 1973, Trustees of the American Psychiatric Association 'ruled that "homosexuality" shall no longer be listed as a mental disorder in its official nomenclature of mental disorders'. The vote was carried unanimously with two abstentions. The Trustees went on to adopt the following resolution by a unanimous vote with one abstention:

> Whereas homosexuality per se implies no impairment in judgment, stability, reliability, or general social or vocational capabilities, therefore, be it resolved that the American Psychiatric Association deplores all public and private discrimination against homosexuals in such areas as employment, housing, public accommodation, and licensing, and declares that no burden of proof of such judgment, capacity, or reliability shall be placed on homosexuals greater than that imposed on other persons. Further, the American Psychiatric Association supports and urges the enactment of civil rights legislation at the local, state and federal level that would offer homosexual citizens the same protections now guaranteed to others on the basic of race, creed, color, etc. Further, the American Psychiatric Association supports and urges the repeal of all discriminatory legislation singling out homosexual acts by consenting adults in private.

This decision of the Board of Trustees was not received with unanimous acclaim by all the members of the Association. Early in 1974, an Ad Hoc Committee, among whose members were Socarides and Bieber, was formed to raise the necessary support to call a referendum of all members of the Association, and 'to petition that the new change brought about in what we consider to be such an undemocratic fashion be undone' (Socarides, 1974:180). In the resulting referendum, 58 per cent of the members voted—about 5800 supported the original decision of the Trustees, and about 3800 opposed it. The removal of homosexuality from the diagnostic list of mental disorders was allowed to stand.

The usual reason given for this change of attitude on the part of the psychiatrists is the mounting evidence that homosexuality was not in fact a 'disorder'. Charles Silverstein pointed out in his address to the Nomenclature Committee of the American Psychiatric Association on 8 February 1973 (Silverstein, 1976/77), that at least since 1957 when Evelyn Hooker published her paper, it had become increasingly evident that homosexuality was not symptomatic of pathology. As early as the 1940s, Kinsey and his associates had discovered far more about the prevalence of homosexual behaviour by refusing to equate homosexuality with pathology, and by sampling the general population rather than allowing conventional prejudice to influence their choice of subjects.

But it was not the 'scientific' evidence alone which was instrumental in effecting the change in the psychiatric definition of 'homosexuality'. In the twenty-odd years between the release of the first Kinsey volume and the American Psychiatric Association's declassification, social, religious and moral definitions exercised a far wider influence than the findings of 'objective research'. To this day, many people remain unconvinced by that research, including some diehard members of the psychiatric profession. In his 1962 volume, for example, Bieber considered the findings of both Kinsey and Hooker, and explicitly rejected them. The work of Evelyn Hooker he dismissed summarily on the grounds that projective tests were notoriously unreliable as measurements of personality. And Socarides continues to assert without qualification that homosexuality is 'one of psychiatry's most severe examples of sexual pathology' (Socarides, 1974).

Other members of the psychiatric profession proved not to be so unbending. But their decision to remove homosexuality from the category of 'mental disorder' was not based solely on the evidence, which was contradictory anyway. That decision was also influenced by the lobbying of the gay activists, who not only demonstrated at conferences and angrily demanded an end to the depreciatory categorisation of homosexuality, but who had also marshalled enough evidence to support their case.

The event which is now regarded as the decisive turning point in homosexuals' resistance to the pejorative labelling process, and the harassment which those disparaging labels were used to justify, is what has become known as the 'Stonewall Riot'. In June 1969 what was a routine police raid on the Stonewall Inn, a male homosexual bar in Christopher Street, New York, turned into a three-day demonstration, as the 'forces of faggotry' fought back (Teal, 1971: 17–23). While this was primarily a blow struck for male homosexual liberation, lesbians were also involved in the three-day storm of protest, although that fact is not evident in most accounts. Lesbians, too, were subjected to harassment and intimidation by the police and by liquor-licensing authorities in the bars—usually the only places where homosexuals could meet. In many parts of the United States, lesbian sexuality was also within the scope of the criminal law because of the vague wording which did not restrict 'crimes against nature' to sexual activity between males as the NSW Crimes Act does. Hence lesbians had as much reason as the homosexual men for joining in the protest. However, since the most violent and frequent incidents of police harassment were directed towards homosexual men, it was the men who were most in evidence on that weekend in June.

With the dawning of the realisation among 'gays'—that is, homosexuals who refuse to accept the negative social definitions—that the 'problem of homosexuality' lay not in their own individual psyches, but in dominant social attitudes from which even the supposedly disinterested professional was not immune, came the decision to challenge the pronouncements of those experts who felt themselves qualified to define homosexuality as pathology. In May 1970 a coalition of gay and women's liberationists disrupted a session of the national convention of the American Psychiatric Association in San Francisco. The chief target of their anger was a paper on aversion therapy by McConaghy (Teal, 1971: 293–5). Most of the 600 psychiatrists present stormed out of the meeting, but a few were impressed with the gay liberationist arguments, and invited them to present a panel on 'Life Styles of Non-Patient Homosexuals' at the next year's conference (Martin & Lyon, 1972: 272).

In December 1972 the New York Gay Activist Alliance interrupted a session at the annual meeting of the Association for the Advance-ment of Behavior Therapy, where once again one of the speakers was a therapist noted for the use of aversion therapy to 'cure' homosexual-ity. In the audience was a member of the Nomenclature Committee of the American Psychiatric Association. This is the Committee which decides what is, or is not, to be classified as a mental illness, and hence included in, or excluded from, the Association's *Diagnostic and Statistical Manual of Mental Disorders*. The Committee member invited the gays to present their case to the full Committee. That meeting, in February 1973, on the topic 'Should Homosexuality be Removed from the Diagnostic and Statistical Manual?', was instrumental in influencing the Association's later decision to withdraw homosexual-ity from its list of mental disorders, just as 'Asocial Trends' like 'Syphilophobia', 'Vagabondage' and 'Pathologic Mendacity' had been withdrawn in the 1950s (Silverstein, 1976/77: 153–4).[10]

In January 1975 the governing body of the American Psychological Association 'voted to oppose discrimination against homosexuals' and 'to support the recent action by the American Psychiatric Association which removed homosexuality from that Association's official list of mental disorders'. The text of the policy statement, which was submitted to the Council of Representatives by the Association's Board of Social and Ethical Responsibility and recommended by the Board of Directors, followed the wording of the American Psychiatric Association's resolution exactly. The statement concluded:

> The council also amended the Association's 'Statement of Policy Regarding Equal Employment Opportunity' to include sexual orientation among the prohibited discriminations listed. APA's employment practices in its various professional placement programs and advertisements in all Association publications will comply with this policy. (Clarke, 1977: 16–7; Silverstein, 1979: 182–4)

The Australian context

The Australian gay movement has staged its own challenges to the helping professions' treatment of homosexual men, and in particular McConaghy's use of aversion therapy to 'cure' male homosexuality. As mentioned earlier, in July 1972, CAMP NSW orgainsed a forum on aversion therapy at the University of NSW, to which they invited McConaghy. At the forum, Dr Robin Winkler, a clinical psychologist in the School of Applied Psychology at the University, put the case against aversion therapy. Although not himself a homosexual, he was asked to speak because of his familiarity with the literature on behaviour modification, and because he was prepared to question certain professional practices, rather than relying on the mystique of professional expertise. His approach in his paper was twofold: to question the assumption that homosexuality was a disorder requiring treatment, and to point out that there was by no means general agreement among psychologists that aversion therapy could do what was claimed for it.

McConaghy did not refute Winkler's arguments, but he remained unconvinced nonetheless. A year later, in 1973, at the 'Psychiatry and Liberation' conference, funded by Geigy, the multinational pharmaceuticals manufacturer, he was still asserting the 'scientific' nature of his work. He had organised the symposium and had invited CAMP NSW, Sydney Gay Liberation and Women's Liberation to attend. These groups had at first refused to participate, on the grounds that neither they nor any other interested parties were to be involved in the planning stages, and that the symposium was not open to everyone. However, at the last moment some members of Sydney Gay Liberation decided to register a protest, and distributed copies of the 'Intellectual Poofter Bashers' article issue of *CAMP Ink*

(1972?), and a leaflet explaining why gay liberationists had refused to participate in the debate. The main theme of McConaghy's paper, called 'Should Psychiatrists Treat the Person or Society?' (1973) was an attack on the 'irrationality' of liberation movements which were in the process of destroying the liberal humanist belief in human progress through reason and its prime exemplar, scientific investigation. When the gay liberationists protested rowdily at these statements, and attempted to counter the accusations (some of McConaghy's ex-patients were in the hall), they were 'rationally' ejected from the meeting.[11]

More recently, in 1981, Sue Wills, author of the critique of aversion therapy, 'Intellectual Poofter Bashers', wrote to McConaghy as part of her PhD thesis on sexual liberation movements in Sydney, asking him if he was still treating (male) homosexuals with aversion therapy; if not, when did he stop and why; and if he still was, did he get as many requests for it as he did ten or more years ago. In his reply, McConaghy said that he and his colleagues still offered treatment to 'people who felt that aspects of their sexual behaviour or urges were out of control'. He added that he did not see this as a 'treatment for homosexuality' any more than the same treatment offered to heterosexuals would be a 'treatment for heterosexuality'. He also said that they had found that forms of desensitisation were as effective as 'aversive therapy', and that this was offered first. If that didn't work, then subjects 'may elect to receive aversive therapy.'

In May 1972, the Australian and New Zealand College of Psychiatrists issued a position statement 'strongly condemning community attitudes and laws which discriminate against homosexual behaviour between consenting adults in private'. In October 1973, two months before the American Psychiatric Association released the Trustees' decision, the College issued a Clinical Memorandum, No. 6, the conclusion of which is as follows:

> Current psychiatric opinion of the nature of homosexuality is largely in accord with the results of controlled studies of non-patient homosexuals. Many psychiatrists consider that homosexual feelings and behaviour are not necessarily or commonly associated with neurotic symptoms, and are compatible with good adjustment and a useful and creative contribution by the individual to society.

> General considerations:
> 1. Homosexuality may distress the individual and may cause him to seek psychiatric help. The aim of psychiatric treatment is usually a better adaptation to life in general and a more satisfactory adjustment to the particular difficulties of being homosexual in a predominantly heterosexual society. Alternatively, when the patient desires it the aim of treatment may be an alteration of his sexual propensity, so that it is

directed less towards his own sex and more towards the opposite sex. The latter aim is sometimes achieved, especially when the patient is relatively young or has experienced some heterosexual desire or activity in the past.

2. The ethics of treatment aimed at change in sexual orientation present difficult problems when the patient asks for such treatment while under the duress of impending trial on a charge of homosexual conduct. Courts may place homosexual offenders on probation or a good behaviour bond conditional on co-operation with treatment to reduce homosexual desire. If such treatment is not offered a prison sentence may be given. In such circumstances some psychiatrists are prepared to offer treatment providing that the individual seems motivated to reduce homosexual behaviour and increase heterosexual behaviour. However, the majority of psychiatrists are not prepared to recommend treatment aimed at change in sexual orientation while the patient is not a free agent. They prefer to delay consideration of such treatment until the patient is no longer under any form of legal constraint.

3. The psychological adjustment of homosexuals and their psychiatric treatment are made unduly difficult by existing community attitudes. The acceptance of homosexuals by society is slowly increasing but could and should be facilitated by reform of existing laws against homosexual acts between consenting adults in private.

This statement illustrates the dilemma of any position which attempts to acknowledge social change while at the same time retaining a foothold in the old order. On the one hand, the Australian and New Zealand College of Psychiatrists made this statement even before the similar stance of the American Psychiatric Association was made public. To that extent, the Australian and New Zealand College's commitment to changing the definition of homosexuality antedated that of the American Association. On the other hand, the Australian psychiatrists continued to affirm that homosexuals 'may' need treatment. It is true that that treatment was 'usually' necessary because of 'existing community attitudes', and that the College recommended law reform as one step towards ameliorating those 'attitudes'. But the emphasis remained on individual adjustment, even to the extent of allowing that changing a (male) homosexual's sexual orientation was a legitimate (although presumably less feasible) alternative to helping him come to terms with his homosexuality and the social opprobrium attendant upon it.

Further, the psychiatrists deplored 'existing laws against homosexual acts between consenting adults in private', and pointed out that it was 'unethical' to treat someone who was forced into treatment by fear of punishment. But they were prepared to accept that 'some psychiatrists' were justified in treating homosexuals who otherwise would face a prison sentence. By doing so, they were either reinforcing those laws which they admitted needed to be reformed by recognising the courts' right to be able to use the psychiatric profession as an alternative to the criminal justice system for enforcing social conformity, or they were being less than straightforward with the courts about what psychiatry could and could not do.

In 1980, when the ADB Report was being researched, the Australian Psychological Society had not issued an official statement expressing their views on homosexuality, although a majority of those who replied to a postal ballot of members of the Society in 1974 condemned discrimination against homosexuals. The ballot did not ask whether or not the members regarded homosexuality as pathology.[12]

5

CHRISTIAN
MORALITY

THE day after the ADB report's release, an irate Christian caller pointed out on Margaret Throsby's 'City Extra' program that it was 'humanist' in orientation, that is, it assumed that morality, specifically the ethical requirements of civil rights, was a human construct, devised by human beings for human purposes. The caller appeared to find this 'humanism' reprehensible. While I do not agree with his disapproving attitude, I will admit that his assessment of the ethical framework of the report was accurate.

The humanist position defined above was not one with which I felt entirely comfortable, since the use of the all-inclusive term 'human' disguises conditions in which some have more privileged access to the means by which they can exercise their 'basic human rights' than do others. Men have a 'right' to work, to organise their own labour power, and bargain for favourable conditions; women who perform 'women's work' in the home do not. White Anglo-Saxon men have a 'right' to own land and exploit it in their own interests; Aboriginal people do not. Business interests have a 'right' to pursue ever-increasing rates of profit, and to 'rationalise' production to maximise those rates of profit; those with only their labour power to sell have no right even to work if their employment erodes profit. Nevertheless, I find a 'humanist' perspective preferable to one which subordinates the human to some transcendental agency beyond the reach of human action.

It is from a position such as this latter one that theological arguments about right and wrong human behaviour flow. Morality is asserted to originate in the extra-human sphere of the divine, devised (if such a term is not too anthropomorphic) by an extra-human agency, the Deity, for purposes which are not always humanly discernible. But as was pointed out in the ADB's report (see below), there were difficulties involved in appraising theological arguments within a secular context.

This incompatibility between a secular discourse and a theological one can be illustrated by examining the objections raised to the ADB's report by the Catholic Education Commission of NSW. The Commission issued a commentary on the report at the end of 1982 (Catholic Education Commission, 1982). The Commission did not disagree with the ADB's argument that (male) 'homosexual' behaviour was not the concern of the criminal law: 'although the Commission holds that homosexual acts are objectively immoral, it does not *for that reason* hold that they should be proscribed by law.' Neither did it object to the ADB recommendation that 'homosexuality' be included within the Anti-Discrimination Act as a ground of unlawful discrimination: 'Homosexuals have been discriminated against, in the past and also at present. This discrimination is unjust whenever the applicant's homosexual orientation has no bearing on the job in question.' The Commission did not even object to the employment of 'homosexual teachers' in Catholic schools and colleges: 'There are those who keep their homosexuality private, and indeed attempt to lead exemplary Christian lives, and in their case homosexuality is not relevant to their employment.'

The Commission had four main objections to the report. First, it objected to what it saw as the ADB's 'commitment to the view that homosexuality should be accepted in law and by the whole community as a valid alternative lifestyle to be granted equal status with heterosexuality'. As a statement of the ADB's commitment that is not entirely accurate. For example, nowhere did we argue in the report for a recognition within law of a homosexual equivalent of heterosexual marriage (although some of the Christian commentators we quoted did). When we did argue for equivalence, the arguments were based on financial or compassionate considerations, for example inheritance rights or hospital visiting rights between partners in a homosexual relationship. And nowhere did we assert either overtly or by implication, the totalitarian view that 'the whole community' be coerced (how?) into accepting the views expressed in the report.

Second, the Commission took the report to task for its 'extraordinary' style, 'more suited', it said, 'to partisan polemics than to objective research'. In doing so, the Commission leapt to the defence of those criticised in the report, in particular those NSW parliamentarians involved in the debate surrounding the Petersen amendment, the Festival of Light, psychiatric 'experts'—it mentioned specifically Caprio and Storr[1]—and the endocrinologist, Gunter Dörner. It did not consider the truth or otherwise of *what* was said about these; it merely stated its objections to the *way* it was said. Neither did the Commission consider that the report's 'polemics' (so-called) might have been an understandable reaction to the appalling quality of much of the material studied, which was on the whole scurrilous, vituperative, and often downright false or just plain silly, as was documented at length in the report. Moreover, when it comes to polemics, the Commission itself need take second place to none. It accused the ADB of arguing 'fervently' and 'with some passion', of 'injecting itself blatantly in a political arena and impertinently (!) speculating on the views and motives of a Minister [of the Crown]', of reacting 'with some disgust' (at Dörner & co's implied suggestion for the eradication of male homosexuality), and of 'unhesitatingly propos[ing] sweeping changes which would profoundly and probably irrevocably alter the mores of the community, the nature of personal, social and legal relationships, the role of the traditional family, indeed the basic nature of our society'. In my opinion the Commission's accusation of 'polemics' is more a case of the pot calling the kettle black than a serious concern for the fate of 'objective research'.

The third of the Commission's objections concerned the fate of Catholic schools if the ADB's recommendations were to be implemented by the NSW Government. In the opinion of the Commission, 'governments must ensure the primacy of the family'. But the 'legislative changes' proposed by the ADB 'would alter the moral basis of society and threaten the traditional family'. In particular, the Commission objected to the report's arguments about the presentation of non-judgmental and non-discriminatory information about homosexuality within Personal Development and sex-education courses in schools, and the employment of lesbian and male homosexual teachers. In the case of the former the ADB's recommendations did not involve legislative changes: there is nothing the ADB or the State government, or even the NSW Department of Education could or would do to interfere with the rights of educational institutions to autonomy in their choice of curricula. The ADB's recommendations on this issue were on the level of suggestions only. If the Commission or individual Catholic schools disagreed with those suggestions, or chose to ignore them altogether, that was their own affair. The ADB made no recommendations about ways and means of forcing Catholic schools to transgress their 'ethos' and break faith with what 'Catholic parents rightly expect Catholic schools to be'.

In the case of the employment of teachers in Catholic schools, the ADB's only legislative recommendation was that private educational institutions should lose their exemptions from the employment provisions of the Anti-Discrimination Act. At the time the report was written, those exemptions allowed non-governmental educational institutions to discriminate with impunity against people on the grounds of sex, marital status and physical impairment, although not on the ground of race. (The exemption from the 'marital status' provision is particularly relevant for employees of Catholic schools and colleges because Catholic educators appear to be as moralistic about people 'living in sin' in de facto relationships as they are about people in homosexual relationships. The ADB has received a number of complaints from people who lost their jobs because their Catholic employers discovered that they were living with a person of the opposite sex without the benefit of holy matrimony.) At the present time, the above exemptions still stand, as do those relating to the subsequent inclusions in the Act—intellectual impairment and homosexuality.

This privileged status accorded Catholic schools was probably the result of the government's concern for 'the Catholic vote' and the strength of the Catholic influence within the government itself. The *Church's* justification for it involved reference to the obligation on Catholic schools to inculcate in their pupils the moral teaching of the Church. According to the Sacred Congregation for the Doctrine of the Faith, this teaching rested on something called 'the objective moral order'. The Commission quoted the Sacred Congregation to the effect that:

> according to the objective moral order, homosexual relations are acts which lack an essential and indispensable finality. In Sacred Scripture they are condemned as a serious depravity and even presented as the sad consequence of rejecting God. This judgment of Scripture does not of course permit us to conclude that all those who suffer from this anomaly are personally responsible for it, but it does attest to the fact [*sic*] that homosexual acts are intrinsically disordered and can in no case be approved of.

It is this 'objective moral order' which would be transgressed, in the view of the Catholic Education Commission, if Catholic schools did not retain the right both to discriminate against homosexual teachers in their employment, and to continue to teach disapproving attitudes towards homosexuality (or, as is more likely, to ignore the issue altogether, thus allowing free rein to prevailing myths and misconceptions). Neither the Commission nor the Sacred Congregation was explicit about the nature of the 'objectivity' of this 'order'.

131

But given its origin in 'Sacred Scripture', and the irrelevance of 'personal responsibility' for actions which this 'order' condemns, it is reasonable to assume that it originates in a sphere which is external and superordinate to the sphere of individual human responsibility; and that in any conflict between personal choice and divine fiat, it is the freedom of the individual which is sacrificed. Within a civil libertarian framework such as that of the ADB's report, such a stance would have been quite inappropriate. Hence, the disagreement between the Church and the ADB is a consequence of their a priori commitment to two incommensurable frameworks. Under most circumstances the two would have nothing to say to each other. But given the Church's interest in the issue of homosexuality, and its involvement with the secular activities of the employment of lay teachers and the education of the young, it was bound to fall within the scope of the ADB's inquiry. That the Church continues to use its considerable political influence to maintain a privileged position outside a law which applies to all other employers in the state, is something to be regretted.

Concerning the 'objective moral order' which constitutes such an important aspect of the curriculum in Catholic schools, the ADB was silent. But any 'moral order' which anathematises 'homosexuality', no matter how many fine hairs are split to give the appearance of accommodation to liberal principles, would be in contradiction to the ADB's commitment to oppose unjust discrimination, a stance which has its own moral justification in the humanist ethic of the rights and responsibilities of the individual. In the absence of any demonstrated harm to others, no democratic state can countenance restrictions on the freedom of the individual if it is to remain consistent with one of the basic principles of democracy. What the Church wants to teach in its schools is not the concern of the state—even state schools have a large measure of autonomy in this area. But in castigating the ADB for its rejection of a moral framework so much at variance with its own, the Catholic Education Commission gives the impression that the 'ethos' of Catholic schools ought to be the rule for all.

In our investigation of the negative social categories which have defined homosexuality over the last century, we have come across an interesting contradiction. Logically, it might be supposed that to define homosexuality as an 'illness' would preclude its definition as a 'sin' or a 'crime'. It is customary to hold the sinner and the criminal responsible for their behaviour, but not the sick person, who is seen as suffering from a condition over which he or she has no control. Indeed, it was this contradiction which was grasped by the liberal thinkers of the turn of the century in their defence of the rights of homosexual men to freedom from legal harassment. If 'inversion' was a 'biological anomaly' (or even a sign of 'degeneracy'), then it was no business of the law. However, logical inconsistency notwithstanding, all three categories—'illness', 'sin', and 'crime'—have continued to coexist and mutually reinforce each other as long as the history of the category of homosexuality itself, as constituent elements of the all-pervasive context for the social condemnation of homosexuality and homosexuals. The 'illness' category has already been dealt with at length in the last chapter. The "crime" category was dealt with in chapter 5 of the ADB report. The category of 'sin', and its various modifications and guises, is the subject matter of the present chapter.

'Sin'

You have requested instances of discrimination against homosexuals. The Bible has several such instances. In Leviticus Ch 20 v 13 God calls them abominable. In Romans Ch 7 vs 24–27, He describes them as unclean and vile. In 1 Corinthians Ch 6 vs 9–10, He excludes them from His Kingdom if they choose to remain in such a state.

As these instances have been clearly documented, what action do you intend to take against God? 'He that sitteth in the heavens shall laugh. The Lord shall have them in derision.' Psalm 2 v 4.

By failing to uphold the standard which God has set against homosexuality, you are resisting God and certainly not benefitting the people concerned. How much better to warn such people of their position before God and then show them God's solution. The very portion of Scripture which excludes them from Heaven tells of this solution and shows also that many people have been saved from such ungodly behaviour. 1 Corinthians Ch 6 v 11 'Such were some of you; but ye are washed.' There is only one remedy to wash away such a degrading sin, 'the blood of Jesus Christ, God's son, cleanseth us from all sin.' 1 John Ch 1 v 7. 'Blessed are all they that put their trust in him.' Psalm 2 v 12.[2]

The concept of 'sin', defined as 'a divergence between the human will and the Divine will',[3] is meaningful only within a religious context. It is not possible for a secular work such as this book to do full justice to arguments which flow from theological premises. It is not customary these days to apply theological arguments to the decision-making processes of the secular state, and the NSW government is unlikely to refer to Holy Writ in justification for its legislative actions (although the consciences of its individual members might).

The problem of the exposition of the religious (strictly speaking, the *Christian*) viewpoint is compounded by the wide divergence of opinion to be found among committed Christians on the question of homosexuality. At one end of the spectrum of Christian attitudes to homosexuality fall the statements which have emanated from the Festival of Light, and the Sydney Diocese of the Anglican Church. The Festival of Light's attitude advocates the retention of every variety of negative sanctions against homosexual men in particular (they rarely mention lesbians), including the relevant sections of the Crimes Act. They have even been known to advocate the use of violence against homosexual men (see p. 142). The Catholic Church's official position is hardly less condemnatory than that of the Festival of Light, although less extreme in its public statements. Further along the spectrum towards a more liberal attitude, are those Christians, such as the Most Reverend Dr K. Rayner, the Anglican Archbishop of Adelaide, who continue to condemn homosexual behaviour as a sin, but who at the same time disagree with the legal intervention of the secular state into what they see as a moral issue between the homosexual individual and his (in this case) Maker. Dr Rayner expressed public support for the South Australian Government's decision in 1975 to repeal the laws against male homosexual acts, because the criminal law was 'not the best way of dealing with the deep and complex problems associated with homosexuality'. At the same time, he recommended that homosexuals refrain from sexual activity, commenting that: 'Certainly no one should pretend that this is easy; indeed, without God's grace it might be too much to ask . . . Of course, it will require moral strength and discipline.'[4]

At the liberal end of the spectrum are those Christians who argue that those whose sexual orientation is primarily or exclusively towards members of the same sex are not thereby automatically excluded from the community of the faithful, nor from the common rights and dignities of humankind. Whether or not homosexuals engage in physical expression of their sexual preference is irrelevant to consideration of the rights of homosexuals to partake fully in all aspects of human existence. Some (although not all) of these Christians are themselves homosexual (Blamires, 1973; Gearhart & Johnson, 1974; Macourt, 1977). Instead of rejecting their religion in reaction to what might be seen as their churches' rejection of themselves, these Christian homosexuals have preferred to remain within the churches, and set up a dialogue with their coreligionists in an effort to change what they see as anachronistic attitudes.

Despite the difficulties involved in appraising theological arguments within a secular context, we have attempted to evaluate these varying (and sometimes contradictory) arguments in their own terms, in so far as that was possible. In the light of the frequently heard assertion that this is a 'Christian society', and to the extent that the Judaeo-Christian heritage remains influential, we found ourselves under an obligation to investigate those arguments which appealed to that heritage as their justification.

The Bible

The following discussion, as indeed the whole of the moral theological debate, is, as ever, largely confined to male homosexuality. No doubt those who condemn the 'immorality' of homosexual behaviour, if pressed, would include lesbian behaviour in that condemnation. However, within this context, as in every other, once again what women do has remained peripheral to the central focus of attention. Whether the discussion involves Old Testament passages imbued with the patriarchal values of the ancient tribes of Israel, or whether it involves the most recent concern for the implications for Christian ethics of homosexual relationships, the debate is largely by men and about men. Once again we have found that in order to reproduce the debate, we have had to reproduce the same male predominance.

The primary authority for the Christian condemnation of male homosexual behaviour is the Bible. As the Anglican Diocese of Sydney put it in their *Report on Homosexuality* in 1973:

> The degree of concern felt by the authors of this report for those who choose homosexual norms of behaviour is heightened by the fact that this is a subject on which the Bible—the Word of God—speaks with explicitness and considerable warning. (The Ethics and Social Questions Committee, 1973)

Two questions arise in relation to the relevance of the Bible to modern Christian views of male homosexuality. The first concerns the intentions of the authors of the texts, the historical context within which they were writing, and the events they were responding to. The second concerns the issue of whether or not what those authorities have been interpreted as referring to as 'male homosexuality' is actually the same phenomenon we refer to when we use the term today.

The Old Testament contains two stories which supposedly condemn the depravity of 'male homosexuals'. The most quoted text cited in support of that condemnation is the Genesis story of the visitation of two angels to the city of Sodom on a mission to ascertain whether or not the city contained 'ten righteous men' (there was no mention of women and children being included among the righteous).

If the angels could find those ten men, the Lord had promised He would not destroy the city.

> But before they lay down, the men of the city, the men of Sodom, both young and old, all the people to the last man, surrounded the house; and they called to Lot, 'Where are the men who came to you to-night? Bring them out to us, that we may know them.' Lot went out of the door to the men, shut the door after him and said, 'I beg you, my brothers, do not act so wickedly. Behold, I have two daughters who have not known man; let me bring them out to you, and do to them as you please; only do nothing to these men, for they have come under the shelter of my roof.' (The Revised Standard Version, Genesis 19:4–8)

Since 'all the people to the last *man*' were implicated in this 'unrighteous' behaviour, the Lord destroyed the city, after first warning Lot to leave with his family. The text does not say what happened to the women and children, but Lot's wife (as is well known) was turned into a pillar of salt as she turned to look back at the city.

An interesting consequence of the exile of Lot and his daughters and the 'death' of his wife, which may have some bearing on the question of the extent to which the Old Testament is relevant to 'timeless principles and patterns of morality' (as the Sydney Anglican Diocese expressed it in their report), is recounted at the end of chapter 19 of Genesis. Lot's daughters, finding themselves living in a cave alone with their father, and isolated from the rest of humankind, were worried that they would never bear children. So they got their father drunk, and 'lay with him'. Both became pregnant, and both bore sons. Nowadays, this is called 'incest', and is condemned out of hand by every Christian denomination. Those who cite the story of Sodom as proof positive of God's condemnation of male homosexual behaviour are silent on other moral issues which that account also raises. For example, what 'timeless principles and patterns of morality' are demonstrated by the casual sacrifice of the honour, and perhaps the lives, of two young women? By the extermination by the Deity of women and children, none of whom were given the chance to prove their 'righteousness' or otherwise? By the transformation into a 'pillar of salt' of a woman who turned to take a last look at her home?

The second story is to be found in Judges 19. A certain Levite was passing through the town of Gibeah on his way home after a long journey to bring back his concubine from her father's house, where she had fled to get away from her master. The Levite was offered hospitality by an old man who was himself a visitor to the town. As in the story of Sodom, the men of the town came and pounded on the door, demanding to 'know' the stranger who had just arrived. Again the householder offered his 'virgin daughter', as well as the Levite's concubine, to the men, so that they might 'ravish them and do with them what seems good to you'. The offer was refused, but the concubine was pushed out anyway, and was raped so brutally that she died. Her master then proceeded to cut her into twelve pieces, 'and sent her throughout all the territory of Israel', except for the Benjaminites (who were the inhabitants of Gibeah), to organise his coreligionists in a war of revenge. All of the Benjaminites, apart from a few hundred men, were killed. But this meant that one tribe of Israel was in danger of dying out, since their wives and children had been massacred. In order to avoid such an eventuality, the 'people of Israel' gave the Benjaminites permission to abduct the daughters of Shiloh for their wives, promising to pacify the fathers and brothers of the women, when they came to complain.

It is stories such as these, and particularly the story of Sodom, which are used at the present time as justification for condemning male homosexual behaviour out of hand. But the behaviour of the men of Sodom and Gibeah was more like attempted pack rape, than the adult consensual male homosexual activity which is still anathematised in the name of Sodom by most of the major Christian churches today.

An investigation of the question of *why* the men of these two towns attempted to rape the strangers sheds an interesting light on the historical times within which the stories were set. The source of the present-day interpretation—that the Sodomites were filled with lustful desire—appears to date back no further than the first century AD, to the writings of Philo and Josephus. Philo described the behaviour of the men of Sodom thus:

> Not only in their mad lust for women did they violate the marriages of their neighbours, but also men mounted males without respect for sex nature which the active partner shares with the passive. (*De Abrahams*, quoted in Treese, 1974)

But this interpretation of Philo's receives no support from the Bible itself. Where the city of Sodom is mentioned in texts in the Old Testament other than Genesis 19, there is no specific reference which suggests that 'the sin of Sodom' was that which is now referred to as 'sodomy'. In both the Old and the New Testaments, Sodom was the primary symbol of wickedness in general. The consensus of biblical scholarship appears to be that the Sodomites' reaction to the angelic strangers was a transgression of one of the basic ethical prerequisites for a beleaguered people—hospitality to coreligionists (The Board of Social Responsibility, 1979). Not only did they fail to offer the travellers food and shelter, they also greeted them with the violence of an undisciplined mob. This interpretation receives some support from the Judges 19 account. The Levite whose concubine was raped and killed by the Benjaminite inhabitants of Gibeah announced to the assembled Israelites on his return home, not that he was threatened with rape, but that he was threatened with murder:

> 'And the men of Gibeah rose against me, and beset the house round about me by night; they meant to kill me, and they ravished my concubine, and she is dead.' (Judges 19: 5)

At least one authority (cited in McNeil, 1977) has suggested a further explanation for the behaviour of the men of Sodom and Gibeah. J. Edgar Brun suggested that the Israelites, like the Egyptians, may have viewed sodomy as an act symbolising the domination of an enemy. It is possible that the strangers—the angels in Sodom, and the Levite and his entourage in Gibeah—were seen by the inhabitants as a threat to the security of their towns. Neither Lot nor the old man were natives of the towns where they lived. It was said of Lot that 'This fellow came to sojourn and he would play the judge!' (Genesis 19: 9). Perhaps the native inhabitants were fearful of an influx of foreigners to the houses of men they did not know (with good reason as it turned out). The surest way to allay that threat was to render the strangers impotent by treating them as women, in other words, by raping them. This interpretation suggests that the abhorrence of male homosexuality is connected with the low status of women. As Brun commented:

> In a society where the dignity of the male was a primary consideration voluntary acts of a [male] homosexual nature could not be tolerated. Both parties would then be undermining the very foundations of a patriarchical society; the one because he uses another [man] as a woman; the other because he allows himself to be used as a woman. The dignity of the male is dishonoured by both. (McNeil, 1977)

To accept the stories of Sodom and Gibeah as presentations of 'timeless principles and patterns of morality' is to regard father-daughter incest and the gang rape, murder, dismemberment and abduction of women, if not with approval, then at least with indifference, in comparison with a perceived threat to the rights and dignity of the male.

In the opinion of many theologians, these are not parables of our 'timeless morality', but events which happened during a specific historical time thousands of years before our own. Then, women were objects of exchange, to be used and abused as a tactical resource in the interactions between their male masters, in the interplay of power and advantage between patriarch and patriarch, between tribe and tribe, between stranger-guest and stranger-foe. Admittedly, it is a simplistic anachronism to accuse the patriarchs of Israel of failing to implement a policy of equal rights for women, which would be to transpose values specific to the modern world to an historical epoch within which they lose all meaning. But it is no less of an anachronism to translate the values of another historical time into our own. If it is true, as the Board for Social Responsibility of the English Church of England asserted in their 'Critical Observations' on the 'Homosexual Relationships' report, that 'abhorrence of [male] homosexual behaviour is entrenched in the text of Genesis', then it is also true that entrenched in the same text are those other values mentioned above which, one hopes, have no relevance today. Some further reference is called for than mere reference to that 'city of the plain' in whose name the age-old condemnation of homosexual men is justified.

The Old Testament does contain further references to what has been interpreted to mean male homosexual behaviour:

> You shall not lie with a male as with a woman, it is an abomination. (Leviticus 18: 22)

> If a man lies with a male as with a woman, both of them have committed an abomination; they shall be put to death, their blood is upon them. (Leviticus 20: 13)

However, according to the English Working Party, care must be taken to place these prohibitions, too, within a wider context. They appeared as part of the Holiness Code, the function of which was the preservation of the kinship groupings which were the basis of the nation of Israel. Any behaviour which threatened the patterns of marriages and alliances which constituted Israelite society had to be rooted out. The death penalty was not so much a punishment for wrongdoing, as a technique for excising potentially destructive elements (The Board of Social Responsibility, 1979). Alternatively, any action which was considered necessary for the survival of any of the tribes of Israel was condoned, if not actively encouraged, as, for example, the abduction of the daughters of Shiloh as wives for the surviving Benjaminite men. The purpose of the Code was to define the distinctiveness and separateness of the Israelite nation, to distinguish the Chosen People from the heathen idolators, and to strengthen ties threatened by the proximity to heathen nations.

Obviously, there is a process of selection operating to sort out those Old Testament principles which remain relevant today from those which are no longer relevant. This process was called by the English Working Party the distinction between 'first-order principles' and 'second-order rules' (The Board of Social Responsibility 1979). The chief criterion for the continuing relevance, or alternatively the irrelevance, of certain Old Testament exhortations is the 'new convenant' of Jesus Christ, the New Testament, which also contains a number of passages, some of which are attributed to St Paul, which condemn homosexual acts, and on one occasion both between men and between women:

> 'Neither the immoral, nor idolators, nor adulterers, nor sexual perverts, nor thieves, nor the greedy, nor drunkards, nor revilers, nor robbers will inherit the kingdom of God.' (1 Corinthians 6: 9)

> For this reason God gave them up to dishonourable passions. Their women exchanged natural relations for unnatural and the men likewise gave up natural relations with women and were consumed with passion for one another, men committing shameless acts with men and receiving in their own person the due penalty for their error. (Romans 1: 26–7)

> The law is not laid down for the just but for the lawless and disobedient, for the ungodly and sinners, for the unholy and profane, for murderers of fathers and murderers of mothers, for manslayers, for immoral persons, sodomites, kidnappers, liars, perjurers and whatever else is contrary to sound doctrine. (1 Timothy 1: 9–10)

According to Treese (1974: 39), the term 'sexual perverts' (or 'homosexuals', which was the translation in the edition of the Revised Standard Version he referred to) in the first of the above passages is a translation of two separate Greek words, 'malakoi' and 'arsenokoitai'. The second word is repeated in the original patristic Greek (the language used by the Greek Fathers of the Church) in the third passage above, where it is translated as 'sodomites'. Both Treese (1974: 34) and McNeil (1977: 52) point out that the original languages of the Bible had no word with exactly the same meaning as our modern English word 'homosexual' (as indeed they could not, since it is an invention of the late nineteenth century). Both authors have reasonably inferred from this that the modern phenomenon of homosexuality, as an intrinsic enduring identity, was also unknown in biblical times. Treese said that the meaning of the Greek terms was obvious— the first referred to those men who engaged in homosexual acts as the 'passive' partner, the second to those who engaged as the 'active' partner. But Treese went on to state that the sinfulness of those acts was a result of their licentiousness, and 'licentiousness is not to be equated with homosexual love'. McNeil pointed out that the Latin Vulgate, the Latin version of the Bible completed by St Jerome in the beginning of the fifth century AD, translated the second term as 'masculi concubitores', which means male cult prostitutes, a more likely meaning than 'sodomites' given the context of the early Christian condemnation of idolatry and the practices connected with heathen worship. This is a concept without meaning in the modern world.

Paul's use of the term which has been translated as 'unnatural' in the second quotation above is also not without problems for the modern interpreter. The context was Paul's condemnation of those gentiles who suppressed their knowledge of God's law which was demonstrated to them 'in the things that have been made', and deliberately refused to adhere to that law. Given what is nowadays regarded as the non-voluntary, and it could be argued, God-given, nature of the homosexual condition, the epithet 'unnatural' in this sense could only be applied to those who engaged in homosexual behaviour against their 'natural' heterosexual inclination. Moreover, the modern usage of the term 'natural' is overlayed with philosophical connotations which did not exist in the first century AD. What is now meant by 'natural' is unlikely to be what Paul meant at the time he was writing.

The relevance of these objections to Paul's condemnation of 'unnatural' sexual practice, however, must be allowed to remain obscure. The philosophical debate surrounding such issues is beyond the scope of this book. However, those who argue for full acceptance of homosexuals by the Christian churches base their arguments on what one commentator (Keeling, 1977) has called 'the fundamental moral structures in the Bible', rather than 'particular Biblical judgments'. Keeling pointed out that recent writings in Christian ethics emphasised the quality of relationships, rather than the nature of certain acts, as the primary consideration in the making of ethical judgments. On this criterion, the relevant moral question was: 'What are my intentions towards this other person?' This was a question, Keeling argued, which could not be answered by appealing to 'any one set of rules' founded on the assumption that 'sexuality can never be separated from procreation'. Hence, it was a question which applied equally to homosexual as to heterosexual relationships.

Treese came to much the same conclusion. He admitted that, 'with regard to homosexuality and homosexual practices the church has maintained (perhaps because it was unexamined) an attitude of condemnation' (1974: 26). The Old Testament verses, which are frequently quoted in support of that attitude, were not relevant, he went on to argue, to the contemporary Church, 'because of their setting in the rules for cultic purification, and because of the lack of clarity in their underlying meaning'. But, he continued, the New Testament verses were unequivocal in their condemnation of homosexual behaviour. Yet he himself had come to know a number of homosexual people whose adherence to Christian ideals in their relationships was in no way inferior to those ideals as expressed in Christian marriage. Finding himself unable to condemn such relationships, Treese spent some time studying the theological issues involved, along with modern theories of the nature and causes of the homosexual condition. He concluded that homosexuals could express their needs for 'self-affirming and other affirming relationships' of 'fidelity, trust and love' to the same extent as heterosexuals could in Christian marriage, although he was not suggesting that the two unions were of the same kind. Nevertheless, he felt that the Church should bless such unions, and provide for homosexuals 'the support of continuing relationships in the worshipping, nurturing community', in the same way as it provided for heterosexual marriages.

The attitudes of the churches

As already pointed out, there is no unanimity of opinion on the question of homosexuality among the various denominations of Christian churches, and often none within denominations either. As yet, no organised Christian denomination has officially endorsed full acceptance of homosexual relationships, although there is a trend among some denominations away from outright rejection, and certainly away from support for the continuation of discriminatory legal penalties for male homosexual acts.

The Festival of Light

However, the increasingly liberal trend of Chistian attitudes towards homosexuality has had no influence on the interdenominational religious lobby group, the Festival of Light (FOL), unless it has been to harden its opposition to such a trend. It is difficult to assess the degree of support for the FOL position, as it is for any group which claims to speak for 'the silent majority', as the National Co-ordinator of the FOL, the Rev. Fred Nile, did in an interview on ABC radio in February 1978,[5] or for the 'moral majority', as it is now being called, after the 'Moral Majority Campaign' in the United States, led by the Baptist minister, the Rev. Jerry Falwell.[6] In a telephone conversation with one of the Board's research officers in 1980, Nile claimed that the FOL was affiliated with 1700 parishes of all denominations. (A parish was regarded as affiliated if it continued to send in annual subscriptions for the literature.) As well, Nile said that 539 individual clergymen were on the mailing list. The FOL opposition to the decriminalisation of consenting adult male homosexual acts has received support from the Anglican Diocese of Sydney, Cardinal Sir James Freeman of the Catholic Archdiocese of Sydney, the Moderator-General of the Presbyterian Church of Australia, the President of the Conferences of Churches of Christ in NSW, the Council of Churches in NSW[7] and the Salvation Army in Sydney.

Sir Marcus Loane, former Archbishop of the Anglican Archdiocese in Sydney, withdrew his support of the FOL in 1977, not because he disagreed with their views in general, but because the FOL had become involved in politics by fielding candidates.[8] The support of the general public would appear not to be as strong as the FOL would like. In 1973 the Australian Festival of Light (South Australia) sponsored a survey administered by its own members. To a question which asked whether homosexuality could be considered 'normal and acceptable', 55 per cent of those who replied answered 'yes'. On this issue, therefore, the FOL would not appear to have as much numerical support as they claim. But then, the FOL are not, in the last resort, so interested in numbers. Their claim is to represent 'the inherent validity of Christian moral standards' which would remain valid—at least for Christians of their own ilk—even if adhered to by only a minority of the population (Hilliard and Warhurst, n.d.: 18–9).

However, that is not the whole of the FOL claim. If it were, it would not fall within the scope of this book, since individual citizens of a democratic state are free to discriminate between one belief and another, and to hold certain opinions while rejecting others. But the FOL not only hold certain opinions—they also claim that their opinions are those of the 'majority', and must be imposed on whatever 'minority' happens to disagree with them. They justify this imposition by appealing to the above-mentioned 'Christian values' as a bulwark against 'the moral and social collapse' of 'our nation'. In order to prevent that 'collapse', the 'over 80 per cent of Australians who believe in God and the over 78 per cent who claim a Christian affiliation' (as Nile put it in *Christian Solidarity* without citing any evidence for this estimate) must impose the FOL's particular narrow fundamentalist version of 'Christian belief' on the rest of the population. The FOL do not take kindly to the rejection of their point of view. In their opinion, the fate of 'our nation' depends on its total acceptance by everyone.

In pursuit of that aim, one of the main campaigns of the FOL has, from the beginning, been directed against attempts to repeal legal provisions which discriminate against male homosexual acts. Their justification for this opposition appears to rest on the assertion that certain consequences would follow upon such a change in the law. One account of these consequences was given by Dr Jean Benjamin, author of a pamphlet disseminated by the FOL (1977). Benjamin asserted that decriminalisation would 'give the word' to 'yesterday's closeted homosexuals' to become 'today's Marxist activists', using 'sexual licence as the weapon for achieving destruction of Western society'. These destructive activists, according to Benjamin, would use Marcuse's *Eros and Civilization* as a blueprint for the proposed Armageddon, because 'they believe what is said'. Her evidence for this credulity on the part of homosexual men was a misquotation from Dennis Altman's book, *Homosexual: Oppression and Liberation,* to the effect that homosexuals read books about themselves and believe them. (Altman's remark had occurred in the context of the dehumanising effect of reading one authoritative tome after another, all of which told the searching homosexual that he or she was sick, immature, deviant, etc.)

This argument is typical of FOL polemics. On another occasion, for example, Benjamin cited a poem by Noel Coward as proof that 'insecurity is characterisitc of the homosexual relationship'. But the lack of sophistication is the least problematic aspect of the FOL polemics. More serious are the vitriolic denunciations and libellous assertions about the personal habits, personality characteristics and moral standards of homosexuals, especially men. The worst example of this kind of unsubstantiated accusation again comes from the Benjamin pamphlet. She states boldly and without qualification:

'Mothers and grandmothers will never accept for example that homosexuals should be allowed to take jobs as baby-sitters and use the sucking reflex of young infants for their own purpose (fellatio) with the added risk of oral syphilitic infection of the baby'. (Benjamin, 1977: 8)

That this kind of fabrication should receive, if not the wholehearted support, then at least the tacit approval, of the church leaders mentioned above is an indictment of their willingness to question the aims and methods of the FOL.

Although extreme, the general tone of this example is not atypical. As a further example, there is the following comment which Nile made about a well-known gay rights activist: 'Our society is a heterosexual society which does have fringe groups like Mr ... He is part of the fringe, perhaps the mentally unbalanced fringe, or morally unbalanced fringe'.[9] And Benjamin characterised (male?) homosexuals thus:

The apparent personal attractiveness of many homosexuals often masks their emotional immaturity, with its lack of self-control; tantrums and rages; with its playfulness; whispering, giggling and mimicry; with its self-righteousness and its preference for adolescents; with its crudity, sordidness and sexual/sensual obsessiveness, and its continual acting and role-playing. (Benjamin, 1977: 3)

Presumably Benjamin intended this description to refer to homosexual men and not to lesbians, since lesbians who 'giggled and whispered' would be within the feminine norm and hence not a cause for complaint. She cited no references in support of her claims about the alleged personality characterisitics of homosexual men. They are not unlike descriptions found in conventional psychiatric/psychological texts until recently, particularly Socarides' *The Overt Homosexual*. But to the extent that those charateristics described by Benjamin comprise a 'mental disorder' they no longer have any place in the recent psychiatric/psychological literature on homosexuality.

The pejorative tone of Benjamin's remarks is also characteristic of the South Australian Community Standards Organisation/Festival of Light (CSO/FOL) submission to the South Australian government, in August 1975, on the government's proposed changes in the laws relating to male homosexual activity. In point 15 of section III of their submission, the CSO/FOL authors began with a reference to 'people manifesting sociopathic disturbances'. They continued with a quotation from a textbook of 'abnormal psychology' published in 1950, which told its readers that 'the psychopath' could be very plausible in presenting 'themselves' as a normal caring human being but that '"they are basically extremely egotistic, selfish and thoughtless of the rights, property and feelings of others"'. The relevance of these statements to the personality characteristics of homosexual men was made clear at the end of the paragraph. The authors of the submission added that 'We are not saying that all homosexuals are sociopaths', but continued by asserting that 'we are saying that the practice of homosexuality is anti-social and does need to be controlled by legal sanctions. Many of the activist spokesmen demonstrate such characteristics'.

One of the most frequent of the FOL accusations to be levelled against homosexual men is a variation of the 'homosexuality is an illness' theme which links male homosexuality with syphilis. For example, Benjamin's 1977 pamphlet said: '70% of syphilis, the most terrible of all venereal diseases, is shown by the Department of Health [*sic*], Sydney, to be transmitted by homosexuals'. Benjamin gave as the source of her information a report in the *Sun* in January 1977 of a statement by 'Dr John [*sic*] Lopez, Deputy Director of Epidemiology, Department of Health [*sic*], NSW'.[10] In 1978, the Board received a submission from the FOL signed by Nile, which contained the following statement: 'We believe it is the duty of Government to protect public health. (Homosexuality leads to a number of diseases including venereal disease'.) In December, 1981, Nile repeated the accusation on the ABC's 'AM' program, saying that 73 per cent of syphilis cases in Sydney are directly transmitted by homosexuals. Exactly what is being alleged in these statements is not at all clear, especially in the light of the inaccuracy with which the source of the information was reported by Benjamin. The original article in the *Sun* read (in part) as follows:

> Seventy per cent of infective syphilis seen in the Sydney VD clinic is homosexually transmitted. Said Dr Lopez, 'It is the same in all big seaports. In Hawaii, it is 90 per cent of cases. Laws against homosexuality have made it very difficult to get men to come in and be treated.[11]

The first point to be made about the FOL allegation is that this statement by Dr Lopez was not a statement about the relative proportion of (male) homosexually transmitted vs. heterosexually transmitted syphilis in Sydney (as implied by Nile), or generally (as implied by Benjamin). It was a statement about the relative proportion of cases presenting to the Sydney VD clinic, and there were a number of reasons why there should have been such a high proportion of men presenting with venereal diseases which were transmitted by means of sexual activity between men, none of which implied any necessary connection between male homosexuality and VD. One reason was suggested by Dr Lopez himself (and ignored by Benjamin)—the high incidence of male homosexually transmitted VD was connected with the fact that Sydney was a seaport. Dr Lopez was not reported as giving the reasons *why* that was a relevant factor (although the VD clinic is situated at Circular Quay), but the implication was that the incidence would be much lower at other centres. A further reason for the high incidence at the Sydney clinic concerned the non-judgmental way in which the staff reacted to the people who presented themselves for treatment. The clinic had a good reputation among the gay male community, because VD was treated as a straightforward medical problem, and not as a moral issue. Furthermore, to say that syphilis is 'homosexually transmitted' (as Dr Lopez did) is not at all the same sort of thing as saying that syphilis is 'transmitted by homosexuals', since non-homosexual men also have homosexual contacts. The FOL appeared to have some awareness of this fact. Benjamin, for example, said in her pamphlet: 'Homosexual behaviour . . . supplies a reservoir of anal syphilis which bisexuals take home to their wives and children', an assertion unsubstantiated by any argument or evidence whatsoever. But even were it the case, then the retention of laws against male homosexual behaviour would be, as Dr Lopez pointed out, an active hindrance to dealing with the problem.

But the FOL is not content simply to recommend that homosexuals continue to be defined as 'sick', and that homosexual men continue to be subjected to discriminatory legal practices. In their zeal to eradicate homosexuality from 'our nation', they also claim that 'poofter bashing' and murder are perfectly reasonable responses to a sexual suggestion from a homosexual man. In a pamphlet issued by the FOL, Janet V. Coombs, a barrister, argued that male homosexual soliciting should be accepted by the courts as a defence against a charge of murder:

> Provocation of this type [a suggestion by one man to another that they engage in sexual activity] at present at least reduces murder to manslaughter and *can* reduce murder to self-defence . . . I want to retain the defence of provocation. My clients need it. (Coombs, 1977)

She made the same assertion in a tape-recording on victimless crime, also issued by the FOL:

> The fact is that once 'these things [consensual adult male homosexual activity] cease to be a crime your right to defend yourself by force from immoral suggestions is reduced, especially where the thing is put that you may do it with consent, because if you do it with consent, then seeking of consent is not longer criminal. And the person who you ask is entitled to punch you, or if they're really terrified, *knife* you.[12]

While it is difficult to be sure about exactly what it is Coombs is claiming here because of the confused way in which she expresses herself, it would appear in the first of the two passages that she is asserting that a man who is charged with murder can have the charge reduced to one of manslaughter, or even dismissed altogether on the grounds of self-defence, if he can demonstrate that the deceased had provoked him to a violent response by suggesting that they engage in sexual activity. This assertion evidently rests on her interpretation of two sections of the Crimes Act. Section 23 (1) states that 'grossly insulting language' or 'gestures' may constitute provocation in the same way as 'a blow'. Section 18 (2) (b) allows for a charge of murder to be dismissed if a homicide occurs in self-defence. However, while a successful plea of provocation *may* reduce a charge of murder to one of manslaughter, it is unlikely that language and gestures, no matter how grossly insulting, would be interpreted by a court as constituting a sufficient threat to the person to justify homicide in self-defence. There *is* a distinction between insulting language, and threatened or actual physical violence, and offended virtue cannot be used as a plea of self-defence.

In the second of the above passages Coombs appears to be arguing that the continued existence of laws against male homosexual acts would enable a man charged with assault or murder to claim provocation, if he could demonstrate that the victim had come up to him and asked him to consent to sexual activity. According to Miss Coombs, the retention of criminal sanctions against male homosexual acts is neccessary if the 'right' of an accused man to plead provocation is not to be 'reduced'. However, in the case of a charge of assault, provocation by 'grossly insulting language or gestures' is not a defence. Apart from the legal considerations, the most obvious response to a man's claim that he was 'provoked' into assault or murder by a suggestion of sexual activity is: Why didn't he just walk away? Recently it was reported that a District Court judge ruled that 'homosexual advances' were 'no excuse' for the behaviour of two young men who punched another man, threatened him with a knife, and stole his car.[13]

A number of objections have been raised to these statements of Coombs. In 1979, one of our informants took the matter up with his local member, who referred the query to the NSW Attorney General. In his reply, Mr Walker said:

> So far as Mr [x]'s question regarding assault and the defence of provocation is concerned, he may be assured that the present law would not condone an aggravated assault in response to any suggestion which might be regarded as offensive. However, as the law in this area is necessarily complex, it would be impractical for me to attempt to explain the complete position in the course of this letter.

Our informant also received another letter from the NSW Department of the Attorney General and Justice, which stated that although his concern was understandable, 'at present there is no law which prevents the Festival of Light publishing literature relating to victimless crimes', and referred him to the Minister responsible for restricting publications.

In December 1979, the Acting General Secretary of the NSW Teachers' Federation, Ms Jennie George, wrote to Nile, requesting the FOL to withdraw the pamphlet and tape from their resource list, pointing out that it promoted anti-homosexual violence. Coombs replied to this request saying:

> Many people are terrified by the mere suggestion of the act of buggery. Moreover when the suggestion is made by a man with the physical strength to force his victim the terror is not without justification especially when one considers that 70% of syphilis in NSW comes from such a contact. Our organization does not promote violence or condone it, but we recognise that it has a place in self-defence.

This denial by Coombs, however, was unconvincing, since it was flatly contradicted by her reiteration of her original argument. In this letter she appeared to be confusing three different kinds of 'provocation' against which she felt her clients needed to 'defend' themselves, but only one of these, physical force, would be recognised in a court of law. As the Attorney General had pointed out in the letter quoted above, the second, 'offensive suggestion', would not be regarded as sufficient provocation to condone aggravated assault. The relevance of the third reference, to syphilis as a form of provocation, remains obscure.

In May 1980, the Inner City Teachers' Association passed a resolution asking the FOL to reconsider their promotion of this material, and requesting the NSW Teachers' Federation to write to the heads of the churches in Sydney which supported the FOL asking them to use their influence 'to end this promotion of violence by the Festival of Light'. In August 1980, letters were sent to Archbishop Loane of the Anglican Archdiocese, to Cardinal Freeman of the Catholic Archdiocese, to the Moderator of the NSW Uniting Church, to the Moderator of the Presbyterian Church, to the President of the Baptist Union, and to the Commissioner of the Salvation Army Eastern Territory. No reply was received from the Catholic Archdiocese, the Baptist Union, or the Uniting Church.

The Rev. Campbell Egan, in his capacity as Convenor of the Church and Nation Committee of the Presbyterian Church, replied that his Church supported the FOL, condemned homosexuality, and opposed law reform and the 'endorsement' of homosexuality in NSW schools. He denied that he and his coreligionists advocated 'violent conduct', but found it 'an elementary fact of life' that 'some people' might react violently to 'certain actions, attitudes, suggestions and approaches'.

Commissioner Leo Ward replied on behalf of the Salvation Army. He said that their FOL representative had assured him that Coombs's statement was 'no longer in circulation', but that if this was not the case, he would like to be informed. He said that the Salvation Army was 'grateful' for the FOL's protection of 'stable society values', but that Salvationists 'would not wish to support any statements which appear to promote or condone violence'.

Archbishop Loane sent two replies. In the first, he pointed out that he had no connection with the FOL and that he did not know anything about the material referred to in the NSW Teachers' Federation letter. In the second reply, he advised the Federation of the name and author of the leaflet they were referring to, and concluded with the comment that not everyone would agree with Coombs's opinion, and that the FOL had 'apparently made it available to its constituency'. The Archbishop gave no undertaking to use his influence with the FOL to get the material withdrawn; nor did he express his own or his Church's disagreement or otherwise with the statements in question.

In September 1980 our informant went to the FOL headquarters to get a new resource list. The leaflet and tape recording were not on the list. When asked about the omission, Nile said he knew that our informant would be pleased, and that the material had been with-drawn because it was 'outdated'.[14] However, Nile again offered the leaflet to the public in his column in the *Sunday Telegraph* on 8 March 1981. He was responding to an accusation made in the letters column of the *Sunday Telegraph* of the week before that the FOL condoned violence against homosexuals, and was offering the leaflet to 'any reader who would like to study this issue'. He denied that the FOL had ever condoned or encouraged physical attacks on homosexuals. However, it is difficult to see how Coombs's argument can be read as anything else but a justification of violence against homosexual men.

But it is not only the content of what the FOL say which is open to criticism—their methods of substantiating their assertions also leave much to be desired. A careful examination of the supporting 'evidence' cited in their publications reveals a tangle of misquotation, distortion and prevarication. One of the authorities quoted by the FOL, Dr Richard Hauser, author of *The Homosexual Society,* was moved to protest in public and in writing at their misuse of his work in their submission to the Royal Commission of Inquiry into Human Rela-tionships (Bureau of Crime Statistics and Research, 1977: 112–3).

Two further examples should suffice to illustrate a practice which is typical in FOL publications. Both are taken from the CSO/FOL submission to the South Australian government. The authors of this submission stated, without qualification:

> In his book, *Crimes Without Victims,* Schur observes: 'It is quite true that control over homosexuality serves to strengthen the position of the family and to reinforce sex-role differentiation'. (Community Standards Organisation, 1975)

However, the authors neglected to point out that Schur continued:

> But this fact hardly provides a basis for wholesale legal and social persecution of inverts. Surely it is fantastic to think that enactment of the proposed reform [of laws against male homosexual acts] would impel hordes of individuals to discard their current heterosexual inclinations and activities for a life of homosexuality, thus precipitating the decline and eventual demise of the conventional family and of civilization as we know it. (Schur, 1965: 110–1)

Quite obviously, Schur was quoted in the context of an argument diametrically opposed to his own. The single sentence quoted in the submission asserted a position which Schur had verbalised in order to oppose it, in order to argue that that point of view could *not* in fact have the consequences which were being claimed for it by the CSO/FOL.

The same kind of distortion occurred in an expurgated quotation from Paul Wilson's book, *The Sexual Dilemma*. The CSO/FOL said:

> Wilson concludes that the medical evidence suggests that 'few would seek treatment if homosexual acts were legal', while for those who seek treatment out of a desire to assume a heterosexual pattern, 'the prognosis is good'. (Community Standards Organisation, 1975)

But Wilson 'concludes' no such thing. The first phrase quoted occurred at the *beginning* of a fairly long argument to the effect that fear of punishment is useless for changing anyone's sexual orientation. The full sentence in which the second phrase occurred was as follows: 'Few seek treatment out of a genuine desire to assume a heterosexual pattern, but for those who do the prognosis is good' (Wilson, 1970: 59).

Such misrepresentations appear to be the rule rather than the exception in the workings of the FOL. Three final incidents illustrate the FOL's perennial failure to substantiate their claims. Two of these incidents are treated in more detail in other places in the ADB report, and will be mentioned only briefly here. The first concerns their invitation to Sgt Lloyd Martin of the Los Angeles Police Department's Abused and Battered Child Unit, to attend to Total Child Care Conference at Macquarie University in 1979. Sgt Martin was regarded as an expert in the field of (male) 'homosexual child molestation' because he had made statements which indicated a high incidence of this offence. However, the fact that he had been forced to retract these statements when they were discovered to be blatantly false, was not information which the organisers of the Conference saw fit to impart to the Australian community leaders they had invited to attend. The second incident occurred in 1981, and involved the Homosexuality Kit which two NSW teachers had received an Australian Schools Commission grant to develop. Nile, in his organised campaign to prevent completion of the kit, confused it, deliberately or otherwise, with the Victorian publication, *Young, Gay and Proud*. Whether Nile had once again not bothered to check the facts or whether it was simply more convenient for his case to retain the confusion, since the kit was not available for inspection, it is not possible to say.

The third incident involved the pirating by Nile of a booklet produced by the Women's Electoral Lobby (WEL) on how to lobby parliamentarians. According to an article in the *Daily Telegraph* in October 1977, a booklet produced by the FOL, with the title *Lobbying for Beginners—1977*, followed by the line 'Compiled by Rev. Fred Nile', reproduced the WEL booklet 'to the end', as the *Telegraph* put it, except for 'a few minor alterations and a few additions that are strictly to do with the Festival of Light lines of thought'. The

Telegraph said that Nile admitted he had 'taken parts of the WEL document', but that he 'had no intention of offending anyone'. He was also reported to have said that he did not 'basically object to WEL', that they just had 'some disagreements on conclusions we made'.[15] However, in saying this, he seemed to have forgotten (or changed his mind?) about his statements in the FOL's *Annual Director's Report—1974/75*. There, his language displayed a marked aversion to WEL:

> These 'exploiters' include . . .—reactionary 'fronts' such as . . . Woman's [sic] Liberation Movement and WEL, whose leaders manipulate members and issues for their own purposes; seeking to turn back human progress to the pre-Christian era with its inhumanity to man.

However, his exposure in the *Daily Telegraph* appeared to have had very little influence on Nile's practice. The 1978 edition of the FOL's *Lobbying for Beginners* was still 'compiled by Rev. Fred Nile'. It *did* 'gratefully acknowledge various lobbying materials' produced by WEL, among others, but at no time had Nile approached WEL for permission to use their material.[16]

Given the FOL's attachment to shaky and misleading 'evidence', and the strings of unconnected assertions in their literature, it is tempting to conclude that they have no case at all. However, despite their inability to sustain their case with coherent argument and rigorous research, they appear to have a disproportionate influence on some parliamentarians—witness the failure of the NSW Parliament at the end of 1981 to pass the Petersen amendment to the Crimes Act, which would have established statutory equality between 'heterosexual' and 'homosexual' offences. Even the Unsworth Bill, which was introduced in the Legislative Council at the beginning of 1982, and which proposed only minor reforms of the 'unnatural Offences' part of the Crimes Act, was rejected by the Legislative Assembly (although passed by the Upper House). According to Mr John Aquilina, MLA for Blacktown, the failure of both bills was a 'clear message . . . that the populace of NSW is not yet in favour of any substantial reforms'.[17] Mr Aquilina did not say what it was that made the populace of NSW so different from the populace of South Australia, Victoria and the Australian Capital Territory. Nor did he mention that the populace of NSW was not given the opportunity to vote on the issue. And if public opinion polls are any indication, his statement was anyway inaccurate. It was not the populace of NSW which influenced the consciences of the majority of parliamentarians. It is more likely that influence stemmed from the small minority of 'swinging voters', which an Australian National Opinion Poll described as 'conservative, selfish and politically ignorant and apathetic'

(Hourihan, 1982), who are prime targets for the FOL's peculiar brand of emotive polemics.

The Anglican Church

As the Bishop of Truro, chairman of the English Church of England's General Synod Board for Social Responsibility, said in 1979, in his Foreword to the report of the Church's Working Party of Inquiry into homosexual relationships: 'Diverse attitudes to homosexuality exist ... within the Church of England, which therefore makes it impossible to contemplate a definitive statement at this moment.' Those attitudes range from the qualified approval of homosexual relationships expressed by the English Working Party, to the unqualified rejection expressed by the Anglican Diocese of Sydney, whose attitude is very similar to that of the FOL.

The views of the Sydney Diocese can be found in their *Report on Homosexuality*, written by the Ethics and Social Questions Committee, and published in 1973. These views were commended by the then Anglican Archbishop of Sydney, Marcus Loane, in the Foreword he wrote to the report. In their report, the Committee condemned homosexual behaviour and relationships out of hand. They explicitly recommended that homosexuals refrain from indulging their sexual propensity, and seek to divest themselves of their condition, which represented 'a most prominent instance of disorder in creation of human relationships'. The Committee based their argument that homosexuality was 'intrinsically wrong', on the biblical passages mentioned earlier in this chapter, and as already noted, rejected any interpretations which suggested otherwise. They also asserted that homosexual behaviour 'deprives those who indulge in it of their ability to take their place within the accepted framework of social relationships', and that the 'practising' homosexual 'adopts a way of life which threatens the social institution of marriage itself'. The Committee expressed concern that homosexuality would become more widespread under the influence of the gay movement, because 'the "coming out" of many folk is not just a making of their homosexual way of life public but a " crossing over" from heterosexuality to homosexuality or a releasing of a previously controlled homosexual propensity'. They supported the retention of criminal laws against male homosexual acts, while recommending that they be made 'more uniform' throughout Australia, as 'the expression of the community's disapprobation of overt homosexuality through legislation'. They saw the existence of these laws as an essential part of a program ... to ensure that marriages are given the maximum chances of success and that the younger generations are not exposed to conflicting models of sexual relationships which in many cases, could lead to arrested sexual development. (Ethics and Social Questions Committee, 1973: 22)

The Committee admitted that 'the law can never include all morality within its scope', but argued that the law was obliged to intervene in the case of male homosexual activity (they did not recommend that lesbian activity be made subject to legal penalties) because that activity affected 'the public good'.

This is the position which lies behind the rejection by the Sydney Anglican Synod, on 12 October 1981 of a motion proposed by Fabian Lo Schiavo, a member of AngGays, a group of Anglican homosexuals. The motion read:

This Synod, noting the many social and legal disabilities which burden homosexual people in our society;
(a) supports such changes in State laws and community attitudes as are necessary to ensure that the homosexual person is treated with justice and equality; and
(b) grants leave to the mover to distribute literature relevant to these issues.

Instead, Synod passed an amendment, proposed by the Rev. R.R. Johnson, Rector of St Michael's, Surry Hills, which read:

This Synod, noting the many spiritual problems facing homosexual persons in our churches, requests Standing Committee to establish a counselling service for:
(a) homosexuals desirous of leaving the 'gay' scene;
(b) potential homosexuals in our congregations, struggling between 'gay' and God; and
(c) clergy trying to minister to homosexuals.

According to the account in *National Magazine,* Johnson, the proposer of the successful amendment, described the 'gay scene' as 'a chamber of horrors', expressed the opinion that young single people were the 'prime targets for the fiery darts of the devil', and recommended that homosexuals seek qualified help to change their sexual orientation.[18]

This is also the position which lies behind the Sydney Anglican Diocese's reaction to Petersen's proposed amendment to the Crimes Act to repeal those sections specifically penalising male homosexual acts. The Church's Standing Committee issued a statement reaffirming its opposition to such a change.[19] And Dean Shilton spoke in St Andrew's Cathedral, saying that the Petersen proposals for 'the legal recognition of sodomy' would divide parliamentarians into 'those who want to return to pagan philosophy' and 'those who want to retain the background teaching of our community'.[20]

This point of view, however, is not shared by the Anglican Synod of the Newcastle Diocese. In October 1981 the Newcastle Synod considered six motions arising out of a study of homosexual relationships conducted by a diocesan subcommittee. Synod passed a motion calling for decriminalisation of (male) homosexual behaviour in private between consenting adults in NSW. They also adopted a motion saying 'that the homosexual condition should not constitute a bar to the exercise of any ministry within the Church'. However, they went on to affirm that 'homosexual acts are not in accordance with God's purpose', and passed another resolution making it a condition of taking Holy Orders that all ordinands must either take a vow of celibacy, or vow to uphold the Christian standard of chastity before, and fidelity within, marriage.[21] One correspondent to the *Newcastle Herald* pointed out that this was cold comfort to those Anglican homosexual men who might feel called to the ministry, since they could be ordained only 'so long as we do not make love nor condone any others of us who make love'.[22]

Neither is the Sydney Anglican Diocese's view on homosexuality in accordance with that of the Melbourne Diocese. In 1971 the Social Questions Committee of the Anglican Diocese of Melbourne released its *Report on Homosexuality*.[23] In this report, the Committee made a distinction between Christian values and those secular values which are upheld by the criminal law. The Committee pointed out that 'homosexual acts, like fornication or adultery, need not be criminal merely because they do not accord with Christian values'. While admitting to disagreements 'on questions of faith and conscience in relation to the personal moral duties of individual Christians', the members of the Committee were unanimous in their recommendations, which included detailed suggestions for law reform to the Victorian State government. In their investigations, the Committee had been surprised to learn that much of what was commonly believed about homosexuality had been brought into question by 'recent surveys and studies'. Among their concluding propositions summarising the material they had studied, the members of the Committee included the following:

> 5. The affection which a homosexually disposed man feels towards another may be of the same order of feeling, in terms of gentleness, admiration, pride and self-denial as the affection of a man for a woman—all these qualities being reinforced by a sexual drive, just as they may be in the case of a man and a woman. (Social Questions Committee, 1971: 31)

The Committee members did not state either their agreement or disagreement with this proposition, but said that the material they had studied was in 'more or less common agreement' with all the propositions listed.

The members of the English Working Party also found themselves unable to reject homosexual relationships out of hand. They expressed a belief 'that Anglicans should continue to teach that the norm for sexual relationships is one of mutual love, expressed and nurtured in life-long exclusive marriage'. Nevertheless, they went on to say, since there was a significant number of people who felt erotic attraction only towards their own sex, it was evident that 'the Church can and should speak pastorally and positively and present the values which can be found in different choices'. The Working Party pointed out the inconclusive, and often 'confused and confusing', nature of the information available on homosexuality, and admitted that 'it is too soon to expect clear and final answers'. They concluded with a plea to Christians 'to soften and reconcile, wherever they can, those who may be tempted to aggressiveness, provocation, scornfulness, bigotry, or malice'. Some of the members of the General Synod Board for Social Responsibility, to whom the Working Party presented their report, agreed with the main conclusions while dissenting from some of the arguments used. The Board's dissenting comments were not directed towards areas of general social concern, such as 'the pressures of society which make life difficult for homosexuals', but towards the biblical and theological arguments. The Board was not convinced by the Working Party's arguments that the Old Testament did not condemn male homosexuality. The Board's comment on the text of Genesis and its condemnation of (male) homosexual behaviour, has already been mentioned. (The Board of Social Responsibility, 1979).

Neither, it would appear, does the Sydney Anglican Diocese's view receive general support in the hierarchy of the Australian Anglican Church. In Sydney, in 1975, the Australian Anglican bishops issued a statement called 'The Politics of Living'. In that statement, the bishops said:

> Participation in a pluralist society means Christians must distinguish between what is applicable to members of the Christian community and what may be expected of the whole society . . . Thus a Christian may hold that homosexual acts are immoral and yet be prepared to recognize that the law should be changed so that homosexual acts between consenting adults should no longer be criminal offences.[24]

The Catholic Church

The Catholic Church's official position is as unequivocal as that of the Festival of Light and the Sydney Anglican Diocese. The Sacred

Congregation for the Doctrine of the Faith, in its *Declaration on Certain Questions Concerning Sexual Ethics*, expressed the Church's position thus:

> At the present time there are those who ... have begun to judge indulgently, and even to excuse completely, homosexual relations between certain people. This they do in opposition to the constant teaching of the Magisterium and to the moral sense of the Christian people ... no pastoral method can be employed which would give moral justification to these acts on the grounds that they would be consonant with the condition of such people ... homosexual acts are intrinsically disordered and can in no case be approved of. (The Sacred Congregation for the Doctrine of the Faith, 1975: 7–8)

The New Family Catholic Catechism makes one reference to homosexuality. In the context of what 'God Forbids' by the sixth commandment, the catechism refers to 'impurity', which is defined as 'letting the sexual powers of the body control our conduct, or using them in some way against God's plan'. Among the examples of 'impure actions which misuse the sexual powers' is homosexuality (along with contraception, and masturbation, which the catechism also calls 'self-abuse') (Tierney, 1981: 180).

Cardinal Freeman, the former Catholic Archbishop of Sydney, came out strongly in opposition to what he called 'any further change in Criminal Law [beyond the Crimes (Sexual Assault) Amendment Act 1981] that encourages homosexual conduct, particularly which may lead to offences directed against boys and girls'.[25] The Cardinal was quoted in the context of the debate on the Petersen amendment, but the exact nature of his objection is not at all clear, since the repeal of sections 79–81B of the Crimes Act would not 'encourage homosexual conduct' in any way which could justify the retention of those sections. Neither would it have led to 'offences directed against boys and girls'. Offences against boys below the age of 16 would have continued to be covered by the recent sexual assault legislation had the Petersen amendment been passed by the NSW Parliament at the end of 1981, as would coercive sexual activity with boys and men above that age. The Cardinal's reference to the 'encouragement' of offences against girls is obscure, firstly, because men who commit such offences can hardly be labelled 'homosexual'. Secondly, if the Cardinal's statement was suggesting that offences against girls are committed by lesbians, then he must be in possession of information that has never been available to legislators in NSW, since there has never been an attempt in NSW to introduce laws framed specifically to penalise lesbian activity. Hence, the Petersen amendment could not possibly have had the consequences the Cardinal was claiming for it. The

Catholic Archbishop of Wollongong, Dr William Murray, has also been reported to be in opposition to repeal, but the consequences Dr Murray alleged were less specific than Cardinal Freeman's. He was quoted in the *Illawarra Mercury* as saying: 'Any change in legislation that would legalise homosexual conduct would be detrimental to the common good and constitute a grave disservice to the community'.[26]

The Church is at pains to make a distinction between a homosexual 'condition', over which the individual has no control, and homosexual 'acts' which the individual can choose to engage in or not. As the Papal Nuncio pointed out in his reply to a letter from CAMP NSW protesting about the views against homosexuality expressed by Pope Paul II in Chicago on 5 October 1979: 'As far as I know, he has not condemned the persons (as persons) who do not want to comply with ... the moral law of the Church.' However, the Nuncio went on to point out, while Christ did not condemn, for example, 'the woman (as a woman) taken in adultery, ... He did say: "Go and sin no more"'.[27]

This distinction between 'condition' and 'behaviour', which is not peculiar to the Catholic Church, but is also made by other Christians who continue to condemn homosexuality, is necessary if that condemnation is to be maintained. If, as seems likely, a homosexual orientation is something over which the individual has no control, the question of its morality (or criminality) does not arise, because the homosexual individual has no freedom of choice in the matter, and hence cannot be held morally (or criminally) responsible. To continue to condemn homosexuals under these circumstances would be an offence against Christian charity and hence itself immoral. 'Hating the sin' while 'loving the sinner' resolves that dilemma, at least for those Christians who condemn homosexuality. For the Christian homosexual, struggling to maintain a Christian commitment in an atmosphere of condemnation, the solution is not so simple. For the Christian homosexual to remain true to the tenets of his or her religion would involve a lifetime of celibacy. On the other hand, to give in to his or her sexual desire, even in a long-term relationship of mutual fidelity and trust, is to fly in the face of the Church's proscription, and in the case of the homosexual Catholic, to live in a state of mortal sin.

The kind of dilemma which the distinction between 'condition' and 'behaviour' poses for the Christian homosexual is described by Father John J. McNeil, a Jesuit priest and author of *The Church and the Homosexual*. McNeil received permission to publish this book from his ecclesiastical superiors. However, that permission implied no more than that the book met the standards of scholarship necesary 'for publication of a book on a controversial moral topic'. It did *not* mean, as McNeil pointed out, that the arguments it contained were 'accepted by the Catholic Church as part of its official doctrine'. McNeil agreed that *if* a lifetime of sexual abstinence was possible 'without serious damage to the person', then the homosexual would be 'prudent' to choose such a course. However, he was not arguing from a position which asserted the sinfulness of homosexual behaviour, and hence the threat such behaviour posed to the homosexual person's 'friendship with God'. Rather, he was arguing that life can be very difficult for homosexuals, considering the sometimes savage reprisals which are meted out to those (especially men) who are known (or suspected) to be practising homosexuals. Hé also pointed out that pious injunctions to refrain from sexual activity, if complied with, could have certain undesirable consequences of their own. For the 'celibacy' which is enjoined on homosexuals, he argued, is not the same kind of continence which is expected of heterosexuals outside marriage (to which it is often compared). 'The heterosexual's abstinence is either a temporary condition or one he [*sic*] has freely chosen; whereas the abstinence the Church would impose on the homosexual is involuntary and unending'.[28]

McNeil continued by drawing out some of the implications for homosexual men of this injuction to sexual abstinence. In the first place, the homosexual man was advised not to associate too closely with women. Given the Church's strictures against all sexual activity outside marriage, together with the strong social pressures to 'cure' the homosexual condition by getting married, the homosexual man could be tempted to get married, should he become close enough to any woman to perceive that it might be possible. As McNeil commented: 'The tragic results for all parties need not be detailed.' Moreover, the homosexual man was also counselled not to associate too closely with men either, since men were for him the occasion of sin. As McNeil pointed out:

> Cut off, then, from all deep and affectionate female and male friendship, the homosexual [man] is literally condemned to living hell of isolation and loneliness. And such a life is not urged temporarily, but must be sustained until death, under threat of possible eternal damnation. (McNeil, 1977: 166–7)

Moreover, McNeil continued, it would be unrealistic to expect homosexuals, who are no better and no worse than anyone else, to exercise a self-control which is beyond the reach of all but the most dedicated and inspired of individuals. He pointed out that the usual outcome of the injunction to abstinence, as 'those clergymen–counsellors who do stay with the persons they direct are well aware', is some attempt at control, followed by bouts of 'promiscuous, even compulsive sex calculated to lead to social ruin and psychological breakdown'. It was for this reason, according to McNeil, that those clergymen who were concerned with the pastoral duty of caring for and counselling homosexual individuals, were loath to condemn outright those committed homosexual relationships which offered the homosexual the equivalent of companionship in Christian marriage.

The Uniting Church

The South Australian Synod of the Uniting Church in Australia sent the ADB the following resolution which had been passed by the South Australian Methodist Conference in October 1972:

Homosexuality
That this Conference endorses the General Conference pronouncement that homosexual acts between consenting adults in private should not be proscribed by law and, in any case, whether present legislation is passed or not, requests the State Government—
1. To provide for adequate research into the causes and nature of homosexuality.
2. To establish a statutory agency or to financially assist a private agency to provide counselling to persons with problems of sexual identity.
3. To establish a significant education program on human relationships including the nature of and reasons for homosexuality.

In relation to the introduction of the Petersen amendment in the NSW Legislative Assembly in 1981, the Rev. Gordon Trickett, secretary of the Board of Social Responsibilities, issued a statement saying that he felt that many people in the Uniting Church would support the amendment.

But support for law reform is evidently as far as a majority of the members of the Sydney Presbytery of the Uniting Church are prepared to go. In September, 1980, the Presbytery voted not to grant a lease for the Kirk Gallery to the Metropolitan Community Church (MCC), a church which had, as its pastor, the Rev. Donald Johnson, put it, 'an outreach into the gay community'.[29] The MCC had been renting space to conduct services on Sunday nights, at the Paddington Village Church, which was also controlled by the Uniting Church. At an initial meeting in May the Presbytery had agreed to lease the Kirk Gallery to the MCC, but in response to a request to reopen the debate, had decided to reverse that decision. The argument which won the day was that the Bible condemns homosexuality in no uncertain terms, and that granting a lease to the MCC would create the appearance of condoning overt homosexuality. The opposing view argued that one shouldn't take ancient texts out of their contexts —the whole of scripture may be taken to suggest a more compassionate stance than the literal interpretation allows. However, the Presbytery did vote to affirm the present arrangement whereby the MCC continued to worship at the Village Church. Evidently this arrangement was not considered to be a condoning of 'overt homosexuality'.[30]

In 1981 a gay fellowship in the Uniting Church, called Unigays, was inaugurated. According to its instigator, Unigays aims 'to express, discuss and understand' the unique experiences of gay people, to provide 'mutual support and pastoral care', and hopefully, to 'benefit the church by playing an educative role'.[31]

The Religious Society of Friends (the Quakers)

The religious denomination which is least condemnatory towards homosexuals is the Religious Society of Friends (the Quakers), although the Society does not wholeheartedly accept homosexual relationships as having the same validity as heterosexual relationships. In 1963 the Friends Home Service Committee in England published *Towards a Quaker View of Sex* (reprinted 1976), which contained a lengthy section on homosexuality. The booklet was written by a group of Friends and the views expressed in it did not necessarily represent the views of every member of the Society. In the chapter on homosexuality, the group discussed the issues of male homosexuality and female homosexuality separately, because, as the authors put it, 'owing to women's nature and to society's different attitude, homosexuality in women takes forms differing from those in men'. However, the greater part of the chapter was devoted to male homosexuality—looking at homosexuality at various life stages among boys, youths and men, at the position of homosexual men in Britain, and at male homosexuality and the law. Even the section on female homosexuality was directed towards male interests rather than deriving from any intrinsic interest in lesbianism itself. Given the situation that female homosexuality was less subject to legal and other social sanctions than male homosexuality, the authors spent almost the whole of the space allotted to female homosexuality in considering the implications for the lives of homosexual men of a modification of the harsher aspects of the social sanctions against them. And those implications, according to the authors, would not be a great improvement on the present situation of homosexual men, because female homosexuality, too, was 'often associated with deep unhappiness', and female relationships displayed many of the same 'harmful features' as male relationships. However, the authors concluded that homosexual relationships should not be dismissed out of hand as being inherently immoral. They commented: 'Surely it is the nature and quality of a relationship that counts: one must not judge it by its outward appearance but by its inner worth. Homosexual affection can be as selfless as heterosexual affection.' (The Friends Home Service Committee, 1963: 41)

In 1973 the Social Responsibility Council of the Society published David Blamires' *Homosexuality from the Inside.* The views in this booklet, which was written by an admitted homosexual man, did not necessarily represent the views of the Society or of the Council. Nevertheless, the Council said that the essay represented 'both the spirit and the method in which we feel such a subject should be approached'. Blamires' aim was to clear up misunderstanding among Friends about homosexuality and to update and extend the material in *Towards a Quaker View of Sex.* His argument was based on the premise that 'homosexual emotions are just as real and good as heterosexual emotions'.

In the same year, *Human Sexuality and the Quaker Conscience,* by Mary S. Calderone, was published in the United States. Calderone argued against passing moral judgments and taking legal actions against homosexuals, and deplored the persecution to which homosexuals were subjected. However, this position was not so much an affirmation of homosexaul relationships, as it was a reiteration of the Quaker belief in the autonomy of the individual conscience, a belief which is central to the Quaker religious life. As Calderone put it:

> The great challenge of being a Friend has always been for me that only one of us may hear, each one for his or her own self, God speaking to us. (Calderone, 1973: 17)

In sum, the non-condemnatory stance the Friends take towards homosexuality is in keeping with the Quaker refusal to impose moral judgments on others.

Homosexuals and the churches

Given the overwhelming tendency among all Christians denominations towards the rejection of homosexuality, it would not be surprising to find that many homosexual Christians resolved the dilemma between their Christian commitment and their sexual nature by leaving the established churches. This was the step taken by most of the members of the small group within 'Cross + Section', the church group within CAMP NSW (this group is no longer in existence) who responded to the Sydney Anglican Diocese's 1973 *Report on Homosexuality*. 'All of the members who had given up being active Christians', the group wrote, 'have done so because the churches have shown such an unenlightened and annihilating attitude towards homosexuals and homosexuality.' Their response, called *Homosexuals Report Back*, and written in 1974, took the Sydney Anglican Diocese to task for their limited and oppressive views. They accused the Anglican Report of being 'narrow-minded and unjust', and the Sydney Diocese of imposing one particular fundamentalist version of Christianity, not only on other Anglicans, but also on the rest of the population, Christian or otherwise, by using its political influence to prevent law change and to suppress any attempts to overcome people's ignorance of homosexuality.

For those homosexuals who want to remain practising Christians outside the established churches, there is the Metropolitan Community Church (MCC), of which there is a branch in Sydney. The MCC was originally founded by the Rev. Troy Perry in Los Angeles in 1968. It was intended as a temporary expedient, to provide a place where homosexuals could worship and socialise openly, until the established churches saw the error of their ways, and could welcome homosexuals back into the fold as fully participating members. So far this has not happened. The existence of the MCC was recently criticised by the Rev. Gordon Moyes of the Wesley Central Mission, who objected to a separate church for homosexuals on 'theological, moral and ecclesiastical principles'.[32] But, as the Rev. Donald Johnson, rector of the MCC in Sydney, pointed out, the MCC was not restricted to homosexuals, but was an ecumenical church open to all. The Rev. Johnson said that he, too, was opposed to separate churches. 'But,' he went on, 'until the denominational churches can adequately serve the homosexual community with acceptance and understanding instead of condemnation and guilt; until they can, in a Christian way, dispense with prejudice, discrimination and persecution, the need for Metropolitan Community Churches is evident.'[33]

But there are some Christian homosexuals who prefer to remain within their own denominations, and work as open homosexuals towards changing their churches' attitudes from within. The formation of AnGays within the Sydney Anglican church, and Unigays within the Uniting Church, have already been mentioned. Acceptance, the Catholic homosexual group, has been in existence since 1973. There is also a group for Jewish homosexuals, called Chutzpah. Orthodox Judaism is no more accepting of homosexual relationships than is Christianity.

Not all those who argue for full acceptance of homosexuals by the churches are themselves homosexual. For example, in 1979, Acceptance circulated a press release which contained a cutting from a Dutch Catholic daily newspaper. The cutting was an article quoting the Bishop of Breda saying that homosexuals 'who live in accordance with their conscience and take the Gospels seriously' should be allowed to participate fully in the life of the Church, including receiving the sacraments. Father John McNeil (1977: 45) argued that 'the only ideals involved in all questions of sexual orientation are the great transcendent questions of justice and love'. And Henry L. Treese, theologian and minister of the United Methodist Church, said:

> The plumbline of judgement must be my own perception of the capacity of these persons for openness to other human beings, for mature and responsible social involvements, and for love in its fulfilling depth. I must in the face of the church's 'no' speak a loud 'yes' to these persons, for I have seen the marks of self-giving Christian love upon their lives. (Treese, 1974: 46)

'A threat to society'

> the target [of the 'militant vanguard of the homosexual movement'] is no less than the total restructuring of society with destruction of the traditional family, its anchor point, as the supreme trophy.[34]

The accusation that homosexuality poses 'a threat to society' is a secularised version of the accusation that it is 'a sin'. Underlying the shift in terminology is the suppressed premise that fundamentalist Christian morality, with its peculiar abhorrence of (male) homosexuality, is the thread whch knits together the whole of the social fabric, and that (male) homosexual acts are breaches in that thread which will, if unchecked, lead to the unravelling of the whole social order. The way in which this will happen is by undermining 'the family', although how 'the family' comprises the whole of the social order, and how that order will disintegrate if (male) homosexuals are left to their own devices, are questions which are rarely addressed.

The context within which 'a threat to society' has been raised most frequently in NSW recently, is around the issue of attempts to repeal or reform the 'Unnatural Offences' sections of the Crimes Act. Hence, the debate has been largely confined to predictions about what will happen to 'society' if the most immediately obvious repressive sanction against homosexuality—anti-male homosexual legislation—were to be lifted. Consequently, the implications of the *absence* of legislative prohibitions against lesbian sexual activity have been rarely mentioned. A rare exception was that of the debate in the English Parliament in 1921 when Frederick Maquisten attempted to introduce legal penalties against 'acts of indecency between female persons'. On that occasion it was argued that the introduction of lesbianism into the Act would have more unfortunate consequences for 'society' than leaving it out, since a single notorious trial, like that of Oscar Wilde, would be enough to inform the female population that 'this vice' existed. It would appear that there is less concern with attempting to 'eradicate' lesbianism by legislative means, than with disguising the fact of its existence. Evidently, there is no fear on the part of those who view homosexuality with distaste that lesbianism per se poses a threat to social stability, since the opponents of the decriminalisation of male homosexual acts do not at the same time argue that lesbians, too, should be subjected to similar legal penalties. Or rather, and perhaps more accurately, having been ignored by the law, lesbianism continues to be ignored by those who argue for or against proposals for legislative change.

The exact nature of the 'threat' which homosexuality allegedly poses to society is rarely spelled out. It appears that it is usually sufficient to reiterate that it does, and to include a list of other nasty habits in the same sentence, without advancing any argument or evidence. Benjamin, for example, asserted:

> it is *Society's choice to protect itself* against homosexual corrupting practices, ambivalent and irrational attitudes, and emotional jags (crying, tantrums and rages) sado-masochism and paranoidal tendencies found in this perversion. (Benjamin, 1977: 4; original emphasis)

But it hardly seems likely that 'society' needs to 'protect itself' from personal idiosyncrasies of behaviour, none of which are peculiar to homosexuals. The exact nature of those 'corrupting practices' supposedly engaged in by homosexuals, and the manner in which the 'corruption' is effected, was not spelled out by Benjamin.

Those arguments which *are* advanced rest on the largely unexamined assumption that homosexuality (or male homosexuality at least) is in some way 'contagious', and would spread like wildfire if any of the social constraints which enforce the present taboo were to be lifted. Indeed, the Sydney Anglican Diocese's report expressed concern that this was already happening under the influence of the gay movement. People were not only 'coming out', they said, they were also 'crossing over' from heterosexuality to homosexuality. According to the FOL, the repeal of anti-male homosexual laws—'legalised sodomy', as Nile put it in a large advertisement in the *Sydney Morning Herald* inveighing against the Unsworth Bill,[35] 'could give the impression of public acceptance', and lead some sexually ambivalent males into thinking 'Well! the law allows it now', and joining 'the ranks of the homosexuals' (Benjamin, 1977: 7). Obviously, the Festival of Light and the Sydney Anglican Diocese see the potential for male homosexual desire to be greater than the actual number of admitted homosexuals.

It is this 'contagious' nature of homosexuality which, it would seem, poses the 'threat to society', by threatening to undermine its 'basic unit', the family. Presumably what would happen if more people, perhaps even *most* people, became infected with homosexual desire, is that they would not marry and found families. But this is by no means a foregone conclusion. Even the FOL is aware that homosexuals do marry sometimes. As they pointed out: 'Many homosexuals marry an opposite sex partner ... either hoping to cure their aberration or to put up a front to the world by demonstrating that they can produce children.' (Parent Responsibility Study Group, 1975: 44)[36] It *is* possible, as the Sydney Anglican report suggested, that the influence of the gay movement has resulted in more people realising their homosexual potential, and establishing themselves in an alternative lifestyle to that of marriage and the family. But it is hardly likely that this constitutes a majority of the population, or even a significantly large minority to pose a threat to the family.

But the wholesale conversion of the population to homosexual relationships is not the only way in which homosexuality threatens the family, according to the FOL. The disintegration of family life which would supposedly be attendant upon any future acceptance of homosexual relationships as a 'valid alternaive' to marriage and the family would also be effected by means of some kind of sex-role confusion which would be engendered in 'normal' people at the sight of ever-increasing numbers of 'out-of-the-closet' gays usurping the prerogatives of the opposite sex: 'homosexual behaviour so profoundly confuses the function of sex in human relationships, its capacity to erode community sex standards is wider than its capacity to attract recruits'.[37] And this confusion would not just happen by accident—it would be a deliberate ploy to throw the whole population into moral chaos by 'proselytising' and/or 'seducing' the impressionable young. Homosexuality, the FOL asserted in their Parent Responsibility Study Group pamphlet, is 'taught by other homosexuals to those who by conditioning during childhood, by isolation or segregation from the opposite sex, etc. have been rendered vulnerable'. And again: 'The predilection of [male?] homosexuals for child partners will ensure that no opportunity is lost to seduce the young ... Your child is their target!' (Parent Responsibility Study Group, 1975: 41) Hence the 'threat to the family' which the FOL and others like them see posed by (male?) homosexuality comes, it would seem, from its erosion of 'community standards' of right and proper sexual behaviour, its confusion of sex roles, and the seductive attraction it offers to the young and impressionable.

Ironically, on this question of posing a 'threat to the family', or perhaps more accurately to the most recent historical form of inter-generational and intersexual relationships, the FOL and the gay move-ment find themselves in agreement. The FOL finds some support for their anxiety that the demands of the gay movement would lead to a weakening of what they regard as the traditional values of marriage and the family, in the writings of the gay activists themselves. Benjamin, for example, cited Dennis Altman's book *Homosexual: Oppression and Liberation,* and quoted from *CAMP Ink* and from Campaign, the Sydney newspaper for homosexuals, as evidence that the gay movement was out to destroy the family, if not the whole of Western civilisation as we know it. The quote from *CAMP Ink* said: 'The nuclear family, the very basis of our society, is our greatest foe. It is the foe we must attack and in force.' The one from *Campaign* said: 'We want to overthrow the Capitalist society, including institutions such as the nuclear family, heterosexism and male dominance. We want to place the struggle for homosexual liberation in the context of total social change.' (Benjamin, 1977: 12).

However, there are no indications that these rousing phrases are any more a blueprint for the future than the FOL's own promotion of the virtues of family life in a period when unemployment and infla-tion render the domestic unit of one male breadwinner with dependent wife and children an impossible ideal. The supposed 'decline' of the 'traditional' family is not a consequence of consciously and deliberately devised strategies on the part of gay activists. It is, rather, a manifestation of changing historical circumstances. What FOL see as God-ordained patterns of family life are in fact peculiar to the modern epoch, and date back no further than the eighteenth century. Both the Festival of Light and the gay activists display an awareness of changing historical conditions as they are manifested in changes in relationships between the sexes and patterns of child-bearing and rearing. But whereas gay activists welcome the changes and attempt to work within an analysis of historical change, FOL seek scapegoats—chiefly feminists and male homosexuals—to blame for what they regard as a disintegration of the God-given social order.

It is hard to believe that arguments such as those put forward by the Festival of Light are taken seriously. Apart from the vituperative accusations levelled at the alleged personal habits of homosexuals, they paint a dour and unpleasing picture of heterosexuality by suggesting that it could be so easily abandoned in favour of an alternative sexual preference simply by virtue of the rescinding of the legal penalties against that alternative. Certainly the Wolfenden Committee were not convinced by arguments of this kind: 'This expectation [that decriminalisation would open the floodgates] seems to us to exaggerate the effect of the law on human behaviour' (Wolfenden et al., 1957: 23). Neither do the 'floodgates' appear to have been 'opened' in South Australia, Victoria and the Australian Capital Territory. The members of FOL display an excessive amount of concern at the prospect that homosexual desire and behaviour (and presumably that also includes lesbianism) would proliferate at the expense of heterosexual relationships. It *is* possible that more people who possess the potential for sexual relationships with the same sex would in fact choose that alternative if it were to become less socially unacceptable. Nevertheless, it is wildly improbable that that alternative would come to predominate. Whatever the preconditions for a homosexual orientation (or a heterosexual one), they are not the kinds of conditions which can be engineered beforehand. If the present situation of heterosexual dominance cannot guarantee that all people will be heterosexual, then it is unlikely that a wider social acceptance of homosexual relationships would revolutionise human sexuality to the extent envisaged by FOL. The suspicion arises that this concern with a supposed proliferation of homosexual tendencies is motivated more by irrational fears than a considered examination of the issue. It would be too sweeping a generalisation (and most likely inaccurate) to accuse all adherents of the FOL position of 'homosexual panic', that is, a reaction against one's own unadmitted and forbidden homosexual desire. Nevertheless, the FOL position does offer a comfortable straightforward (and simplistic) explanation of social change, and provides a convenient scapegoat whose exclusion from 'society' will, they hope, halt the 'decline in moral standards' and the disintegration of those moral values which hold the 'community' together.

6

CONCLUSION

A
T the present time the task which gay liberation set itself in the early seventies is by no means completed. The first fine flush of revolutionary fervour has long died down in the face of cold hard political reality. 'Changing society' is not an enterprise which lends itself to the 'art of the possible'. Nonetheless, the gay movement has had a noticeable influence on attitudes and practices concerned with the social definitions of 'homosexuality'. There is now more public awareness of prejudice against 'homosexuals' and of the problems they face because of that prejudice. The misconceptions are now less easy to justify since 'homosexuals' have 'come out' and declared themselves. The 'medical model' which defined 'homosexuality' as pathological has been shown to be an anachronistic hangover of the nineteenth century. Gay men now have a milieu (at least in the cities) where they can meet and socialise openly. 'Homosexuality' is now enshrined in NSW statutes as a ground of unlawful discrimination. And recently, the situation of adult homosexual men in relation to the criminal law improved in NSW.

In May 1984 the NSW Government passed the *Crimes Amendment Act* 1984. This legislation repealed sections 79–81B, the 'Unnatural Offences' Part of the *NSW Crimes Act* 1900, sections which referred to the commission or attempted commission of buggery, indecent assault, acts of gross indecency, and the procuring, soliciting or inciting of such activities, by male persons upon male persons. In place of the repealed sections, the legislation inserted sections 78g–t, all of which related to offences committed by and with male persons under the age of eighteen. The bill had been introduced as a private member's bill by the Premier, Neville Wran, and it was the prestige of his sponsorship which ensured the bill's passage through parliament. (The fate of previous private members' bills on the same issue is detailed in the ADB's report, in chapter 5.)

However, the Premier's sponsorship was not sufficient in itself to guarantee its acceptance by the consciences of the parliamentarians of NSW, who could not be soothed to the point where they would agree to statutory equality between (male) 'homosexual offences' and (male) 'heterosexual offences'. The 'age of consent' was set at eighteen whereas it is sixteen for equivalent offences against girls. Moreover, the legislation did not resolve the existing anomalies between the penalties prescribed under this Part of the Act, and those prescribed under the amendments introduced into the Act by the *Crimes (Sexual Assault) Amendment Act* 1981. The 1984 amendments still prescribe higher penalties for consensual sexual activity than for the non-consensual activity (sexual assault) specified in the 1981 amendments.

But the most worrying aspect of this latest attempt at law reform is what is known as 'the Yeoman's amendment', which prescribes a maximum penalty of two years' imprisonment for anyone who 'solicits, procures, incites, or *advises* any male person under the age of 18 years to commit or be a party to the commission of an act of gross indecency with another male person'. There is no definition of 'advises'. Does it mean that those who are concerned with the counselling, reassuring and *advising* of young gay males, for example, the Gay Counselling Service of NSW, the ADB, school counsellors, are subject to this provision of the Act, and hence liable to a term of imprisonment? At the moment, no one seems to know.

The fight goes on, though diminished in fervour and without that initial intense commitment which brought at least an appearance of cohesion in the early days. There is no general agreement among gay groups about what is still to be done, or even what constitutes a problem. For example, some groups see the above-mentioned Crimes Act amendments as a final victory, while others continue to struggle against the remaining anomalies. And whatever their political commitments and affiliations (or lack of them), gay groups are still male-dominated. At the same time, public opinion is not all good. Police harassment continues, and the grand old sport of 'poofter bashing' seems to be on the increase with the greater visibility of the 'gay scene'. The criminal law does not provide statutory equality for gay men; and the churches remain adamantly opposed. There is still plenty for gay groups to do. But none of it is likely to result in 'revolution'. And that might not be such a bad thing after all is said and done, because I have a more than sneaking suspicion that, faced with a fully-fledged 'revolution' tomorrow, we wouldn't know what to do with it.

NOTES

Introduction

1 The ADB's report was released in June 1982. I was principal author of the report, although the ADB, in the person of Christine Burvill, its research co-ordinator, maintained a continuous editorial watch on what I produced, and the 3-member Board itself retained the final right of veto over the material. (That is not an implication of censorship, since in fact there was none. We worked together harmoniously, and were in accord on all the major issues.) I wrote chapters 1, 2 and 3, a first draft of chapter 4 (of which only the "Child Custody" section was retained in its entirety), the final draft of chapter 5, and chapter 7. The vast bulk of the research had been done by the time I arrived at the Board to start writing up the project in March 1980, including the 'Homosexual Phone-In', although I also took over the research then going on, as well as writing up the immense amount of information I was faced with on my arrival

2 From November 1980 to October 1981

3 The ADB's terms of reference were stated in section 119(a) of the *NSW Anti-Discrimination Act* 1977 as follows:

119. For the purpose of eliminating discrimination and promoting equality and equal treatment of all human beings, the Board may—
(a) carry out investigations, research and inquiries relating to discrimination and in particular discrimination against a person or persons on the ground of . . .
(x) homosexuality;
(xi) a characteristic that appertains generally to homosexuals;
(xii) a characteristic which is generally imputed to homosexuals.

The areas within which it is unlawful under the Act to discriminate against individuals are specified as: employment, education, and goods and services. At the end of 1982, 'homosexuality' was included within the Act as a ground of unlawful discrimination

4   After the release of the ADB's report, this approach was criticised by fundamentalist Christians on the grounds that it was 'biased'. What these critics (who would be hard put to substantiate any claim that they themselves were *un*biased) failed to perceive was that the same 'bias' (if such it was) was already presupposed within the legislation itself. The very inclusion of 'homosexuality' within anti-discrimination legislation in the first place suggests at least the strong possibility that individuals labelled 'homosexuals' are discriminated against. Given that initial presupposition, it is only logical that any subsequent research will be directed towards uncovering the nature and extent of that discrimination, and an obvious starting point is to investigate the experiences of those people who fall into the category specified. Nonetheless, despite this 'bias' a large part of the ADB's report was devoted to serious (on the whole) discussion of arguments that discrimination against 'homosexuals' was justified, even necessary. If at times the report's language verged on the derisive (chiefly in response to attitudes expressed by the Festival of Light), that was because the 'arguments' being considered hardly merited serious consideration

5   In chapter 2, 'Defining Homosexuality'

6   Nevertheless, I have retained this usage in this book, and more consistently than I did in the report. The patriarchal tendency to define everything human with reference to the male alone must be resisted at all costs, even at the risk of appearing (perish the thought!) 'militant', 'strident' or 'rabid'. The quotation marks around 'homosexual' and 'homosexuality' are intended to emphasise the problematic status of the concept

7   Specifically in reference to chapter 3, the chapter on religious objections to homosexuality

Chapter 1

1   In Part I, I have omitted the quotation marks around the word 'homosexual', because to use them here would be anachronistic. At the time these events were happening, and to the people involved in them, there was nothing problematic about the word

2   Conversation with Lex Watson. Lex is at present working with Garry Wotherspoon on a history of these male homosexual groups

3   The 'Inc.' was dropped fairly early on, and 'NSW' was added after the establishment of branches in other states

4   The 'Joanna' of David Widdup's 'Minnie Drear' column in *CAMP Ink,* for the first few of which she was a co-perpetrator

5   *Australian* 12 November 1981

6   A report of the meeting was written up in *The Bulletin* 13 March 1973, p. 28

7   The second interview in the *Australian,* 19 September 1970. Of course, a

newspaper article is a fitting context for the 'apt phrase', and not at all appropriate for 'detailed theoretical analysis'

8 *CAMP Ink* 1, 12 1971; 2, 1 1971. The *Australian,* 4 and 6 October 1971, ran two short articles before the demonstration. However, in a letter to Paul Foss, John Ware wrote: 'One sour note was the refusal of the media to give us any publicity [of the event itself]. Perhaps our next demo will be against the media.'

9 By the end of the first year, this aim had been largely achieved, with approximately 1500 members nationwide, and branches in Melbourne, Perth, Brisbane and Canberra. See Ware (1971)

10 By the hiring of club rooms, where functions could be held, members could drop in and socialise, and John and Michael could live on the premises so that there would be someone available 24 hours a day

11 *CAMP Ink* 2, 10, pp. 4–5; and 2, 12, p. 11

12 *CAMP Ink* 2, 11, p. 11; and 2, 12, pp. 2, 4–5. See also: The Tribunal on Homosexuals and Discrimination, Exhibit No. 21; and John Lee's article in *Sydney Gay Liberation Newsletter,* 1, 5 1972

13 The premises at 393 Darling Street, Balmain

14 *CAMP NSW Newsletter*, 2, 2 1973

15 *CAMP Ink* 4, 3–4 1975

16 Conversations with Jan Davis and Col Eglington, who worked in PAF from the beginning until 1975

17 Printed in the *CAMP NSW Newsletter,* March–April 1976. Margaret McMann's health had forced her to take a less active role

18 *CAMP Ink* 5, 5, pp. 5–12. The incident was also reported to the Tribunal on Homosexuals and Discrimination

19 *Daily Telegraph* 20 November 1975, 'Church Move to Gag Teacher'

20 *Australian* 20 December 1975, 'Homosexual Wins Battle to Appear at Inquiry'; *Sydney Morning Herald* 26 December 1975, 'Homosexuals Give Evidence: Human Relations Inquiry'

21 *CAMP Ink* 4, 3–4, pp. 6–8, for a report on the first seminar; 4, 5–6 for a report on the second

22 Conversations with Robyn Plaister and Margaret McMann

23 *CAMP Ink* 4, 5–6

24 *CAMP Ink* 5, 2, no.37, June 1976, pp. 4–6

25 *CAMP NSW Newsletter,* August-September 1976

26 Report of Deputation to Premier Wran, Supplement to *CAMP Ink*, no. 38, September 1976. From the files of Mike Clohesy and Peter de Waal

27 *CAMP Ink*, no. 38, September 1976, pp. 4–5

28 *National Times*, 28 March–2 April, 1977, 'How the Religious Schools Lobby Rolled Over Wran'. The following account is based on that article

29 Conversations with Jan Davis, and Sue Rawlinson, who was one of those psychologists and was with HGS as long as it existed

30 *CAMP NSW Newsletter* 2, 1, 11 May 1973

31 *CAMP Ink* 4, 1 1974

32 *CAMP NSW Newsletter*, no. 40, September 1978; no. 42, November 1978

33 A particularly nasty little Trotskyist sect, who leech onto other people's

causes because they see themselves as the Vanguard of the Revolution—all six of them

34   Conversation with Margaret McMann
35   Conversation with Di Minnis, the Gay Trade Unionist member
36   *CAMP NSW Newsletter* no. 43, December 1978
37   *CAMP NSW Newsletter* no. 49, August 1979
38   That is, gay liberation as a social analysis, not the comparatively short-lived group which called itself 'Sydney Gay Liberation' (see chapter 2), which was even less successful than CAMP in influencing 'the wider society'

Chapter 2

1   The probable date of this opus is the end of 1970. This is the date ascribed to it by Paul Foss, who cited it in his own paper, and who lent it to me. Its source is obscure. The group which produced it had no connection with Sydney Gay Liberation, which did not get off the ground until the beginning of 1972. The handout gave as their address 67 Glebe Point Road, which at that time was a centre for a number of 'subversive' activities, including Women's Liberation.
There was also another 'Gay Is Good' pamphlet produced at this centre. This one reproduced at the whole of Martha Shelley's paper, with adaptations for the Australian context. Its probable date is 'approximately early 1971' (dated by John Lee, who lent it to me), and it appeared in one issue of a short-lived radical newspaper called *Playgue*. Its origins, too, were a mystery to those former SGL members I spoke to. It supplied a contact phone number and the name 'Kate' for anyone interested in Gay Liberation, but, according to John Lee, no one ever answered. However, in May 1971, at least one aspiring gay liberationist (Richard Jessop) managed to contact 'Kate'. He had seen a notice about Gay Liberation in the window of the Third World Bookshop. He met 'Kate', who introduced him to Dennis Altman. Dennis took him along to CAMP. So by that time at least, this early gay liberation group had ceased to exist
2   The other speakers at the Forum were Liz Fell, Germaine Greer and Gillian Leahy. The text of Dennis's talk on that occasion is reproduced in Altman, 1979
3   *SGL Newsletter* 1, 4, 1972
4   *SGL Newsletter* No. 9, 1973
5   The first of these quotes is taken from the Manifesto. The second is from Martha Shelley's 'Gay Is Good', as it was reproduced in *Playgue*
6   From SGL's first handout, March 1972
7   *The Bulletin* 8 July 1972, an interview with Dennis Altman
8   *SGL Newsletter* 1, 5, 1972
9   Conversations with John Lee and Tim Carrigan
10   *SGL Newsletter* 1, 2, 1972
11   *SGL Newsletter* 1, 3, 1972

12 *SGL Newsletter* 1, 1, 1972
13 *SGL Newsletter* 1, 6, 1972
14 *SGL Newsletter* No. 8, February–May 1973
15 ibid, and No. 9 July(?) 1973
16 That McConaghy may subsequently have changed his mind about the pathological nature of homosexual desire is suggested by some of his more recent research (McConaghy et al., 1979). This study found that 60 per cent of a sample of 204 second-year medical students could recall being aware of homosexual feelings in adolescence, and 40 per cent were still aware of these feelings. The researchers were inclined to the belief that their study supported the biological theory that homosexuality was established before birth, at least in the case of men, because there was a correlation between their adult homosexual orientation, and 'female sex dimorphic behaviour' in childhood, i.e. they were sissies. It would appear that McConaghy's long historical search for scientific truth was nearly over—with this conclusion, he had reached the nineteenth century
17 *SGL Newsletter* No. 11, August 1973
18 ibid.
19 *Sun* 15 September 1973: ' "Gay Lib" Brawls at Cenotaph'; *Sunday Mirror* 16 September 1973: 'Gay Lib, Police in Punch-Up'; *Sunday Telegraph* 16 September 1973: 'Gay Libbers Arrested'; *Honi Soit* 20 September 1973: 'Poofters Arrested for Coming Out'; *Tribune* 18–24 September 1973: 'Militant Gay Lib March'; *Arena*, n.d.: 'The Gay Pride March—And Police Brutality'
20 A pamphlet containing three discussion papers prepared for the meeting: 'Part of a Solution' by Craig Johnston; 'What's Right and Wrong with Sydney Gay Liberation?' by Denis Freney; and 'What's Wrong with Gay Liberation' by Jeff Hayler. See also: *SGL Newsletter* November 1973

Chapter 3

1 Gilbert Ryle (1949) defined a 'category-mistake' as the representing of certain facts 'as if they belonged to one logical type or category...when they actually belong to another'
2 This was not the definition used by Bebbington and Lyons. See below
3 *Australian* Weekend Review, 19 September 1970, p. 15
4 *CAMP Ink* 1, 3, 1971, p. 15
5 According to a list of coming events included with the May 1971 issue of *CAMP Ink*
6 See one of the Letters to the Editor in *CAMP Ink*, 2, 1, 1971, p. 16
7 In the March 1971 issue, and the July 1971 issue
8 That this strategy contained further and, finally, insoluble contradictions between the interests of women and those of men, was to become obvious later. See below
9 Minutes of CAMP executive meeting, 9 March 1973. Supplied to me by Robyn Plaister

10 *CAMP NSW Newsletter* 25 June 1979
11 *CAMP Ink* 5, 1, 1976, p. 4
12 Kenneth Pitchford was married to Robin Morgan, American radical feminist, poet, editor of 'Sisterhood Is Powerful', and author of *Going Too Far*. She writes at some length about their relationship in the latter volume. Pitchford appeared in the Canadian feminist film, 'Not a Love Story: A Film about Pornography', with Robin and their son
13 These are holes in the partitions between the cubicles in men's public lavatories, the exact size and height for the insertion of an erect penis

Chapter 4

1 The Shorter Oxford English Dictionary
2 'Homophile' is the term used to describe those organisations which were the predecessors of the recent gay liberation movement, and which agitated for the social acceptance of homosexuals
3 After Sappho, the Greek poet
4 A 'tribade' is still defined by the Shorter Oxford as 'A woman who practises unnatural vice with other women'
5 Havelock Ellis informs us in *Sexual Inversion* that the term 'homosexuality' was invented by a German, Dr Benkert, who wrote under the pseudonym, 'Kertbeny'. Ellis himself did not approve of the term on the pedantic ground that it was a bastardised mixture of Greek and Latin
6 The *Australian*, 10 February 1979, letter to the Editor from Dr L. Rogers, Pharmacology Department, Monash University, and Dr M. Ross, Psychiatry Department, Flinders University
7 Ware called the procedure 'cingulo-trachotomy'. The term in the Gould Medical Dictionary is 'cingulotractomy', but the term used in the published papers is 'cingulotractotomy'. The dictionary also says that the procedure is 'used rarely, in control of psychotic disorders'
8 The ADB's Homosexual Phone-In was conducted in February 1980. Approximately 200 people phoned in during the three-day survey, and 174 of the completed interview schedules were used for data analysis. All respondents identified themselves as homosexual, or felt that they had a homosexual component in their make-up. Anyone who rang who was not homosexual was asked to ring back at another time. The interview schedule contained a combination of closed- and open-ended questions, so that the research team was able to obtain both statistical data and individual case study material. The schedule was divided into a number of sections, each of which covered a different area. Respondents were asked to specify two areas which were of major concern to them personally, and were then asked questions specifically concerned with those areas. They were (in order of decreasing frequency): public attitudes, employment, law and law enforcement, education, accommodation, and access to and custody of children. For a detailed discussion of the Phone-In, see the ADB Report (1982)

9   The debate occurred in the *Journal of Consulting and Clinical Psychology* 44, 2, 1976, and in the *Journal of Homosexuality* 2, 3, 1977
10 The Manual still lists, under the heading 'Other Psychosexual Disorders', the designation 'Ego-dystonic homosexuality', which we assume refers to those people who have failed to come to terms with and accept their homosexuality. In that sense, this designation locates the cause of the problem in the anti-homosexual society rather than the homosexual individual, in so far as it is possible for a discipline such as psychiatry, which is essentially concerned with the individual, to locate problems in the wider social context
11 *SGL Newsletter* August 1973
12 *Australian Psychologist* 9, 2, 1974, p. 207

Chapter 5

1   Treated in the report but omitted in the present book
2   A submission to the Board received from an individual—February, 1979
3   By the Board of Social Responsibility of the English Church of England, in their 'critical observations' on the report of the Church's Working Party. See: The Board of Social Responsibility of the Church of England Working Party (1979)
4   *Adelaide Advertiser* 8 March 1980—'The Sins of Sexuality' by Chris Milne. Quoted from an article by Dr Rayner in the *Adelaide Church Guardian*
5   2Bl, 3 February 1978
6   See the first issue of the recent newspaper format publication of the FOL, *Australian Christian Solidarity* 1, 1, 17 April 1981, p. 1
7   ibid
8   *Sydney Morning Herald* 14 February 1977, p. 12
9   In the ABC interview mentioned above
10 In fact, the doctor's first name is 'William' not 'John', and the department is the Health Commission of NSW.
11 *Sun*, 10 January 1977
12 From a transcript of the recording. Emphasis in the original
13 *Campaign* No. 59, November 1980
14 *Gaytas Newsletter* no. 11, September–October, 1980
15 *Daily Telegraph* 12 October 1977
16 For a more detailed account of the practices of the FOL, see: *Nation Review*, 29 September–5 October, p. 9; 6 October–12 October, p. 11; 13 October–19 October, p. 11, 1978, for a series of articles called 'Festival of Lies' by Michael Glass
17 *Daily Mirror*, 7 April 1982
18 *Nation Magazine*, February–March, 1982, 'God Against Gays?'; *Sydney Morning Herald* 13 October 1981
19 *Sydney Morning Herald* 7 April 1981
20 *Australian* 23 November 1981

21   *Newcastle Herald* 19 October 1981
22   *Newcastle Herald* 31 October 1981
23   Strictly speaking this is a report on *male* homosexuality
24   Reprinted in *Australian Presbyterian Life* no. 238, 19 November 1975, p. 7
25   Quoted in *Australian Christian Solidarity* 1, 1, 17 April 1981, p.l. See also: *Daily Telegraph* 4 April 1981
26   *Illawarra Mercury* 7 April 1981
27   *CAMP NSW Newsletter* 10 December 1979, p. 1
28   McNeil was aware of the male bias of the Church's moral pronouncements—see, for example, p. 83–7, 143–4—but found himself unable to avoid that same bias because those pronouncements were the subject matter of his own discourse
29   *Sydney Morning Herald*, 22 July 1980, 'The Church in Harmony with Homosexuals'
30   *Horan Hall Walker Notes*, Week 38/80, 'Homosexuals Rolled by Uniting Church'
31   From a letter to *Forward*, the journal of the Uniting Church, by the instigator of Unigays. Copy received at the Board
32   *Sydney Morning Herald* 16 July 1980
33   *Sydney Morning Herald* 21 July 1980
34   *Age*, 28 November 1980, Michael Barnard's 'Comment' column
35   *Sydney Morning Herald*, 15 March 1982
36   One chapter of this pamphlet, 'Homosexuals and Homosexuality', by a 'medical specialist', was reproduced as a background paper to the NSW Government Seminar on Victimless Crime
37   Rev. B.L. Smith, *The Church Record*, quoted in Benjamin, 1977

BIBLIOGRAPHY

Abbott, S. and Love, B. (1978) *Sappho Was a Right-On Woman: A Liberated View of Lesbianism* New York: Stein and Day

Agel, J. ed. (1973) *Rough Times* New York: The *Rough Times* Staff, Ballantine Books

Altman, D. (1972) *Homosexual: Oppression and Liberation* Sydney: Angus and Robertson

—— (1979) *Coming Out in the Seventies* Sydney: Wild and Woolley

Antolovich, G. (1973) 'Women's Commission 1973' *CAMP Ink* 3, 4, n.d. (April? May? 1973)

Armon, V. (1960) 'Some Personality Variables in Overt Female Homosexuality' *The Journal of Projective Techniques* 24, pp. 292–309

The Australian Union of Students (1978a) *Homosexual Research Project: Attitudes & Experiences of Lesbians and Male Homosexual Students in Tertiary Education* Carlton, Victoria: The Australian Union of Students, n.d. (1978?)

—— (1978b) *Homosexuality: An Action and Resource Guide for Tertiary Students* Carlton, Victoria: The Australian Union of Students n.d. (1978?)

Bardwick, J. (1972) *Readings in the Psychology of Women* New York: Harper and Row

Bates, E.M. and Wilson, P.R. (eds) (1979) *Mental Disorder or Madness?* Brisbane: University of Queensland Press

Bebbington, L. and Lyons, M. (1975) 'Why Should We Work With You? Lesbian-Feminists versus "Gay" Men' *Papers and Proceedings of the First National Homosexual Conference* Melbourne

Begelman, D.A. (1977) 'Homosexuality and the Ethics of Behavioural Intervention' *Journal of Homosexuality* 2, 3, pp. 213–9

Bell, A.P. and Weinberg, M.S. (1978) *Homosexualities: A Study of Diversities Among Men and Women* The Institute for Sex Research, Indiana University: The Macmillan Co. of Australia

Bene, E. (1965a) 'On the Genesis of Male Homosexuality: An Attempt at

179

Clarifying the Role of the Parents' *British Journal of Psychiatry* 3, pp. 803–13

—— (1965b) 'On the Genesis of Female Homosexuality' *British Journal of Psychiatry* 3, pp. 815–21

Benjamin, J. (1977) *Homosexuality: Its Victims and the Value of Legal Deterrence* Sydney: Festival of Light

Bieber, I. (1976) 'A Discussion of "Homosexuality: The Ethical Challenge"' *Journal of Consulting and Clinical Psychology* 44, 2, pp. 163–6

Bieber, I. et al. (1962) *Homosexuality: A Psychoanalytic Study* New York: Basic Books

Blachford, G. (1981) 'Male Dominance and the Gay World' in Plummer ed. (1981)

Blamires, D. (1973) *Homosexuality from the Inside* London: The Social Responsibility Council of the Religious Society of Friends

The Board of Social Responsibility of the Church of England Working Party (1979) *Homosexual Relationships: A Contribution to Discussion* London: The Church Information Office

Bradstock, M., Dunne, G., Sergeant, D. and Wakeling, L. (eds) (1983) *Edge City on Two Different Plans: A Collection of Lesbian and Gay Writing from Australia* Leichhardt: Sydney Gay Writers' Collective

'Brain' (1981) 'Coming Out in a Catholic School' *Gaytas Newsletter* 18, July

The Bureau of Crime Statistics and Research (1977) *Background Papers to the Research Seminar on Victimless Crimes* Sydney: The NSW Bureau of Crime Statistics and Research

—— (1978) *Homosexual Offences: Research Report no. 3* Sydney: The NSW Bureau of Crime Statistics and Research

Calderone, M. (1973) *Human Sexuality the Quaker Conscience: The 1973 Rufus Jones Lecture* Philadelphia: Friends General Conference

Camp NSW (1976a) *Background Papers and Submissions to the Tribunal on Homosexuals and Discrimination* Sydney: CAMP NSW

—— (1976b) *Report to the Nation: '76* Sydney: CAMP NSW

—— (1977a) *Comments on the NSW Public Service Board's Background Paper, No. 16: 'Homosexuals in the Public Service'* Sydney: CAMP NSW

—— (1977b) *Report to the Nation: '77* Sydney: CAMP NSW

Canadian Human Rights Commission (1979) *Annual Report* Ottawa

Caprio, F.S. (1954) *Female Homosexuality: A Psychodynamic Study of Lesbianism* New York: The Citadel Press

Carrigan, T. (1977) 'The Political Relationship Between Gay Men and Lesbian Women' Paper presented at the Third National Homosexual Conference, Adelaide

Catholic Education Commission of NSW (1979) *A Critical Review of Some Aspects of the Anti-Discrimination Act 1977 and the Anti-Discrimination Board* Sydney: Catholic Education Commission

—— (1982) *Catholic Education and Homosexuality: A Commentary on the Report 'Discrimination and Homosexuality'* Sydney: Catholic Education Commission, n.d. (but released late in 1982)

Clark, T.R. (1973) 'Homosexuality as a Criterion Predictor of Psychopathology in Non-Patient Males' *Proceedings of the 81st Convention of the American*

Psychological Association 8, pp. 405–6

Clarke, D. (1977) *Loving Someone Gay* California: Signet Books

Clohesy, M. and de Waal, P. (1974) *Oppression on Reflection* Sydney: CAMP NSW

Community Standards Organisation/Festival of Light (1975) *Submission to the South Australian Government* Sydney: Festival of Light

Conway, T. (1977) unpublished paper presented at the Victimless Crimes Seminar, University of NSW

Coombs, J.V. (1977) 'Victimless Crime?' A paper presented to the Bureau of Crime Statistics and Research Centre' Sydney: Festival of Light

Davison, G.C. (1976) 'Homosexuality: The Ethical Challenge' *Journal of Consulting Clinical Psychology* 44, 2, pp. 157–62

Delaney, M. (1972) 'Sex Lib Demonstration' *William and John* 1, 6, August.

De Luca, J.N. (1967) 'Performance of Overt Male Homosexuals and Controls on the Blacky Test' *Journal of Clinical Psychology* 23, 4, p. 465

Dörner, G. (1969) 'Hormonal Induction and Prevention of Female Homosexuality' *Journal of Endocrinology* 42, pp. 163–4

Dörner, G., Rohde, W., Stahl, F. and Masius, W.-G. (1975) 'A Neuroendocrine Predisposition for Homosexuality in Men' *Archives of Sexual Behaviour* 4, 7, p. 18

Dworkin, R. (1978) *Taking Rights Seriously* Cambridge, Massachusetts: Harvard University Press

Ellis, H.H. (1915) *Studies in the Psychology of Sex, II: Sexual Inversion* 3rd edn, Philadelphia: F.A. David and Co.

—— (1950) *My Life* London: William Heinemann Ltd

Ethics and Social Questions Committee to the Synod of the Church of England, Diocese of Sydney (1973) *Report on Homosexuality*

Feldman, P. (1977) 'Helping Homosexuals With Problems: A Commentary and a Personal View' *Journal of Homosexuality* 2, 3, Spring, pp. 241–9

Foss, P. (1972) 'Gay Liberation in Australia' *William and John* no. 8, December

Foucault, M. (1976) *Histoire de la Sexualité, I—Volonté de Savoir* Paris: Gallimard

Frank, J.D. (1972) 'Treatment of Homosexuals' in The National Institute of Mental Health Task Force on Homosexuality

Freedman, M. (1971) *Homosexuality and Psychological Functioning* Belmont, California: Brooks/Cole Publishing Co.

Freeland, J. (1979) 'STOP! CARE TO COME and PROBE the Right-Wing PIE: Behind the Attacks' *Radical Education Dossier* 8, Autumn

French, R. (1981) 'Gay Issues in the Australian Press: 1953 to the Present' *Gay Information* no. 6, Winter

Freud, S. (1905) 'Three Essays on the Theory of Sexuality' in *On Sexuality* vol. 7, The Penguin Freud Library

—— (1912) 'The Universal Tendency to Debasement in the Sphere of Love' in *On Sexuality*

—— (1910) 'Leonardo da Vinci and a Memory from His Childhood' in *The Standard Edition of the Complete Psychological Works of Sigmund Freud (The Standard Edition)*, vol. 11 London: The Hogarth Press

—— (1920) 'Psychogenesis of a Case of Homosexuality in a Woman' in *The*

Standard Edition, vol. 18

—— (1925) 'Some Psychical Consequences of the Anatomical Differences Between the Sexes' in *On Sexuality*

—— (1931) 'Female Sexuality' in *On Sexuality*

—— (1933) 'Femininity' in *The New Introductory Lectures on Psychoanalysis* vol 2., The Penguin Freud Library

Freund, K. (1960) 'Some Problems in the Treatment of Homosexuality' in Eysenck, H.J. (ed.) *Behaviour Therapy and the Neuroses* Oxford

—— (1977) 'Should Homosexuality Arouse Therapeutic Concern?' *Journal of Homosexuality* 2, 3, Spring, pp. 235–40

Friends Home Service Committee (1963) *Towards a Quaker View of Sex: An Essay by a Group of Friends* London: The Religious Society of Friends (reprinted 1976)

Gay Task Force (1979) *Submission to the Australian Broadcasting Tribunal Inquiry into Television Stations' Licence Renewals* Sydney: Gay Task Force

—— (1980a) *New Directions: Proposals for Change* Balmain: Gay Task Force

—— (1980b) *Submission to the NSW Inquiry into Police Administration: Publication No. 6* Balmain: Gay Task Force

Gearhart, S. and Johnson, W.L. (eds) (1974) *Loving Women/Loving Men: Gay Liberation & the Church* San Francisco: Glide Publications

Grier, B. and Reid, C. (eds) (1976) *Lesbians' Home Journal; Stories from the 'Ladder'* Oakland, California: Diana Press Inc.

Halleck, S.J. (1976) 'Another Response to "Homosexuality: The Ethical Challenge"' *Journal of Consulting and Clinical Psychology* 44, 2, pp. 167–70

Hammersmith, S.K. and Weinberg, M.S. (1973) 'Homosexual Identity: Commitment, Adjustment and Significant Others' *Sociometry* 36, 1, pp. 56–79

Harris, G. (1980) 'Notes on the New Puritanism' *Gay Information* no. 2, May–June

Hawkins, P. (1975) 'Effeminism' *Papers and Proceedings of the First National Homosexual Conference* Melbourne

Hay, B. and Goulden, T. (eds) (1982) *Gays and Their Families* Surry Hills: Gay Counselling Service of NSW

Hilliard, D. and Warhurst, J. (n.d.) 'Festival of light' *Current Affairs Bulletin* 50, 9

Hooker, E. (1957) 'The Adjustment of the Overt Male Homosexual' *Journal of Projective Techniques* 21, 1, pp. 18–31

—— (1965) 'Male Homosexuals Their Worlds' in Marmor

Hopkins, J. (1969) 'The Lesbian Personality' *British Journal of Psychiatry* 115, pp. 1433–6

Hourihan, M. (1982) 'The Compleat Candidate' *Refractory Girl* no. 23, March

Human Relationships Commission (1977) *Final Report* Canberra: Australian Government Publishing Service

Humphreys, L. (1970) *Tea Room Trade: Impersonal Sex in Public Places* London: Duckworth

Hurley, M. and Johnston, C. (1975) 'Campfires of Resistance: Theory and Practice for the Liberation of Male Homosexuals' *Papers and Proceedings of the First National Homosexual Conference* Melbourne

BIBLIOGRAPHY

Hyde, H.M. (1970) *The Other Love: An Historical and Contemporary Survey of Homosexuality in Britain* London: Mayflower Books
Jay, K. and Young, A. (eds) (1972) *Out of the Closet: Voices from Gay Liberation* USA: A Douglas Book
Johnston, C. (1980) 'Radical Homosexual Politics into the Eighties' *Gay Information* no. 2, May–June: no. 3, August–September
Karlen, A. (1971) *Sexuality and Homosexuality: A New View* New York: W.W. Norton and Co. Inc.
Keeling, M. (1977) 'A Christian Basis for Gay Relationships' in Macourt ed. (1977)
Kinsey, A.C. (1941) 'Homosexuality: Criteria for a Hormonal Explanation of the Homosexual' *Journal of Clinical Endocrinology* 1, pp. 424–8
Kinsey, A.C., Pomeroy, W.B. and Martin, C.E. (1948) *Sexual Behavior in the Human Male* Philadelphia and London: W.B. Saunders Co.
Kinsey, A.C., Pomeroy, W.B. Martin, C.E. and Gebhard, P.H. (1953) *Sexual Behavior in the Human Female* Philadelphia and London: W.B. Saunders Co.
Lee, J. (1977) 'A Working Relationship Between Lesbians & Homosexual Men? or In Defence of Poofters' Paper presented at the Third National Homosexual Conference, Adelaide
Llewellyn-Jones, D. (1978) *Everywoman: A Gynaecological Guide for Life* 2nd edn, London and Boston: Faber and Faber
Loftus, M. (1972) 'Women in Gay Liberation' *Sydney Gay Liberation Newsletter* 1, 3, p. 12
Loney, J. (1971) 'An MMPI Measure of Maladjustment in a Sample of "Normal" Homosexual Men' *Journal of Clinical Psychology* 27, 4, pp. 486–8
McConaghy, N. (1971) 'Aversion Therapy of Homosexuality: Measures of Efficacy' *American Journal of Psychiatry* 127, 9
—— (ed.) (1973) *Proceedings of the Geigy Psychiatric Symposium: Liberation Movements and Psychiatry*, Sydney
—— (1977) 'Behavioral Intervention in Homosexuality' *Journal of Homosexuality* 2, 3, Spring, pp. 221–7
McConaghy, N., Armstrong, M.S., Birrell, P.C. and Buhrich, N. (1979) 'The Incidence of Bisexual Feelings and Opposite Sex Behavior in Medical Students' *The Journal of Nervous and Mental Diseases* 167, 11, pp. 685–8
McNeil, J.J. (1977) *The Church and the Homosexual* London: Darton, Longman and Todd
Macourt, M. (ed.) (1977) *Towards a Theology of Gay Liberation* USA: Student Christian Movement Press
Mannion, K. (1976) 'Female Homosexuality: A Comprehensive Review of Theory and Research' *Journal Supplement Abstract Service* The American Psychological Association
Marmor, J. (ed.) (1965) *Sexual Inversion: The Multiple Roots of Homosexuality* New York: Basic Books
Martin, D. and Lyon, P. (1972) *Lesbian/Woman* New York: Bantam Books
Masters, W.H. and Johnson, V.E. (1979) *Homosexuality in Perspective* Boston: Little Brown and Co.

Meyer-Bahlberg, H.F.L. (1977) 'Sex Hormones and Male Homosexuality in Comparative Perspective' *Archives of Sexual Behaviour* 6, 4, pp. 297–325

Money, J. (1972) 'Sexual Dimorphism and Gender Identity' in Bardwick, (ed.)

—— (1977) 'Bisexual, Homosexual and Heterosexual: Society, Law and Medicine' *Journal of Homosexuality* 2, 3, Spring, pp. 229–33

Morgan, R. (ed.) (1973) *Sisterhood is Powerful: An Anthology of Writing from the Women's Liberation Movement* New York: Vintage Books

—— (1978) *Going Too Far: The Personal Chronicle of a Feminist* New York: Vintage Books

Myrick, F.L. (1972) 'Homosexual Types: An Empirical Investigation' *Journal of Sex Research* 10, 3, pp. 226–37

National Institute of Mental Health Task Force on Homosexuality (1972) *Final Report and Background Papers* Maryland: US Department of Health Education and Welfare (reprinted 1976)

NSW Anti-Discrimination Board (1978a) *Discrimination in Government Policies and Practices* Sydney: NSW Government Printer

—— (1978b) *Discrimination in Legislation* Sydney: NSW Government Printer

—— (1980) *Discrimination and Political Conviction* Sydney: NSW Government Printer

—— (1982) *Discrimination and Homosexuality* Sydney: The NSW Anti-Discrimination Board

NSW Public Service Board (1977) *Review of NSW Government Administration: Homosexuals in the Public Service: Background Paper No. 16* Sydney: NSW Government Printer

Parent Responsibility Study Group (1975) *Sex Education, the School and Your Child* Sydney: The Festival of Light

Plummer, K. (ed.) (1981) *The Making of the Modern Homosexual* New Jersey: Barnes and Noble Books

Poll, C. (1970) 'Gay Liberation' *The Old Mole* no. 7., Sydney University, 26 October, p. 5

Roazen, P. (1975) *Freud and His Followers* London: Peregrine Books

Robertson, G. (1972) 'Parent and Child Relationships and Homosexuality' *British Journal of Psychiatry* 121, pp. 525–8

Ruitenbeck, H.M. (ed.) (1973) *Homosexuality: A Changing Picture* London: Souvenir

Ryle, G. (1949) *The Concept of Mind* London: Penguin Books, 1976

Sacred Congregation for the Doctrine of the Faith (1975) *Declaration on Certain Questions Concerning Sexual Ethics* Homebush, NSW: The Society of St Paul

Saghir, M. and Robins, E. (1971) 'Male and Female Homosexuality: Natural History *Comprehensive Psychiatry* 12, 6, pp. 503–10

Schur, E.M. (1965) *Crimes Without Victims: Deviant Behavior Public Policy* Englewood Cliffs, N.J.: Prentice-Hall Inc.

Siegelman, M. (1972) 'Adjustment of Homosexual and Heterosexual Women' *British Journal of Psychiatry* 120, pp. 477–81

—— (1974) 'Parental Background of Male Homosexuals and Heterosexuals' *Archives of Sexual Behaviour* 3, 1, pp. 3–18

Silverstein, C. (1972) 'Behavior Modification and the Gay Community' Paper presented at the Annual Convention of the Association for the Advancement of Behavior Therapy, New York City
—— (1973) *Society and the Healthy Homosexual* New York: Anchor Press/Doubleday
—— (1976–77) 'Even Psychiatry Can Profit from Its Past Mistakes' *Journal of Homosexuality* 2, 2, pp. 153–8
—— (1977) 'Homosexuality and the Ethics of Behavioral Intervention' *Journal of Homosexuality* 2, 3, pp. 205–11
—— (1979) *A Family Matter: A Parent's Guide to Homosexuality* New York: McGraw Hill Book Co.
Socarides, C.W. (1968) *The Overt Homosexual* New York: Grune and Stratton
—— (1974) 'The Sexual Unreason' *Book Forum* 1, 2, p. 180
Social Questions Committee (1971) *Report on Homosexuality* Melbourne: Anglican Diocese of Melbourne
Snortum, J. et al. (1969) 'Family Dynamics and Homosexuality' *Psychological Reports* 24, pp. 763–70
Stanley, J.P. and Wolfe, S.J. (1980) *The Coming Out Stories* Watertown, Massachusetts: Persephone Press
Stein, P. (1972) 'Women's Oppression' *Sydney Gay Liberation Newsletter* 1, 6
Teal, D. (1971) *The Gay Militants* New York: Stein and Day
Tierney, B.J.H. (1981) *Catholic Family Catechism* Parramatta, NSW: Newman Catechist Centre
Thompson, D. (1980) ' "Neo-Puritanism?" Or the Failure of the Sexual Revolution' *Gay Information* no. 4, October–November
Thompson, N.L., McCandless, B.R. and Strickland, B.R. (1971) 'Personal Adjustment of Male and Female Homosexuals and Heterosexuals' *Journal of Abnormal Psychology* 78, 2, pp. 237–40
Treese, R.L. (1974) 'Homosexuality: A Contemporary View of the Biblical Perspective' in Gearhart and Johnson (eds) (1974)
Tripp, C.A. (1977) *The Homosexual Matrix* London: Quartet Books
US Commission on Civil Rights (1981) *Affirmative Action in the 1980s: Dismantling the Process of Discrimination*
Vida, G. (1978) *Our Right to Love: A Lesbian Resource Book* New York: Prentice-Hall
Ware, J. (1971) 'Twelve Months Past' *CAMP Ink* 1, 11
—— (1973?) 'Psychosurgery in Australia' *CAMP Ink* 3, 4
Watson, L. (1979) 'Homosexuals' in Bates and Wilson, (eds) (1979)
Watson, L. and Wills, S. (1972) 'Where Are We Going?' *CAMP Ink* 2, 7
Weeks, J. (1977) *Coming Out: Homosexual Politics in Britain from the Nineteenth Century to the Present* London: Quartet Books
Weinberg, G. (1975) *Society and the Healthy Homosexual* Gerrards Cross, Bucks: Colin Smythe
West, D.J. (1955) *Homosexuality* London: Penguin Books, 1974
—— (1977) *Homosexuality Re-examined* London: Duckworth
Westwood, G.A. (1960) *Minority: A Report on the Life of the Male Homosexual in Great Britain* London: Longmans, Green and Co.
Widdup, D. (1971) 'The First Year of the Movement' *William and John* (I do

185

not have an issue or volume number for this article)

—— (1973?) 'In the Category of Women and Other Trivia' *CAMP Ink* 3, 1

Wilbur, C. (1965) 'Clinical Aspects of Female Homosexuality' in Marmor (1965)

Wills, S. (1972?) 'Intellectual Poofter Bashers' *CAMP Ink* 2, 1

Wilson, M. and Green, R. (1971) 'Personality Characteristics of Female Homosexuals' *Psychological Reports* 28, pp. 407–12

Wilson, P. (1971) *The Sexual Dilemma: Abortion, Homosexuality, Prostitution and the Criminal Threshold* Brisbane: University of Queensland Press

Wilson, P.R. and Chappell, D. (1968) 'Australian Attitudes Towards Abortion, Prostitution and Homosexuality' *The Australian Quarterly* 40, 2

Wolfenden et al. (1957) *Robert of the Committee of Inquiry into Homosexual Offences and Prostitution* London: HMSO

Young, W. (1969) *Eros Denied* Corgi Books

INDEX

191